South Bronx Battles

South Bronx Battles

STORIES OF RESISTANCE,
RESILIENCE, AND RENEWAL

Carolyn McLaughlin

Foreword by David Gómez

UNIVERSITY OF CALIFORNIA PRESS

University of California Press, one of the most distinguished university presses in the United States, enriches lives around the world by advancing scholarship in the humanities, social sciences, and natural sciences. Its activities are supported by the UC Press Foundation and by philanthropic contributions from individuals and institutions. For more information, visit www.ucpress.edu.

University of California Press
Oakland, California

Library of Congress Cataloging-in-Publication Data

Names: McLaughlin, Carolyn, author | Gómez, David, writer of foreword
Title: South Bronx battles : stories of resistance, resilience, and renewal / Carolyn McLaughlin, foreword by David Gómez.
Description: Oakland, California : University of California Press, [2019] | Includes bibliographical references and index. |
Identifiers: LCCN 2018050297 (print) | LCCN 2018056144 (ebook) | ISBN 9780520963801 (ebook and ePDF) | ISBN 9780520288973 (cloth : alk. paper) | ISBN 9780520288997 (pbk. : alk. paper)
Subjects: LCSH: Bronx (New York, N.Y.)—History—20th century. | Urban renewal—New York (State)
Classification: LCC F128.68.B8 (ebook) | LCC F128.68.B8 M28 2019 (print) | DDC 974.7/275—dc23
LC record available at https://lccn.loc.gov/2018050297

Manufactured in the United States of America

26 25 24 23 22 21 20 19
10 9 8 7 6 5 4 3 2 1

For my wonderful grandchildren, Hana and Sora Karanja, Jordan and Shaun McLaughlin, and Nathan Turner, with hopes that this book will inspire you to choose careers that work, in some manner, for a more just world

Contents

Illustrations

Foreword

"The Bronx is burning." That phrase, often attributed (by urban legend) to Howard Cosell during his broadcast of Game 2 of the World Series on the night of October 12, 1977, encapsulates the image that was projected across America in both the sports and mainstream media for almost half a century. As an endless parade of presidential aspirants posed atop piles of rubble in nondescript abandoned lots, the Bronx became synonymous with urban decay, poverty, crime, and hopelessness. An entire borough of New York City (one that would be the seventh largest city in America were it an independent city), home to a population larger than those of Dallas, San Antonio, San Diego, or San Jose, the Bronx became a punchline in the national consciousness.

As the Goodyear Blimp hovered above the Bronx on that October night and projected images of burning buildings into the living rooms of America, did anyone consider who were the people a thousand feet below and what was happening in that community? Several questions were seldom asked and never answered: How did this happen? How did a thriving community with a rich history assume the identity of the national symbol of urban blight? More importantly, were this community and others like it relegated to such a dire status in perpetuity? What lessons, if any, could be drawn from the experience that might serve other communities in this nation?

These questions and more are explored in the compelling portrayal of the South Bronx presented here by Carolyn McLaughlin. From the perspective of a true insider, Ms. McLaughlin weaves historical fact, personal narratives, community activism, political intrigue, and stories of courage and triumph into a complex tapestry that tells the story of the South Bronx as few have or could. Make no mistake, however—this is not a story of personal triumph or a David-and-Goliath allegory designed to convince the reader that good triumphs over evil. Instead, it tells the complex and nuanced story of how one community began its descent and, more importantly, how it began its present ascent. It is also a cautionary tale of journeys both down and up the ladder of success.

McLaughlin came to the Bronx as a self-described naive idealist—in many ways truly a stranger in a strange land—coming from small-town America to the very definition of gritty urban life in the late 1960s. As a young professional trying to do the right thing, she was faced with the harsh realities of urban politics, public social services policy, human suffering, socioeconomic forces, the AIDS epidemic, powerful real estate interests, and entrenched racism. Through her work and life in the Bronx, she sees both the power and the potential of the human will, including her own.

McLaughlin's introduction to the Bronx began much like that of many young people in that era, with a firm belief that social justice was not only an aspirational goal but a human right. As a young caseworker for the NYC department of welfare, she truly reflected the "Kennedyesque" idealism of the '60s. Unlike many of the young idealists of that era, however, who became disillusioned by the seemingly insurmountable obstacles posed by the city's power brokers and who ultimately abandoned their dreams of social justice for more lucrative professional careers, she heard the voices of human courage and redoubled her efforts at making a difference in the lives and futures of the people of the Bronx. And in this book, those people—who were known to most Americans only as vague shadows somewhere in the background of fires seen from a thousand feet—come alive.

The Bronx in the '60s, much like the Bronx of today, was a study in contrasts. This county of New York State includes affluent communities like Riverdale (once the childhood home of John F. Kennedy as well as the residence of Theodore Roosevelt, Mark Twain, and Arturo Toscanini) and lower-income areas like Mott Haven that attracted, and still attract, new immigrants and working-class families, like the Piccirilli brothers who, working on 142nd Street in the South Bronx, carved the statue of Abraham Lincoln for the Lincoln Memorial in Washington, D.C. Millions visit Yankee Stadium, the Bronx Zoo, the New York Botanical Garden, and Fordham University each year. Yet, at the beginning of McLaughlin's story in the '60s, the Bronx was on the brink of disaster.

As she set out to build what would be her life's work (the Citizens Advice Bureau, later to become the BronxWorks organization), McLaughlin recognized that the issues challenging the Bronx were not poverty or substance abuse alone. It was not housing or the economy alone. Nor was it politics or institutionalized racism alone. All of these factors and more, acting in concert, drove this community to a state of near ruin. *Near*, however, is the operative term here. In a true case of "fight or flight," she shares the stories of individual and organizational courage that have contributed to the beginning of the Bronx's comeback.

As one who knew and worked with the power brokers, from mayors to city and statewide elected officials, McLaughlin witnessed firsthand the challenges facing people in poor communities and helped craft the strategies that both led to short-term improvements in the community and set the stage for continued improvement and growth in the long term. She describes the battles waged to save the Bronx through the narratives of families, workers in community agencies, and community leaders and activists. These stories, which at the time were viewed by many as quixotic battles against unbeatable foes, speak to the persistence and unyielding faith of leaders like McLaughlin in making the inexorable climb out of the abyss. They show the collective impact of small victories on solving large problems.

The description of the conditions and the plight of the people of the Bronx is not where this book draws its strength. Even the unique "insider's" perspective is not its value. Rather, it is the ability to present a highly complex story of sociopolitical turmoil and survival through the unapologetic voices of those who lived it and who are part of the story of the borough's resurgence. Reading this book, you will clearly hear the voices of dismay and defiance. You will hear calls for the creation of social, religious, and educational infrastructures that sustain communities. You will hear the message to policymakers that communities, if well supported, are more than capable of solving their own problems.

It is telling that McLaughlin avoids the historical clichés that are so often the story line of the Bronx. Robert Moses, while often and legitimately demonized for the impact that his "urban renewal" projects had on the Bronx, is given only passing notice in this story. Rather, the confluence of factors that Moses and others of that era set in motion receive primary attention: white flight, the rise in communities of color, discrimination in housing and employment, fiscal and banking policies, the failing national economy along with the City's precarious fiscal situation, educational policies, and insurance and housing practices that led to incentivizing arson over the development of affordable housing.

Just as the decline of the Bronx was the result of a series of complex factors contributing to the perfect storm of urban decay, the rebounding of the Bronx and the triumphs of its people came through a combination of forces that were driven by organizations like BronxWorks and small community-based groups, by individual community activists and individual acts of courage, by more progressive public policies, and, yes, even by some courageous and forward-thinking political leaders who helped reshape the policies, politics, and narrative of the South Bronx. As someone who was not only there but who knew, and knows, the principals in this still unfolding drama, McLaughlin strikes a cautionary note on the Bronx's renaissance. The issue is not framed in stereotypical terms of gentrification versus local residence but rather as a matter of balance.

As with all stories of perseverance, McLaughlin reminds us that there are lessons and challenges for the South Bronx that are no different from those of many urban communities in this nation as they wrestle with the downside of economic recovery. That is, is it possible for those who helped save the community to benefit from its recovery? Is it possible for the Bronx to avoid the pitfalls of other cities and, instead, lift the community up rather than push people out? While the answer seems to be yes, McLaughlin cautions that the same forces that led to the Bronx's decline can, if left unabated, cause harm to communities during periods of economic turnaround.

New industries and businesses moving into the community bring the prospect of jobs and economic viability. With livable wages, residents and political leaders believe that they will be able to sustain their families, send their children to strong schools, and retain the cultural and social qualities that made their communities attractive and unique within the city. New businesses also threaten to bring increased commercial traffic to areas with the highest asthma rates in the state. An influx of new residents brings with it the threat of higher rents and the prospect of displacement.

Developers continue their efforts to brand neighborhoods in an attempt to attract young professionals and increase real estate values. New construction is booming throughout the South Bronx, and promises of affordable housing are bandied about. Absent from these proclamations is any definitive answer to the question "Affordable for whom?" How will thirty- and forty-story housing complexes impact the character of the community? Will the factors that contributed to the decline of the Bronx—the lack of religious, educational, recreational, and social support systems, health services, and full-service supermarkets—be repeated in the haste to take advantage of the last frontier of real estate development?

The answers to these questions are more likely the subject of Ms. McLaughlin's next book. For now, she leaves us with the prospect of community-based organizations and leaders expanding their role from advocating for social reform and justice to include advocacy for residents to share in the potential of the new catchphrase "The Bronx is booming." As you read *South Bronx Battles* and reflect on the stories of its people, you will no doubt be inspired and troubled. The story is still unfolding.

David Gómez
Bronx, New York, August 2018

South Bronx Timeline

1920s–1950s	The South Bronx provides stable neighborhoods for primarily European immigrants.
1930s–1960s	Robert Moses constructs four highways, three bridges, and major housing developments, causing massive dislocation in the South Bronx.
1940s–1960s	Increasing numbers of Puerto Rican, African American, and West Indian families move to the South Bronx as whites move out. South Bronx nightclubs feature major black and Latino musicians.
1947–1981	NYC loses half of its manufacturing jobs, making it increasingly hard for newer residents to find employment.
1960s–1970s	Heroin use explodes and crime increases, causing neighborhood instability. Starting in the late 1960s, Bronx nonprofits form to start rebuilding housing and neighborhoods. Arts agencies are founded to support Bronx artists.
1960s	Women start to organize for better schools and more services.
1970s	Fires increase, causing devastation in many areas. Residents clean vacant lots to use as community gardens.
1970	Activists take over Lincoln Hospital, demanding a new building and a drug detox department.

1972   Citizens Advice Bureau (CAB) is founded.

1973   A new music, hip hop is created; over the years, it will rise to become the world's most popular music.

1975   The NYC fiscal crisis causes huge cuts in City services and jobs; poor areas suffer most.

1975–1976   Community members fight to keep Hostos Community College from closing.

1977   Widespread looting and arson during a twenty-five-hour blackout cause major damage to commercial areas.

1980   Due to fires and building abandonment, the South Bronx population has fallen by 315,000 in ten years. The South Bronx is declared the poorest congressional district in the United States.

1980s–present   More immigrants from the Caribbean, Africa, and Central America settle in the South Bronx.

1985–1990   During the height of the crack epidemic, HIV rates rise rapidly.

1986   Mayor Koch issues a $5 billion plan to build or rehabilitate one hundred thousand units of low- and moderate-income housing and redevelopment takes off.

1988   To meet emerging needs, CAB opens free immigration and HIV/AIDS programs.

1990s   Crime declines. Neighborhoods rebuild. Available funding allows CAB and other agencies to expand, offering help to homeless people, people facing eviction, seniors, and, to some extent, children. Residents fight against incinerators and waste transfer stations and advocate for new parks.

1992   Nos Quedamos, Borough President Ferrer, and City agencies plan together for the Melrose Commons development, providing a model for cooperative planning.

1997   The Bronx wins the All-America City Award, demonstrating the borough's progress.

2000–2018   Preschool and after-school programs expand significantly, as do options for public schools, providing greater educational and social opportunities for children and teens. New arts groups are formed and existing ones expand. Groups advocate for the removal of the Sheridan Expressway and to keep trucks off local streets on their way to Hunts Point. The city struggles with increasing homelessness.

2001   The Bronx River Alliance is formed and cleanup of the river accelerates.

2014   Mayor de Blasio pledges $41 billion to preserve or build two hundred thousand units of affordable housing.

2015–present   Developers build luxury housing in Mott Haven. Community groups raise concerns about displacement and seek solutions. Many new large residential buildings are constructed throughout the South Bronx.

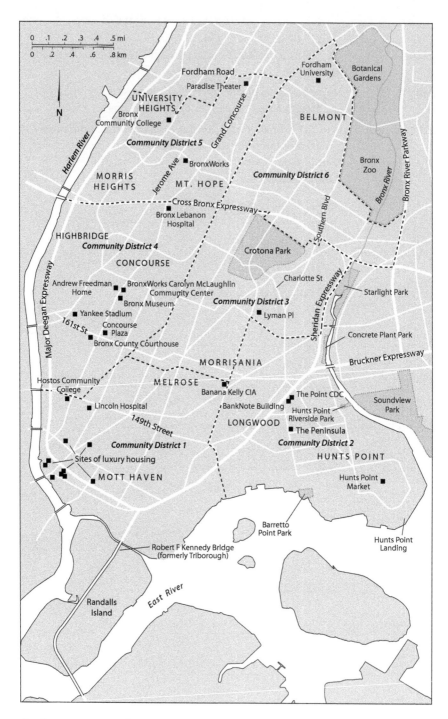

South Bronx, New York (2018).

1 The South Bronx

Kathryn Speller has been a community activist and concerned citizen in the West Bronx for over sixty years. She is an interesting, outspoken, energetic eighty-six-year-old. Although slender, pretty, and only four feet eleven inches, she is imposing, her gray hair in an "Afro," her mind active. In her living room, games stand ready for play when family or friends visit. At the end of one of our meetings, she calls a neighbor to remind her to take her medicine. Discussing her community's past, present, and future, she told me:

> My husband, my mom, and I bought a house in 1968 in the West Bronx. When we moved into the neighborhood, it was very nice, very multiethnic. When the area started getting rough, the African Americans and Hispanics stayed. My friends and I marched against the terrible hospital closings. I worked to organize tenants' organizations. I advocated for many, many years for parks and services for youth and senior citizens. I was active with the precinct advisory council, which worked to promote better relationships between the police and the community.
>
> Overall, I welcome the new immigrants but worry they might be less socially active than I and my friends were. I worry about the proposed rezoning of Jerome Avenue, and whether the rezoning will cause displacement. Will there be enough schools or will current schools become more

Kathryn Speller at home, discussing one of her favorite topics, the Bronx. An activist and outspoken observer of community life, she has lived in the West Bronx for sixty years, through the hard times and the rebuilding. Her mother was part of the Great Migration of African Americans to the north. Raised in Harlem, Ms. Speller moved to the Bronx as a young woman. Photo by author.

overcrowded? With taller buildings, are plans being made for open space? What will happen to neighborhood stores? I particularly worry about the effect that gentrification would have on the poor, although I welcome improvements to the area. I am afraid that the poor will be told, "Get out of here."[1]

THE SOUTH BRONX TODAY

So near and yet so far. The South Bronx, the poorest half of New York's poorest borough, is separated from Manhattan's wealthy Upper East Side by a few subway stops, and yet these two areas couldn't be more different. The South Bronx grapples with New York's highest school dropout rates[2] while the Upper East Side boasts an average household income of $311,000.[3] The South Bronx is 1 percent white while the Upper East Side is 80 percent white.[4] The South Bronx has blocks of aging, overcrowded housing with numerous violations while the Upper East Side contains posh Park Avenue high-rises and Prada, Gucci, and other luxury stores along Madison Avenue. Alluding to this kind of stark inequality that he is fighting, Mayor Bill de Blasio refers to New York as a "tale of two cities."[5] In short, the South Bronx has been a place for the poor while the Upper East Side and areas like it are for the wealthy.

The Bronx is a world unto itself, covering over forty-two square miles, including the two largest parks and the only freshwater river in New York City. To the north stretch the primarily suburban areas, the City of Yonkers, and, further north, the cities of Albany, Syracuse, and Buffalo—all referred to generically as "upstate." Manhattan lies over small bridges to the south and west, and the borough of Queens on Long Island over major bridges to the east. To the people of the Bronx, the rapidly gentrifying borough of Brooklyn is somewhere on the other side of Manhattan. The fifth borough, Staten Island, is over that way too. The Bronx communicates mainly with Manhattan.

The Bronx contains cultural treasures, many of them highly touted. The Bronx Zoo, the sixth-largest zoo in the world, has four thousand animals; the New York Botanical Garden, with 250 beautiful acres, sponsors a Christmas train show and a yearly orchid spectacular; and the new Yankee Stadium, rebuilt in 2009 at a cost of $1.6 billion,[6] holds hopes for another World Series win. Near the zoo is Belmont, with its numerous, much-loved Italian restaurants.

Perhaps the Bronx's most outstanding treasure is its residents themselves. Over 1.4 million people call the Bronx home, more than live in the entire state of Alaska. And they are so diverse—this is the most diverse county in the United States. Any two people randomly meeting on the street have a 90 percent chance of being of different races or of different ethnic backgrounds. Puerto Ricans, African Americans, and European Americans mix with people from the Dominican Republic, Mexico, Jamaica, and other countries in the Caribbean, West Africa, South America, and Asia.[7] Most amazingly, people generally get along. This diversity infuses the Bronx and New York City with energy and vitality.

The people of the South Bronx work at rates comparable to the rest of New York State, at all kinds of jobs, though too many of them are very low-paid service jobs, contributing to the high poverty rate. But not everyone is poor: while 38 percent of the people of the South Bronx meet the official definition of poverty, 62 percent do not.[8]

In the mornings, the subways are packed with people commuting to work in Manhattan: civil servants, teachers, office workers, security guards, and construction workers. Many others find work in the Bronx. A surprising 45 percent of the people who work in the Bronx work for non-profits, including hospitals and other health-related facilities.[9] Many others work in mom-and-pop businesses, such as hair salons and retail stores, or drive taxis.

The Bronx's residential landscape is dense and full of life. In older sections of the South Bronx, many of the apartment buildings appear tired and worn, despite the flow of young mothers and children in and out of their front doors. Barbed wire remains atop some fences, a reminder of the high crime of years past. Residences for people who are homeless appear well kept from the street and blend in with the neighborhood. In once dev-astated areas, attractive, renovated five-story apartment buildings mingle with two- and three-family houses that allow for home ownership.

The commercial landscape in the South Bronx is also busy, offering a range of stores, from "99 cent" and inexpensive clothing stores to restau-rants, check-cashing and money-transfer services, beauty and barber shops, and laundromats, all with colorful signs. Bodegas—little grocery stores whose signs usually say "Deli" but that everyone refers to as bodegas—liven many corners, offering snacks and essentials such as bread, bananas, milk, beer, and coffee. Full-scale grocery stores can be hard to find, contributing to the epidemic of obesity and diabetes.

An abundance of churches and mosques reflect the religious passion of South Bronx residents. The edifices range from traditional, steepled stone Catholic and Protestant churches built over 120 years ago to large Pentecostal churches, often in converted movie theaters and catering halls, to a profusion of other churches, sometimes in transformed houses and storefronts. Mosques number about thirty, and the members often spill out the storefronts onto the sidewalks for prayer.

In sharp contrast to the South Bronx, Riverdale is a middle-class to wealthy area in the northwest Bronx. With co-op apartments, multimillion-dollar houses, and three exclusive private schools, it is physically and economically separate from the rest of the Bronx. The northeast Bronx, with its many private houses, is home to a large Jamaican community. Throughout this book, I will distinguish whether I am talking about the South Bronx or the entire Bronx, which includes several middle-income areas and, in the case of Riverdale, upper-middle-class and wealthy areas.

The old industrial areas lie near the waterfront. Many of the factories that once employed large numbers of people closed years ago, but waste transfer facilities remain, as do companies such as the *New York Post,* Coca-Cola, and Jetro Cash & Carry (a supplier of bodegas). Other commercial ventures such as FreshDirect (online grocery delivery) have recently built new facilities.

The huge Hunts Point produce, meat, and fish markets, through which most of the food for New York City passes, have annual revenues of more than $2 billion a year and employ thousands of unionized workers, many from the Bronx.[10] But like so many things in life, it is a mixed blessing. Residents of Hunts Point have the highest rates of asthma in New York City, which they attribute to the market's very heavy truck traffic rumbling through their neighborhood.

New hotels, ritzy market-rate housing along the Harlem River, and plans for the world's largest ice-skating complex indicate profound change. Big money is investing in the Bronx. Add in the Trump Golf Links, a few craft breweries, and new shopping malls, and a picture of a different kind of Bronx starts appearing, one that appeals to people with resources. Gentrification is on the horizon.

MY LIFE IN THE SOUTH BRONX

I came to the Bronx as a naive but determined idealist in 1968, accompanied by my Kenyan husband, David Karanja, and my infant son, Kamau

Karanja. I arrived from small-town America and found an urgently needed job working as a caseworker in the Bronx for the welfare department. It was a good fit with my evolving interest in social justice, which had started when I was in high school and increased in college when I was an exchange student at Fisk University, a historically black college. The welfare job, which I kept for three years, required making frequent home visits (and climbing lots of stairs in old apartment buildings) and determining clients' eligibility for benefits. I divorced at the age of twenty-four. At various times, I lived in Highbridge, near Bronx Lebanon Hospital, and near Fordham Road. After earning a master's degree in social work with a concentration in community organizing, marrying Jim McLaughlin, and having another son, Jimmy, I organized activities in senior citizen centers in the Bronx for six years. Then I settled into my life's work.

For thirty-four years, I worked on the ground, building BronxWorks (originally called the Citizens Advice Bureau, or CAB), an organization that helps tens of thousands of low-income Bronx residents improve their lives. Initially, working from a one-room office on the Grand Concourse and Burnside Avenue with one other employee and two interns, I saw people in crisis, families without food or on the verge of being evicted, children with the odds stacked against them, and seniors in untenable situations. Slowly, but with determination and high standards, we resolved individuals' problems and found resources to build programs to help greater numbers of people—including senior citizen centers, shelters for the homeless, early childhood education, after-school programs, job placement, homelessness prevention, and support for people with AIDS and other major illnesses. We helped families stabilize their lives and take steps to move out of poverty. In the course of doing so, I built a highly regarded organization. When I retired in 2013, BronxWorks was helping thirty-five thousand people a year, with a skilled and dedicated staff of six hundred who worked at twenty-seven locations in the South Bronx.

During the course of my career, I witnessed the South Bronx at its most desperate, when blocks and blocks of abandoned buildings were interspersed with rubble-filled lots where apartment buildings once stood. The devastation spread north and the definition of the South Bronx expanded from 138th to 149th to 161st Street, to the Cross Bronx Expressway, and finally all the way to Fordham Road, subsuming the West Bronx and most of the Grand Concourse. I participated in the South Bronx's rebirth, the rebuilding of both the physical structures and the social infrastructure. I worked closely with four city administrations, with mayors and commissioners, and with local community leaders and residents. I struggled for funding and learned how to manage government contracts, solicit foundations and individuals for money, and develop a board of directors. Over the years, CAB made significant progress in learning how to resolve many of the problems that plague poor people. We developed expertise in entitlements and housing, youth development, gerontology, workforce development, immigration, and mental health. I saw families move up economically and leave the Bronx, to be replaced with new immigrants, bringing cultural diversity and new energy to the borough. The South Bronx changed dramatically, yet it remains a place that cares about low-income people. Hopefully, it will remain a place for low-income families far into the future.

I was blessed with the opportunity to have an extremely meaningful career that actually changed lives, working in a place that I love with people I admire. I did so while raising three children with my husband, a remarkable daughter, Johnicka, having joined our family along the way.

WHAT THIS BOOK IS

The journey described in this book demonstrates that the South Bronx's revitalization is a great American success story. Far from being a desperate no-man's-land, the South Bronx, to me, represents the future of American cities as sites of struggle, immigration, innovation, and mobility. In these chapters, I show how the Bronx's embrace and support of the poor and immigrants makes it a national model as an essential urban haven.

Based on my nearly five decades of working in the Bronx for social change, I've been compelled to write an insider oral history of this misunderstood, understudied, and undervalued slice of New York City. As a social worker and as someone who lived in the Bronx for twenty years during the hard times, I've penned a work of journalism, not a scholarly volume, that draws upon a range of primary and secondary sources, including interviews of longtime residents, published and unpublished reports, oral histories, and newspapers and books. I write as a participant observer who has the perspective of a social worker and a community activist. My aim is to provide a broad overview of the decline and resurrection of this borough, with a focus on lower-income residents of the South Bronx, using my experiences and those of my informants to provide a visceral guidance through the narrative. I have drawn upon people I worked with for decades, including community residents, service providers, artists, environmental activists, academic experts, and policymakers, as well as more recent contacts. By bringing together these multiple points of view, I hope to give the reader a feel for the people of the South Bronx, their accomplishments and challenges. Some people are quoted many times at various points in the book when their experience relates to the topic being discussed. Many other people and organizations that I was unable to include in this book have made remarkable contributions and have compelling stories as well.

This book seeks to fill a gap in writings about the South Bronx by focusing on problems residents face and the response from communities, government, and human services agencies. It does not attempt to be a comprehensive history of the Bronx, but rather features selected issues I think are important, based on my experiences and on conversations with people whose opinions I value. In sections of several chapters, I describe the progress of CAB/BronxWorks in developing comprehensive programs to support families as one example of the positive role that social services can play in a low-income community. Other social service agencies have their own histories and achievements, but I focus on the organization that I know best. Not enough has been written about the evolution and impact of human services on communities.

My adult life has been spent working to improve the lives of the people of the Bronx, and I write as a determined community activist who cares deeply about what happens to this storied and complicated borough and its residents. I also write as someone who is concerned about the tendency to blame society's ills on poor people, rather than seeing these people as assets who contribute greatly to our communities. The resilience and strength that the people of the South Bronx showed in living through the hard times— and their contributions toward its rebuilding—should be widely acknowledged and respected. The same resilience and strength resides in people living in other poor areas, and they can, if nurtured with resources and opportunity, contribute substantially to reclaiming their communities.

In this work, I take a hard but empathetic look at the South Bronx, chronicling its fall and rise since the 1960s. I look at factors that caused the collapse of residential real estate, as well as the barriers faced by Puerto Ricans and African Americans as they moved to the Bronx. The stories in this book describe the role residents played in reclaiming their neighborhoods, including the many contributions of immigrants. The Bronx, in turn, provided a route to upward mobility for many. The mixing of people from many backgrounds created music and culture that had worldwide impact.

Based on my years of experience developing and leading a major social service nonprofit and serving on the boards of directors for several other Bronx nonprofits, I make a case that the Bronx plays an important role in New York City, offering less costly housing to low-income native-born residents and immigrants who are priced out of the rest of the city. Indeed, the South Bronx is poor and, in many ways, needs to stay so in order to remain an affordable home for over six hundred thousand New Yorkers. This is not to say that individuals who are poor should remain so—quite the contrary. My whole career was devoted to helping people move out of poverty. This is also not to say that we don't need to improve the Bronx, from schools to housing to basic infrastructure. Poor communities need and deserve an investment of resources available to residents in higher-income areas. As an activist, I've worked day in and day out to improve education for children and adults, prevent homelessness, increase job options, lower crime rates, and offer resources for healthier lives, and I will show how current initiatives in these areas are essential urban projects. This is also not to say that everyone in the South Bronx is poor (the majority are not) or that the South Bronx should be home primarily to low-income people.

Rather, I want to raise a clarion warning about the danger of the "Brooklynization" of the Bronx, an incipient phenomenon rapidly gaining momentum especially in the South Bronx. Thousands of units of luxury and affordable housing targeted to families with significantly higher incomes than those who now live in the area are being constructed, raising concerns about displacement. People in the Bronx want a community that includes diversity of income as well as ethnicity, but only up to a point. That point arrives when people who move in are wealthy enough to change the economics of the area, to rapidly drive up residential and commercial rents. The Bronx should not become unaffordable for its current residents.

This book is a plea to keep the Bronx moving forward as a diverse area full of immigrants from the Dominican Republic, Nigeria, Mexico, Sierra Leone, and dozens of other countries while sustaining important African American and Puerto Rican communities. These latter two groups, who suffered the most during the Bronx's worst years and played leading roles in building the new Bronx, are vulnerable to displacement along with the new immigrants.

And it is not just the families that meet the official federal definition of poverty that are vulnerable to displacement. Close to 60 percent of Bronx residents pay over a third of their income for rent, and a third pay over half of their incomes.[11] These high rent burdens, the worst in New York State, make it very hard for families to have enough money for their other essential expenses, food, utilities, transportation, and clothing. High rent burdens also make families susceptible to loss of their housing. Displacement has huge social costs, for the families who lose their homes and jobs and for the city as a whole.

Yes, the South Bronx is the poorest urban county in the country.[12] But this does not mean that low-income people in the South Bronx are poorer or worse off than those in other parts of the country. It just means that there are more people who are poor. Many people think poor areas are bad areas that need to be radically fixed, usually by people of wealth and influence. But poor neighborhoods are not necessarily bad neighborhoods. The Bronx has many assets that are particularly crucial to low-income people, such as good public transportation, basically sound housing stock, comparatively low crime, accessible health care, higher educational opportunities, improving parks, relatively high life expectancy,[13] and a robust social service support system. These assets make the Bronx, although far from perfect, a place that low-income families want to continue to call home.

The South Bronx was poor forty years ago and is still poor, but many of the current residents are not the same people who lived here in past decades. For most of its history and continuing to this day, the Bronx has been a place where families work to build futures that are better than their pasts. As they join the middle class, they decide to stay or they move to a higher-income area. If they stay, they are likely to invest in the community and help family, friends, and neighbors who are still struggling economically. If they move, their apartment is likely to be re-rented to an immigrant family or to another low- to moderate-income family. In neither case is there a disruption to the local economy. The neighborhoods continue to evolve at a reasonable pace. Rents rise but not astronomically. Locally owned businesses are not forced out to make room for posh stores and restaurants. Families can continue to work toward their dreams of a better future.

In recent years, though, neighborhood groups and individuals are actively raising concerns about displacement and gentrification. They are pushing back against proposals for "affordable housing" that would not be affordable to current residents. They have concerns about increasing density and the loss of mom-and-pop businesses. They are worried that the people who move into apartments now being constructed on the waterfront, which will rent for $3,500 a month, will change the fundamental nature of their communities. They feel they helped the Bronx by staying during the bad times and have contributed toward the new Bronx. They are worried that if they are priced out, they will have no place to go.

Many Bronxites really care about their communities. As in previous generations, they are fighting to preserve their neighborhoods. Their ideas on how to mitigate the displacement crisis facing the borough should be taken very seriously by all levels of government, as the power of government is needed to counteract speculation in the real estate market.

I hope this book will be of interest to people of the Bronx who know little of the borough's recent history, to students of social welfare issues and policy, to visitors who are startled to see what the new South Bronx looks like, and to everyone who is interested in what makes communities strong. It is my conviction that other urban areas currently facing problems of disinvestment, crime, and building abandonment can learn from the Bronx's successes. Perhaps the South Bronx can also be the place that deals successfully with the threats posed by gentrification, while continuing to provide a path for many to upward mobility.

THE SOUTH BRONX: A BRIEF HISTORY

The land in the South Bronx was transformed from forest to large estates, small farms, and villages, and later to dense urban residential and industrial use. A snapshot of the history of the South Bronx is illustrated by the successive uses, by different groups of people, of the Bright Temple African Methodist Episcopal (AME) Church building on Faile Street. I became familiar with the church when a pastor joined CAB's board of directors. The historic building was constructed in 1859 for the Hoe family, as a mansion called Sunnyslope. In 1919, it became the Temple Beth Elohim Synagogue, and later it was used as a Hebrew school. During the Great Depression, a Works Progress Administration teacher provided art classes there for neighborhood residents. Bright Temple AME Church acquired the building from the Jewish congregation fifty years ago. The church has an active social ministry, including a soup kitchen and a food pantry. The building is listed on the National Register of Historic Places.[14]

With its natural beauty and resources, the Bronx has always attracted newcomers. In 1639, Jonas Bronck, a Swede, bought land in what is now Mott Haven to create a homestead. Within twenty years of the arrival of Europeans, the Siwanoy, a band of Algonquian, suffered major losses from bloody battles and disease. Their numbers decimated, the Native Americans left to live in upstate New York and Connecticut.[15] The land they left behind became known by the river that ran through it, named after Jonas Bronck. Bronck's River became the Bronx River and the whole area became the Bronx.

The wooded hills and valleys gave way to farms in the early nineteenth century. Small towns grew around the farms, with names like Morrisania, Mott Haven, Hunts Point, Morris Heights, and Claremont. The early immigrant settlers, somewhat in this order, were Dutch, English, Irish, German, and Italian. Later, Jews from Germany, and then from Russia and Poland, settled in the Bronx. Industry developed in the waterfront areas of Mott Haven, Port Morris, and Hunts Point. Nearby tenements housed the workers.

The extension of elevated trains from Manhattan, starting in 1886, sped the development of the Bronx. As a train line unfolded into an area, land values increased and land that had been farms became housing, private houses and then apartment buildings. In 1895, planners set aside four thousand acres for parks, including the two largest parks in New York City, Pelham Bay Park and Van Cortlandt Park. The third large park, Bronx Park, was divided to become the Bronx Zoo and the New York Botanical Gardens.[16] The huge BankNote Building in Hunts Point, which printed stock certificates and currency for many foreign countries, was built in 1909.[17]

The Grand Concourse, the main north–south street in the West Bronx, was based on the famed Champs Élysées in Paris. Opened in 1909, its center lanes were originally planned for use by horses and carriages; other lanes were for bicyclists and pedestrians. Now trees in the medians of the six-lane roadway struggle to survive because of the high volume of traffic and the subway rumbling underneath. Because the Grand Concourse was built on a series of ridges, twenty-three of its cross streets were tunneled underneath the roadway.[18] Years later, homeless adults slept on the sidewalks of these underpasses, sheltered in the tunnels from the rain, wind, and extreme cold.

The 1920s saw major institutions of the West Bronx constructed: Yankee Stadium, the opulent Concourse Plaza Hotel (now housing for senior citizens), New York University (now Bronx Community College), Fordham University, the Andrew Freedman Home, Loew's Paradise Theatre (now called the Paradise Theater), a New York Society for the Prevention of Cruelty to Children shelter (now BronxWorks), and the Tremont Temple Gates of Mercy synagogue (now Union Baptist Church). Many of the large apartment complexes on the Grand Concourse and its side streets were also built in the 1920s. Apartments on the Concourse are widely known for their Art Deco and Art Moderne architecture.[19]

During this time, a pattern of movement was set up that lasted for seventy years. Families, often immigrants who had secured a foothold in the squalid, overcrowded Lower East Side of Manhattan, moved up to the South Bronx, the area of the Bronx with the oldest and least expensive housing. These families, when they were financially able, would then move from the South Bronx to more upscale areas in the borough, such as the West Bronx or Pelham Parkway.

Each neighborhood had its stores, schools, synagogues, and churches. Immigrants often found a route to the middle class by owning a local store or business, a barber shop, a bakery, a tailor or butcher. Others traveled to the industrial areas of the Bronx or into Manhattan to find work. Significant loss of industrial jobs started in the 1930s with the Great Depression, but massive public building under President Roosevelt lessened the suffering. The Public Works Administration funded the construction of many of the other well-known features of the Bronx, including the Bronx County Building and the main post office, Orchard Beach, highways, and the Whitestone and Triborough (now Robert Kennedy) bridges. With the completion of the subway under the Grand Concourse in 1933, the design of the Bronx was largely set.

Eugene Oliva (called Gene), a family friend who grew up in an immigrant Italian family and had an exciting career in public relations, remembers his lively West Bronx neighborhood near Burnside Avenue in the 1930s and '40s when it was "primarily Jewish, Italian, and Irish." With great enthusiasm, he describes the joy he had playing sports, including parks-department-supported baseball:

> I had many friends, we all got along, and played lots of sports together—hockey in the street on roller skates, stick ball in the street, and, as we got older, on teams. One year, we won the baseball championship for the Bronx in the park where the new Yankee Stadium is now. Harrison Avenue with its apartment buildings and private houses was a good place to grow up.

In addition to recreational activities, Gene also had employment opportunities:

> About twenty of us worked as ushers at the beautiful Loew's Paradise Theatre. I loved watching the movies and memorized many of the lines.[20]

When Stan Freilich, a successful actuary, grew up in the 1940s, the Bronx was half Jewish. Stan's grandparents and his mother came to New York City in the early twentieth century when many Jews were fleeing persecution in Eastern Europe and Russia. As with many immigrants, the family was central and the living conditions overcrowded. Stan became a BronxWorks board member after he retired, in order to give back to the borough of his childhood:

> I lived with my parents, my sister, my grandfather, and my aunt in a two-bedroom, one-bath apartment. The apartment was crowded. People were all over me. My friends and I would play on fire escapes in order to have room to play. My extended family lived nearby. My family usually shopped right in the neighborhood, at the bakery, the fruit and vegetable market, the butcher, the fish store. There was a strong focus on family and one that I haven't felt since that time.

Stan received an excellent education from adequately funded schools. He particularly values the music lessons:

> Luckily my school had a special music program with a classically trained pianist and I learned to play the clarinet. I took the test and got into Bronx High School of Science. Science was mainly Jewish at the time, although a classmate was Stokely Carmichael, who later led the Student Nonviolent Coordinating Committee. My high school graduation was at Loew's Paradise Theatre, very grand.[21]

Joan Allen Canada's father, a craftsman who did needlework, was from the Caribbean and her mother was from the South. Like other families of that era living in overcrowded sections of Manhattan, they sought better housing in the Bronx. When the family moved to Reverend James A. Polite Avenue near Lyman Place in the Morrisania section, the area was a rare, stable integrated area for over a decade. It became a flourishing African American community, full of music blended from several cultures:

> We moved to the Bronx in 1945 looking for a better and larger place to live. We lived in a five-story walkup. Our tenement was directly across from a Jewish synagogue. I remember when we arrived in the Bronx, it was so bright. Also, the air seemed better. The synagogue was purchased and became our church.

In Joan's community, music and the arts were a very important part of children's experiences and led to rewarding careers:

> I was being trained by a man from the Metropolitan Opera House on piano, classical music. It was the culture, everyone had a musical instrument, a violin or piano. When you walked through the neighborhood you'd hear children practicing. As a child, Emilio Antonio Cruz, the abstract expressionism artist, lived next door. My brother, Leopold Allen, became Mikhail Baryshnikov's personal makeup artist at the American Ballet Theatre. My sister, Glenda Allen Hooker, became famous, sculpting miniature dolls. Later Elmo Hope, the great jazz musician and composer, lived nearby.[22]

As a young adult, Joan ran a shop on Boston Road that sold African American clothing and jewelry.

Like Joan Canada, Jacqueline Smith Bonneau remembers the music of Morrisania flowing out of apartments and churches. Her family had moved to Lyman Place in the early 1940s when she was a young girl. Her uncle Thelonious Monk, the famous jazz pianist and composer, stayed with her family for a few years.

> My parents listened to jazz, show tunes, classical, and religious music. And there was music in the street. I could hear it coming from other people's apartments because at that time we felt safe enough to leave our door open. [My uncle Thelonious] would go to Mr. Elmo's apartment and take turns playing the piano. Other musicians from the neighborhood would come by and jam with them. They'd sit there and listen and laugh with each other.[23]

Most of Joan Canada's family, like other middle-class families, moved out of the Bronx. In her case, they moved to California in the 1960s. Jacqueline Smith Bonneau's family moved from the area in 1965.

Gene Oliva had to return to his parents' house for several years after he graduated from college. Only when he received his master's degree and found a higher-paying job could he afford to move to his own apartment. As it is in most immigrant families, the support of the extended family was essential:

> After the Marines and college, I married and we lived with my parents in the house in order to save money. An aunt who was blind and confused lived with us. After our first two children were born, we moved in 1959 to a large apartment in Queens and had two more children. My parents sold the house and moved to an apartment near us.[24]

For Stan Freilich's family, again like many immigrants, upward mobility was the prized goal. For many families of his generation and the following ones, this meant moving out of the Bronx:

> The goal of everyone in the family was always to move up, educationally, but also to leave the Bronx and move to a better place. Parents would say, "You will do better than I did." Our parents did not want the children to run their businesses but rather insisted we go to college and be professional. The move had nothing to do with the Bronx changing, it was still the same as it had always been but we had a desire to move up.[25]

Within ten years after Stan moved out of the Bronx to finish college, the borough was in serious decline. By the late 1970s, much of the South Bronx had been destroyed by abandonment and fires. Over three hundred thousand people felt they had to flee.[26] Some blocks lost virtually all of their buildings.[27] The South Bronx became known throughout the world as the symbol of urban decay. Residents formed groups to fight the spreading destruction and to start to rebuild. Luckily the City, which had largely given up on the South Bronx, pulled out of recession and found the commitment and resources to fund reconstruction (the government of New York City, hereafter referred to as "the City," is headquartered in Lower Manhattan). The Bronx stabilized, rebuilt, and repopulated, returning to its historical roots as a place where low-income families and immigrants are welcome and can work toward their goals. Still, the resources that Gene, Stan, Joan, and Jacqueline had growing up are only slowly becoming more available to children in the South Bronx today. But now the residents may face a new threat: displacement.

LITERATURE REVIEW

For readers who are interested in a detailed history of the Bronx, there are three excellent books: *The Bronx* by Evelyn Gonzalez (2004), *South Bronx Rising* by Jill Jonnes (2002), and *Boulevard of Dreams* by Constance Rosenbaum (2009). The historian Lloyd Ultan has written nine books on the Bronx, including a comprehensive history, *The Northern Borough: A History of the Bronx* (2009). Robert Courtney Smith's *Mexican New York: Transnational Lives of New Immigrants* (2005) describes the lives of immigrants in New York from Puebla and their relationship to their hometown in Mexico; many of the Mexican Americans in the Bronx are from Puebla. Harry DeRienzo's *The Concept of Community: Lessons from the Bronx* (2008) discusses the decline and rebuilding of the South Bronx from the perspective of a community organizer and nonprofit housing developer.

Several books of oral histories have recently been published, including *Before the Fires: An Oral History of African American Life in the Bronx from the 1930s to the 1960s* (2016) by Mark Naison and Bob Gumbs, *Just Kids from the Bronx* (2015) by Arlene Alda, and *Bronx Faces and Voices* (2014) by Emita Brady Hill and Janet Butler Munch. Fordham University's Bronx African American History Project, now online, is an invaluable resource of over three hundred personal stories. Lehman College and the Bronx Historical Society have extensive resources.

Justice Sonia Sotomayor's autobiography, *My Beloved World* (2013), poignantly describes the challenges many Puerto Ricans faced during the time of her childhood. Books such as Allen Jones's *The Rat That Got Away* (2009, with Mark Naison), Adrian Nicole LeBlanc's *Random Family: Love, Drugs, Trouble, and Coming of Age in the Bronx* (2003), and Fernando Laspina's *Mis Memorias, Mis Raices* (2017) describe in dismaying detail the lives of Bronx people affected by the heroin epidemic and gangs.

Mel Rosenthal's documentary photographs from 1976–82, reproduced in the book *In the South Bronx of America* (2001) along with telling commentary, illustrate the spirit and courage of the people in a backdrop of poverty and devastation. *Jerome Ave* (2016), by the Bronx Photo League of the Bronx Documentary Center, is a collection of beautiful photographs and short narratives that describe the people who earn their living on Jerome Avenue (most of whom will be displaced with the rezoning plan described in chapter 8).

The short stories in Nicholas Mohr's *El Bronx Remembered* (1973) provide a glimpse into the day-to-day life of Puerto Ricans in the Bronx. *Bitter Bronx: Thirteen Stories* by Jerome Charyn (2015) offers fictional stories of people from the borough. The *Bronx Memoir Project* (2014) from the Bronx Writers Center of the Bronx Council on the Arts has short stories written by over fifty Bronxites.

Ladies and Gentlemen, The Bronx Is Burning (2005) by Jonathan Mahler describes what New York City was like in 1977, emphasizing the politics behind the fiscal crisis. Kim Phillips-Fein's *Fear City: New York's Fiscal Crisis and the Rise of Austerity Politics* (2017) explains how the financial austerity imposed by the Financial Control Board in the 1970s fundamentally altered the City's ability and willingness to pay for the social and human services that aided so many earlier generations. Carol Lamberg's *Neighborhood Success Stories: Creating and Sustaining Affordable Housing in New York City* (2018) describes her experiences as a nonprofit housing developer in the Bronx and in Manhattan. *The Poor among Us: A History of Family Poverty and Homelessness in New York City* by Ralph de Costa Nunez and Ethan G. Sribnick (2013) provides a broader context for understanding poverty in New York City.

Robert Caro's *The Power Broker: Robert Moses and the Fall of New York* (1975) has two chapters devoted to describing the destruction of neighborhoods caused by the construction of the Cross Bronx Expressway. *The Political Icon: José E. Serrano* by Carlos Velasquez (2007) has a detailed chapter on the environmental battles in Hunts Point and the restoration of the Bronx River. Jonathan Kozol's books, such as *Amazing Grace: The Lives of Children and the Conscience of America* (1995), describe his experiences and his views on education in poor areas of the Bronx. Dennis Smith's *Report from Engine Co. 82* (1972) relates experiences and perceptions of firemen in the South Bronx in what was the busiest firehouse in the United States at the time. Finally, many newspaper articles pose the issue of development and gentrification of the South Bronx.

ROAD MAP

This book begins in the "dark era" of the 1960s and '70s, when, indeed, the South Bronx was burning. In the midst of Game 2 of the 1977 World Series, with the Dodgers beating the Yankees, famed sportscaster Howard Cosell is widely (but perhaps incorrectly) quoted as saying, "There it is, ladies and gentlemen, the Bronx is burning."[28] The camera swept the horizon and smoke could be seen rising from what was later determined to be an empty school building. This was a few days after President Carter's visit to Charlotte Street. Newspapers throughout the country showed pictures of the president standing in a rubble-strewn lot, often compared to scenes from bombed-out Dresden, Germany, at the end of World War II. The Bronx's deplorable state became a fact known throughout much of the world.

Chapter 2 describes events that caused the South Bronx to become so poor. The South Bronx has carried the distinction of being the poorest congressional district in the United States for over thirty years. A great storm of factors—including massive construction projects that tore neighborhoods apart, the upward mobility of the once dominant Jewish population, the construction of many public housing projects, the GI Bill that made home ownership in the suburbs affordable, and fear of living among people who were seen as "the other"—led to rapid middle-class, primarily white, flight.

Most of the community's newer residents—Puerto Ricans, African Americans, and a relatively small number of immigrants—were very poor when they came, as were most of the immigrants before them. They discuss the reasons they came to New York City and the challenges they faced as they moved to the South Bronx. They tell of the loss of factory jobs, difficulties they had dealing with the school system, substandard housing, the lack of services, drugs, and overt racial discrimination. Despite these problems, they worked to build communities for themselves and their families. Many moved into the middle class—if not them, then their children. Others were pulled down by the lack of opportunity and by the drugs and crime.

Chapter 3 debunks the myth that poor people caused the destruction of the Bronx. Contrary to popular opinion, low-income African Americans and Puerto Ricans did not cause the decline but suffered greatly during those years. As an old ballad laments, "It's the same the whole world over, it's the poor what gets the blame." The devastating changes in the economics of residential real estate are examined, as are the management practices of disreputable landlords. Other factors, such as the "redlining" of most of the South Bronx by banks and insurance companies, contributed to the decline. The incidence and causes of arson are explored.

In chapter 4, we look at how the people of the South Bronx fought back in the 1960s and '70s to try to save and then to rebuild their neighborhoods. They protested and demonstrated against bad policies. They confronted banks and landlords. They forced the banks to stop redlining their communities and, instead, to reinvest in them. Residents advocated for the housing, hospitals, and other services needed. During the City's fiscal crisis and brush with bankruptcy, people rallied against disinvestment, such as hospital and firehouse closings, and the layoff of thousands of City workers. They fought for quality education for their children. Some squatted in abandoned buildings and started to rebuild. Residents organized tenant and neighborhood organizations. Organizations that served the prior population groups closed, and newer organizations gradually took their place. For example, CAB was formed to provide practical help to residents of the West Bronx. Our slogan was "Whatever your problem, we are here to help." Local community development agencies emerged to manage housing on a nonprofit basis. New art forms flourished, including some that expressed the harsh reality of young people's lives. Hip hop was born.

Chapter 5 describes the progress and setbacks of the 1980s. The fires finally stopped, but some people remained in dangerous housing situations. CAB helped senior citizens and others relocate. Housing affordability became an issue because residents' income from employment and public assistance did not keep pace with rapidly escalating rents. Family homelessness rose. Lawyers and social workers increased their advocacy. Housing conditions and availability started to improve as the City turned over buildings to nonprofits to manage. Community groups initiated projects to improve neighborhoods, such as community gardens and adoption of parks. The population started increasing, with large numbers of Latin American and West Indian immigrants moving into the Bronx. Bronx arts expanded and flourished as galleries opened. Hip hop put its stamp on the world's perception of the Bronx. CAB offered free legal services and English classes to immigrants. Crack and AIDS hit the Bronx very hard, causing more misery. CAB and other groups responded with social services and medical help. The Bronx was rocked but survived corruption scandals among some of its top political leaders. And finally, in 1986, Mayor Ed Koch published a ten-year, $5 billion plan to rehab and rebuild housing. The Bronx responded quickly with plans to secure its share of the funds.

Chapter 6 describes the 1990s, which saw a decline in crime and the intense rebuilding of neighborhoods. Community members continued the fight for educational equity. More immigrants settled in the Bronx, both documented and undocumented. West African immigration grew rapidly. Residents put the brakes on one large housing development until they had a significant voice in the design. Despite all the new housing, homelessness remained a problem and more services and shelters were provided. The City's decision to contract out human services that it had been providing directly became the base for future high-quality, community-based programs. The social service infrastructure in the Bronx strengthened but still lagged in resources compared to other parts of the city. CAB became a major provider of senior centers and other programs for the elderly. Through a merger with another agency, CAB was able to expand its services for children and youths. Residents worked on issues of environmental justice, forcing the City to stop using the Bronx as a dumping ground. By 1997, enough progress was made in enough areas that the Bronx was able to win the All-America City Award of the National Civic League.

Chapter 7 describes how the environmental movement has gained strength as residents worked for green space and access to waterways in the early twenty-first century. As big commercial projects were approved by City officials, groups tried to negotiate community benefits agreements. The human services infrastructure expanded significantly, much as housing construction did in the 1990s, providing residents with more resources. New child-care and after-school programs, as well as new high schools, provide expanded educational opportunities to young people. Welfare reform, passed several years earlier, placed an increased emphasis on employment services and financial work supports. As homelessness continued to increase citywide, CAB expanded its services and was able to dramatically decrease the number of people living on the streets. CAB changed its name to BronxWorks to reflect its expanded programs. Reacting to the epidemic of obesity and diabetes, interest in healthy eating and active lifestyles increased.

Chapter 8 looks to the future. The landscape of the Bronx is rapidly changing—will the borough be gentrified and thousands of poor people displaced? The City is investing billions in affordable housing, much of it in the Bronx.[29] Community groups are working feverishly to prevent displacement of current residents by providing more legal protections. Some advocate to ensure that more of the "affordable" housing being built will be truly affordable to current residents. It is unclear to what extent they will succeed. Others are suggesting innovative housing models. Some experts fear that real estate speculation is becoming overheated and will cause a new round of neglect. Can resources that are likely to accompany development projects help low-income residents move out of poverty more quickly? The Bronx's large immigrant communities are worried about rising anti-immigrant policies throughout the country, although New York City is very strong in support of these new Americans.

Chapter 9 provides a summary of my perspective and of the book's major points. It also describes the work musicians and artists are doing to preserve the Bronx's Puerto Rican and African American heritage while they continue to incorporate new influences.

Carmen Cordova, a close friend, came to the Bronx with her parents and sister when she was very young. Her family was typical of the thousands who fled the poverty of Puerto Rico to start anew in New York in the late 1940s and early '50s:

> At that time, the husband would come ahead and save enough money to send for the rest of the family. My family settled in the Bronx in 1952. Before airplanes, people migrated by ship, the *Marine Tiger*, the banana boat. Later people came on the airplane. Family on both sides came, they would say, "Oh it is working out, you can come." My father was very frugal, and it was only a few months until he brought my mother, my sister, and me.[30]

2 How the South Bronx Became the Poorest Congressional District

Upon moving to the Bronx in 1968 and taking an urgently needed job with the welfare department, my first client was a reserved, elderly African American woman. She lived in a fourth-floor walk-up apartment on Union Avenue. It was a rough area, but no one ever bothered me when I climbed all those stairs in that tired building to visit her. She, however, having arthritis, being a bit overweight, and using a cane, had a great deal of trouble managing the climb. I worried if she would be able to evacuate quickly in an emergency, such as a fire. The astounding thing about her apartment was the number of roaches. Her walls were crawling with dozens of them. Her kitchen table was covered with cans of spray and the air was heavy with the smell. The apartment was not dirty, nor was there food around. The roaches must have come from other apartments. We battled a lot of roaches where I lived, but the problem was minor compared to what that poor woman lived with. I don't know how she breathed. I felt that if she had to live in these conditions, I could surely visit her for an hour every few months to make sure she was getting her benefits.

Such was the reality of living in the Bronx during that period, when a stark landscape of poverty was settling in on its inhabitants. In fact, the South Bronx was well on its way to becoming the poorest congressional district in America, an unfortunate status that arrived twelve years later, in 1980, when the population had shrunk so much as a result of building abandonment that two congressional districts had to be combined to meet the mandated population requirement.

Sometimes the abandoned buildings were left standing, the glass in the windows broken, the front doors open, garbage abounding. Other times, especially if there had been a fire, the structure was knocked down, leaving a useless rubble-filled lot, which was not good for playing ball or making a community garden, just a home for rats as the garbage increased with time. Other buildings were still occupied, perhaps with some upper-floor apartments vacant because of fire, the black stains still on the outside walls, the windows knocked out, derelict cars parked in front, their windshield wipers filled with parking tickets, the wheels and battery gone. The cars were likely to have been stolen, stripped of certain parts, and left to be towed away months or years later by the sanitation department. Fire hydrants spilled water into the street and were likely to run for weeks. Stray dogs and cats scavenged for food. Young men stood on corners, engaged in some aspect of the drug trade. Some blocks were better, some worse.

My first job with the welfare department presented certain challenges. It had two main responsibilities, each in conflict with the other. One was to determine whether the person was eligible to receive public assistance benefits. Caseworkers had to visit people within a few days of their application, get them emergency assistance if needed, and determine their eligibility for public assistance. With ongoing cases, we had to visit every few months to recertify their eligibility. Many welfare clients referred to the case managers by their previous title, investigator. Did the person really live there, was she paying her rent, may I see the rent receipts please? Were the children really hers, birth certificates and school records please? Were the utilities paid, Con Ed receipts please? Are you able to work, are you trying to find a job? Other case managers took the investigator role further and looked under beds and in closets (no asking "please" about those searches) to see if there was any sign of a man living in the household, which would likely make the family ineligible. We helped families avoid crises, such as evictions, added babies to the budget once the birth was verified, and helped process changes of address.

The other expectation of the job, conflicting with the first, was that the case manager should help the family with other issues they were having, but generally both trust and resources to do so were lacking. The recipient saw the case manager as an investigator, not someone to trust with personal problems. Many of the case managers, like me, were very young, not even able to offer much advice from life experience. We could, at times, get approval for special grants for the family, and this was one way our idealism could be fulfilled, giving money to needy people. (Studies later showed that an effective way to reduce poverty is simply to give people money. A pilot antipoverty project that BronxWorks undertook with the Bloomberg administration confirmed that when families had more money they spent it wisely, they ate better, and their stress levels were lessened.)[1]

The caseload in the late 1960s was rapidly increasing, as more poor people moved to the Bronx, displaced by urban renewal in other areas and the availability of apartments for rent within the allowable welfare rent levels. Others lost their jobs in factories as entry-level employment dried up. Our caseloads surpassed the union-approved maximum and continued to climb. The welfare rights movement was in full swing. Bomb threats frequently forced us to evacuate the office and wait on the sidewalk until the police gave us the all clear.

I met my friend Carmen Cordova at the welfare department. She worked as an assistant to the director. Her relative Bacha was the babysitter for my two sons, a life saver for me. Carmen's daughters and children of her relatives spent many years with my sons at Bacha's.

After three years with the welfare department, my last assignment before I went to graduate school was to help prepare the case records of those deemed the "worthier poor"—senior citizens, people who were elderly, disabled, or blind—for transfer out of the welfare system and into the Social Security system. Thereafter, these recipients (including my elderly client with the roaches) would no longer carry the stigma of being on welfare; instead they would receive Supplemental Security Income (SSI), meet with workers at Social Security offices, and not have their privacy invaded with home visits. Since its founding, America has been trying to figure out who are the "worthy poor," how they should be helped, and what should be done with those deemed less worthy.

After I left, the welfare department went through other changes, primarily to separate the role of determining eligibility and that of providing case management assistance. Over the years, generic case management faded away. Specialized case management services were enhanced in the child welfare system, adult protective services, homeless services, and contracted employment services.

The leader of the welfare rights movement in the Bronx, with whom I had become friendly, wrote one of my references for graduate school. I applied to only one school, Columbia University School of Social Work, which awarded me a full scholarship. Afterward, I worked in a senior citizen center located in a synagogue that was later demolished. It was one of over 270 synagogues in the South Bronx that closed as the demographics in the South Bronx changed, from primarily Jewish to Puerto Rican and African American. Next, I worked for an agency that provided weekly outings for blind senior citizens. The seniors insisted on knowing my ethnicity. In New York, apparently, everyone had to have an ethnic identity, something I was unfamiliar with.

CITIZENS ADVICE BUREAU: WHATEVER YOUR PROBLEM,
WE ARE HERE TO HELP

In March 1979, I assumed the position of executive director of Citizens Advice Bureau (CAB), a small nonprofit agency, which over the years would grow much larger; it changed its name to BronxWorks in 2009 (throughout this book, I use the name CAB when referring to the years prior to the name change). This was an identity I would carry for the next thirty-four years. I had no idea where the agency was going when I arrived, nor did I have any grand plans for its growth. I saw what was in front of me and took one step at a time, always trying to do the right thing. I didn't know I would be working during such crucial times of great change.

CAB had rented a large front room in a cavernous old building on the Grand Concourse that had been the main Elks Club location in the Bronx.

Like many institutions at that time, it had just changed hands and was now an African American Masonic Lodge.

The Grand Concourse, the boulevard that runs north and south in the West Bronx—with its Art Deco apartment buildings with large rooms, elevators, sunken living rooms, and stately lobbies—was definitely starting to feel the strain of the decline occurring in other parts of the Bronx. The West Bronx had not yet deteriorated to the point when it would be reclassified as part of the South Bronx, the ghetto immortalized in the public media. That happened a few years later. But the area had changed, as most white people had left for the suburbs, leaving behind some elderly whites who lacked the inclination, family assistance, or money to move out. For the first time in the Bronx's history, Hispanics and African Americans were allowed to rent apartments on or near the Concourse. Previously, discriminatory practices had ensured they were confined to areas with less desirable housing.

The CAB office employed one other staff person besides me and two trainees. The concept of the service was very simple and practical: open the doors each morning, let people tell you their problems, and then do what you can to resolve them. Our motto was "Whatever your problem, we are here to help." People with low incomes, mostly Jewish senior citizens, Puerto Ricans, and African Americans, brought us their severe housing and income problems.

The office was ideal in some ways and certainly challenging in others. Being located on a major corner, in a first-floor room with large windows facing the Grand Concourse, provided excellent visibility and accessibility. Although electric typewriters came in a few years, the Wite-Out and eraser tape didn't work well when typing though several layers of carbon paper. The mimeograph machine was a pain. When we later bought a Xerox machine, it broke frequently. But most challenging of all, there was only one, very old, bathroom. Located across the large, unheated "grand ballroom," it was used not only by our staff and clients, but also by party attendees who rented the ballroom on weekends. We dreaded seeing what it would look like on Monday morning after a rental. And, inexplicably, the toilet often flushed hot water.

I guess I may not have been sufficiently tuned in to the staff's needs in the early years. Mary Sheehan, a young social worker who had done her fieldwork internship with me when she was a graduate student, joined the staff as assistant director for a few years. She was both caring and competent. She remembers:

> The staff appointed me to get you to agree to get us a water cooler. It took some work. You had reservations—the expense and concern that roaches would infest it—but I finally prevailed. I also persuaded you to close the office for half a day on Friday so that we could clean up. Then I got you to agree to get an exterminator service. You were always putting the needs of the clients first but you listened to me. I liked systems and was able to bring order and sanity to the office. But your commitment to the clients was key to the success of the agency.[2]

Our clients' housing problems included lack of heat and hot water, lack of ability to pay the rent, disputes with landlords as to whether or not the rent had been paid, and questions about the legality of rent increases. Clearly landlords were neglecting their buildings. Often it was hard to figure out who the landlord was or how to reach him. Especially for some older tenants, frightened and in despair as their buildings declined further and were abandoned by the landlords, the need was for emergency relocation, a move to a safer, habitable apartment.

Kathryn Speller worked as an administrative assistant at Community Board 5 in the Bronx in the early 1980s. Community boards were set up to give community residents a voice in local government decisions. Ms. Speller recalls:

> During the years I worked for the community board, CAB was the place I called when a senior needed help. This was when the area was getting bad. The district manager would tell me to "call Carolyn" when we had a bad situation. I particularly remember a call from a man who was hysterical because his wife was very ill and needed home care. The home care worker wouldn't enter the building because it was in such bad condition. He said they would just lie down in bed and die. I was relieved when you called to tell me you were able to get them rehoused. I feel the shopping trips CAB arranged for the seniors were a wonderful help when people were afraid to go shopping on their own and there were no good grocery stores in the area.[3]

The income problems we helped residents with often had to do with welfare cases being closed, leaving the family in crisis without any money.

Lack of public assistance left families at immediate risk of homelessness and food crisis. We called, wrote letters, advocated, and found help for the family. In the words of Mary Sheehan:

> Housing, housing court, and food referrals. Not much domestic violence came to us. People were hungry and that amazed me. They didn't have heat—food and shelter were the two main issues. The office was always packed with people needing help. I was shocked about the food referrals most of all—that people would go hungry in the United States. I think I felt helpless with the severity of the problems we dealt with every day and probably could not handle the sadness, particularly the young mothers and children. I believe you never gave up hope about solving those problems.[4]

FACTORS THAT SHAPED THE SOUTH BRONX

Changes to the built environment in the South Bronx during the 1950s and '60s caused hardship during the time of construction and, in the case of the highways, still have harmful effects to this day. Much of it was due to Robert Moses, the master builder who reshaped New York City during five mayoral administrations from 1924 to 1968. Sections of the Bronx were destroyed to benefit other parts of the greater metropolitan area. Unquestionably, Moses did much good for New York in setting aside large tracts of land for parks on Long Island and in Upstate New York. He oversaw the 1937 construction of Orchard Beach in the Bronx, a heavily used and much-loved beach in Pelham Bay Park. But overall, he ran roughshod over the interests of the Bronx.

Lots of Public Housing

The South Bronx was simultaneously blessed and bedeviled by one of the largest concentrations of public housing in the country. While the New York City Housing Authority (NYCHA) built public housing throughout the city from the 1930s to the '60s, the South Bronx received a disproportionate share. In the '50s, five large projects consisting of ninety-six tall buildings were constructed with a total of 12,486 apartments, much of it under the direction of Robert Moses.[5] Neighborhoods were destroyed and residents uprooted to make room for the new housing. The projects were initially designated as either middle income or low income, an example of how government policy supported segregation.[6] Four of the five in the South Bronx were low income, targeted to blacks and Hispanics. Middle-income projects were largely for whites. Despite promises, the families displaced by the construction of urban renewal projects were rarely offered an opportunity to move into the new units. Too many people were being displaced, there was no good way of tracking them, and other people were already on waiting lists. Generally, families were left on their own to squeeze into some overcrowded housing elsewhere.[7]

The tall project buildings changed the character of the area and made it less neighborly—no more front stairs to sit on while chatting with friends, little ability to call out the window to a child or neighbor passing by, limited or no capacity to influence the city to allow one's relatives to move in next door. There were fewer local stores and a loss of small-business opportunities.[8] But for the families who moved in, it was good-quality housing, better than what they had lived in before. New schools were built. A sense of community often developed, and in the early years, people of varied racial and ethnic backgrounds appreciated the opportunity to live in stable, decent, affordable housing.

John Sanchez had a long career as a professional social worker, including serving as the executive director at Catholic Big Brothers and later at East Side House Settlement. His family lived in the Mott Haven section of the Bronx and moved into the projects in the East Bronx area called Throgs Neck when John was in fourth grade:

> You know how you had a big celebration when you got your first TV. We had a big celebration when we got accepted to public housing. It was a step up. Living in public housing was a tremendous boost to our chances of making it. We got to live in a better community and in better housing. NYCHA had a big role in improving the lives of many people.[9]

Dorothy Howell, always welcoming, well dressed, and articulate at age ninety-one, feels fortunate to have lived in public housing for most of her adult life. She was one of the first African Americans in St. Mary's housing in Mott Haven:

St. Mary's was a middle-income public housing project, very hard to get into. I even had to get a letter from my children's school about their behavior in school. The area was primarily Jewish when I moved in, although some of the stores were Italian. The schools were pretty good. The projects were beautiful, dogs were not allowed. They have great views of the water and the Empire State Building. It was like a private condominium.[10]

Gladys Echevarria, age seventy-nine, also lives in public housing, in the E. Roberts Moore houses. She remembers the high standards, the welcome diversity, and some ethnic rivalry:

When I moved in 1967, there were only two Spanish families. The rest were Jewish, Irish, Czech, and Chinese. The children were not allowed to play on the grass. We kept our children primarily in the apartment. Parents would get a note if their children were hanging around. When my daughter was in high school, I had to be sure to pick her up every day at three because there were fights between the Italians and the Spanish, not really gangs, just kids fighting.[11]

The Archibald family moved to the Patterson Houses in 1950. The family had been living in one room in the grandmother's apartment. Victoria Archibald, the sister of NBA star Nate "Tiny" Archibald, remembers aspects of her childhood in the projects:

The saying "It takes a village to raise a child"—it was absolutely true in the Patterson Houses. They didn't hesitate to speak to you about dropping garbage in the hallway or talking too loud. All a neighbor had to do was say, "Don't let me tell your mother."[12]

Bobby Sanabria, a well-known Latin jazz percussionist, composer, and bandleader, grew up in the Melrose projects in the late '50s and '60s. He recalls:

Before drugs people knew each other. The Rodríguez family lives here, the Sanabrias live on the twelfth floor. Knock on their door if you need some sugar. There was a real sense of community. I remember hearing Yiddish, Italian, Spanish of course, and the sound of African Americans speaking in the southern drawl. We played the street games of the day—skellzies, Johnny-on-the-pony, ringolevio, Chinese box ball, stick ball, stoop ball, marbles, etc. We all watched girls doing double Dutch.[13]

With upward mobility and incentives to move to the suburbs, more white families, who represented the majority of the middle class at the time, started moving out of the southern part of the Bronx in the '50s, including the public housing projects.

Neighborhoods Sliced and Diced

Robert Moses allowed little input from residents into decisions that would have profound effects on their lives. He didn't subscribe to the concept that the built environment should foster a sense of community. Forced through by Moses, who favored highways over public transportation, the construction of four major expressways—Major Deegan (completed in 1956), Sheridan (1963), Cross Bronx (1963), and Bruckner (1973)—and three major bridges—Triborough (1936, renamed Robert F. Kennedy in 2008), Bronx-Whitestone (1939), and Throgs Neck (1961)—contributed greatly to the decline of the South Bronx. Major highways and the access roads for the huge new bridges to Queens and Manhattan cut up neighborhoods. As apartment buildings, homes, and businesses were torn down to make space for these massive projects, thousands of people were displaced and vast areas were left in shambles during construction. The displaced families were promised that they would be rehoused, but this promise was almost never fulfilled. As a result, families were forced to jam into existing housing, causing already overcrowded conditions to worsen.[14]

In addition to destroying existing neighborhoods, the highways hurt in other ways. They hastened the development of the suburbs, as did the GI Bill, which gave World War II veterans low-cost mortgages with little or no down payments. Middle-income residents left cities throughout America. From the Bronx, families bought houses in nearby suburban areas of Westchester, New Jersey, and Long Island. Many Bronxites felt that their borough became a place for others to drive through, traveling from Westchester to Manhattan, from New England to New Jersey, and from New Jersey to Long Island. With the traffic came lots of pollution—and little else.

The most egregious Moses project was the construction of the Cross Bronx Expressway. Its purpose was to link the George Washington Bridge to the Bronx-Whitestone and Throgs Neck bridges (which lead to Queens and the rest of Long Island) and also to the New England Thruway. To do so, the seven-mile highway bisected the Bronx, displacing two thousand families and eight hundred businesses and destroying stable, primarily Jewish, neighborhoods. Groups of residents fought hard to have their neighborhoods spared but lost to the implacable Moses. The emptying of buildings, the blasting through bedrock, the noise and dirt, went on for fifteen years, from 1948 to 1963. The expressway aided interstate transportation and the growth of the suburbs at the expense of the Bronx. That legacy continues as the pollution from this heavily traveled road contaminates the center of the Bronx.[15] The Cross Bronx Expressway was named the most congested highway in the United States in 2016.[16]

Co-op City and Rapid Population Changes

Another Moses project was America's largest cooperative housing complex, consisting of thirty-five high-rise buildings, constructed in the North Bronx in the late 1960s and early '70s.[17] Co-op City, boasting over fifteen thousand brand-new apartments at a reasonable monthly fee with utilities included, finalized the exodus of thousands of middle-class families from the South and West Bronx. The effect of its opening was often described as "sucking the middle class out of the [rest of the] Bronx." Some residents who moved to Co-op City sought to escape encroaching poverty and its problems. For many others, it was a simple economic decision.

Elba Cabrera, a lifelong Bronx resident and community leader now in her eighties, made her notable career in arts and education. She is honored frequently by Bronx institutions as one of "Las Tres Hermanas" with her sisters, Evelina López Antonetty, the founder of United Bronx Parents, and Lillian López, the first Puerto Rican administrator in the New York Public Library system. Elba describes her family's decision to move to Co-op City from public housing:

> We went to Co-op City when it opened. It made economic sense. We were paying $90 for the projects, and because I was working part time, our rent was going up. We had a two-bedroom apartment with two sons. In Co-op City, we paid $157 for three bedrooms, one and a half baths, with light and gas and air conditioning included. A lot of our friends from the projects moved too.[18]

Meanwhile, the dominant population in the Bronx, the Jewish population, was ready for its next step up—to Riverdale (the wealthy section of the Bronx), to upscale areas of Manhattan, to the suburbs, or to Co-op City. Living on or near the Grand Concourse may have fulfilled the dreams of people who were young adults in the 1930s and '40s, but their children, who came of age in the '50s and '60s, wanted more. It was always assumed that they would move somewhere "better."

But once African Americans and Puerto Ricans starting moving into the Bronx in significant numbers, many of the whites felt an urgency to move quickly, as though it would be thought that something was wrong with them, that they would be stigmatized, if they stayed once the neighborhood had changed. Many neighborhoods changed populations very rapidly. A building I lived in had a 100 percent turnover in tenants within one year, even though many of the Irish families living in it couldn't really afford to move.

Middle-income Puerto Ricans and African Americans, previously denied access to good housing, rented apartments and bought houses vacated by Jews, Italians, and Irish. They were followed by lower-income Latinos and African Americans, including a disproportionate number of people on welfare. I remember that most of our clients who were on welfare lived in apartments whose rents matched the maximum amount welfare would pay.

William (Bill) Frey, a graduate of Fordham University, worked for the Northwest Bronx Community and Clergy Coalition (NWBCCC) at its founding in 1974. Bill is now the senior director of Enterprise Community Partners, which works to create low-income and affordable housing. He discusses the very rapid increase of the people on welfare in the Bronx:

> Some owners recruited people on public assistance as tenants because at that time welfare was paying more than the market rent. They decreased services to scare longer-term tenants out so they could re-rent the apartments at a higher amount to people on welfare.[19]

Thus, the South Bronx became an area where large numbers of poor people and people of color lived.

By 1970, the fires started. Just as many factors coalesced to make the South Bronx the poorest urban area in the United States, many factors converged to cause the fires that in some neighborhoods burned down the majority of the apartment buildings. The poverty and the fires were related, but they were not a single phenomenon. There is very little, if any, evidence that people who were poor caused the fires or the building abandonment. Poor people had been moving to the Bronx for a hundred years, and those families often joined the middle class in less than a generation.

What was different this time was that as large numbers of Puerto Ricans and increasing numbers of African Americans moved to the South Bronx, they were hit with rapid loss of entry-level jobs, a collapsing New York City economy, an aging housing stock, racial discrimination, disinvestment, and an influx of illegal drugs. The South Bronx's dramatic decline took a toll on families, although many of the new residents (or their children) did eventually manage to progress economically.

AS IN THE PAST, PEOPLE CAME SEEKING OPPORTUNITY

In the twenty years following World War II, a million people fled the harsh poverty of Puerto Rico to come to the mainland. Some had worked in agriculture, cutting sugarcane or picking coffee or tobacco. Others had toiled in factories. Many had been unemployed, hampered by low levels of literacy and a dismal economy. Puerto Ricans were American citizens as declared in the Jones Act of 1917, but comparatively few had migrated before the war. The postwar availability of cheap airfare made the trip possible for tens of thousands. Most settled in New York City, in East Harlem in Manhattan and the neighborhoods of the South Bronx.[20]

Eric Soto spent much of his childhood and most of his career working in the Bronx. Educated primarily in the Bronx, he then attended Harvard University and afterwards worked as a street banker for Chemical Bank. The bank, at the urging of Mayor John Lindsay after the riots of the 1968 blackout, created an urban affairs department to reach out to community organizations and leaders in intercity neighborhoods. As a street banker, Eric provided grants to nonprofits, including CAB, as well as encouraging groups and individuals to establish banking relationships. Eric has been the director of Bronx Public Affairs for Con Edison for many years. He sums up the economic impetus for the Puerto Rican migration:

Most Puerto Ricans who left Puerto Rico were poor, not like the Cubans. The Puerto Rican rural populations were pushed into the cities as conglomerates took over the small farms and farm work was done by machines, not people. There were no jobs in the cities, so people came to New York.[21]

My friend Carmen Cordova interviewed her mother, Santa Garcia, at the of age eighty-seven in Fajardo, Puerto Rico, about the family's migration to the Bronx. Carmen summarizes:

> My parents, my sister, and I were born in Puerto Rico. We came to New York as part of a big migration from Puerto Rico to the U.S. in the 1940s and 1950s. People couldn't get jobs. My father was taken out of school when he was in the second grade to work in the sugarcane fields, and my mother was taken out of school in the third grade.[22]

From 1915 to 1970, six million African Americans left the poverty, discrimination, and humiliation of the South in hopes of finding work for decent pay, education, and a measure of respect and fairness in the Northeast and Midwest. The Great Migration was hastened by the exploitation inherent in the South's sharecropping system and the availability of factory work in the North. More settled in NYC than in any other city.[23] Currently, over six hundred thousand people of African ancestry call the Bronx home.[24] Kathryn Speller's family was among the early migrants:

> My mother, Pearl Stewart, was born in 1912 in South Carolina. She came north with her family in 1925. My mother's father worked building roads and followed the work north. Unfortunately, he was killed when hot asphalt from the back of a dump truck spilled on him. His brother who worked building railroads was also killed at work when a crane fell on him. I was born in 1932 on Welfare Island, now called Roosevelt Island. My mom and I lived in Harlem before I moved to the Bronx.[25]

Sallie Smith is an active, well-informed, longtime homeowner in the West Bronx. She has been a supporter of BronxWorks for forty years and now attends a BronxWorks senior citizen center. Her family was also part of the Great Migration:

> I was born in 1937 in North Carolina, one of eight children. Everything was very segregated. My father was a sharecropper. He knew education was important and wanted a better life for his children. In North Carolina, seventh

grade was as high as school went when my father attended school. Then the only option was college. We migrated north one at a time. I came second and worked as a live-in governess. I then helped my siblings come. Everyone in the family was able to get some form of higher education. Our family instilled in each of us a good work ethic, honesty, and respect for others.[26]

ENCOUNTERING BARRIERS

The Burden of Discrimination

Life for the new residents was not easy. Although they were not immigrants, they faced the myriad challenges that earlier immigrants in the Bronx had faced. Certainly Jews, Irish, and Italians faced serious hardships caused by discrimination. But African Americans and Puerto Ricans faced a more virulent and enduring form of discrimination, based on their skin color. Discrimination greatly limited opportunities for employment, housing, and education, making the move into the middle class much harder than it had been for previous groups of Bronxites. Kathryn Speller describes her mother's difficult work situation:

> The discrimination we faced was in Harlem as well as in the Bronx. We could shop on 125th Street but not work here. We couldn't go to major movie theaters or eat at restaurants. Because of discrimination against African Americans, the only work my mother could get was cleaning houses. My mother had to enter the house or apartment she worked in through the service entrance. African Americans were not allowed to use the front door. My mother always left the house dressed in a hat and gloves—you wouldn't know she was going to clean houses. It pained me seeing her on her knees scrubbing floors.[27]

Avis Hanson, an educator who taught in several Bronx high schools, came to the Bronx from Harlem as a child in 1930. In an interview with Mark Naison of the Bronx African American History Project, she describes what she calls the "Bronx Slave Market" that women like Kathryn Speller's mother had to participate in. Women would gather in certain places, often close to a subway:

> The women would sit on milk crates. Whoever needed a day maid would come by, pick up somebody, and take her for a price.[28]

Sallie Smith's story also underlines the role discrimination played in the lives of African Americans:

> My husband, James Smith, was a jazz musician but he stopped playing because of discrimination. [Because he was black] it was too hard for him to travel out of New York to give concerts. He became a full-time college student and when he graduated, he worked for the NYC Department of Social Services. I worked at various jobs to support my children after my husband died. I had mortgages to pay. I worked at a consulting firm, as a cosmetologist, a domestic, at a catering service.[29]

A group of Puerto Rican women in the South Bronx, whom I spoke to at a senior center, claim that Puerto Ricans were the pioneers for the other Hispanic populations that came later—Dominicans, Mexicans, and Central Americans:

> We opened the door for them. We didn't have it easy. There was no one who spoke Spanish at hospitals, schools, we had to bring an interpreter. We took the brunt of the discrimination.
>
> It was a curse to be Puerto Rican. People were horrible. It is not so bad anymore. Now people come to the Bronx from all over the world and there are other people to blame for problems.[30]

Of course, racial discrimination was not unique to the Bronx or to New York City. Throughout the United States, even the government fostered discrimination. Eligibility for Social Security was set up so that it excluded domestic and farm workers, often the only jobs people of color could get. Low-income housing projects were often placed next to highways, isolating the residents and exposing them to polluted air. Policies made it difficult for African Americans to get federally backed home mortgages, home ownership being a key to building wealth. Low-income areas typically get fewer government services, ranging from sanitation pickups to nice parks to new public buildings.

A 2018 study of twenty million children, based on census data, illustrates the damaging effect of racial discrimination on black boys. The study was conducted by researchers from Stanford, Harvard, and the U.S. Census Bureau and controlled for factors such as family income and wealth, family structure, and parents' education. When they grew up and were in their thirties, these black men earned considerably less than their white counterparts. Even among those who grew up wealthy, more ended up poor than stayed wealthy. Many fewer black boys who were raised poor advanced to middle or upper income levels than was the case among comparatively situated white boys.[31]

Lack of Decent Housing

The difficulty of finding decent housing was an ongoing struggle that lasted for years. Carmen Cordova's family moved every few years, each time to slightly better but still very substandard housing:

> The first place we lived in when we arrived in the Bronx was St. Ann's Avenue. Like most of the people who migrated from Puerto Rico, we first lived in a furnished room. The apartment owners would have an apartment and rent out individual furnished rooms. The apartment was like a railroad car, so besides the shared kitchens and baths, people would have to walk through other people's rooms to get to the kitchen or bathroom or exit door. Back in Puerto Rico, my sister and I were used to running around in the open country and now we had to stay quiet and be confined in a single room.

Carmen describes the next steps of their housing journey, each one a slight improvement made possible by hard work and frugality:

> We were not at St. Ann's Avenue for too long. In 1953, we moved to Claremont Parkway off Webster Avenue, into a basement apartment in a five-story apartment building. Three families, my grandparents, my aunts and uncles, my parents, and a cousin shared that basement apartment. This was quite an improvement from being cramped in one tiny room. This area was mainly Latino and African American.
>
> The next apartment we lived in was a "real apartment" on Brook Avenue, shared with our grandparents. There were African Americans, whites, and Latinos living in the building. The problem with this apartment was we did not have heat, nor hot water, most of the time. My parents always paid the rent on time, regardless of the lack of services. I am not exaggerating, the rats were the size of cats, and the apartment was infested with roaches. The ceiling would collapse in the bathroom, so we couldn't use the bathtub. We used steel tubs and would heat up the water to bathe in the kitchen. The

Carmen Cordova with her husband, Alfonso. Carmen's family
came to the Bronx from Puerto Rico when Carmen was a young
girl. With both parents working in factories, the family was able to
slowly improve their housing situation. Carmen found a route to
the middle class through civil service employment. Photo courtesy
of Carmen Cordova.

conditions were deplorable, but regardless of how bad it was in New York, it
was still better than back home in Puerto Rico. I remember in the winter
there would be vapor coming out of our mouths—that was how cold it was.
We would dress under the bedcovers.[32]

For African Americans, the search for housing was very difficult. Howie
Evans, a sportswriter for the *Amsterdam News* and a basketball coach, in
an interview with the Bronx African American History Project, describes
how he lived in several different buildings growing up, but always in the
basement. One area of the South Bronx he describes living in was 99 percent Jewish, with a few Italians and nine black families. The few other
black families in his neighborhood also lived in basements. One of the few
ways African Americans could get housing in a "good" area was to work as
the "super" of a building. He felt there were so few black families that they
were not a threat to the whites.[33]

The Hanson family was also able to find a place in the Bronx. They rented from the Jacob sisters, who surprisingly had a large sign on their building that said "We accept select colored tenants." Avis Hanson, then a young girl, asked her father, "Are we select colored tenants?" And he responded, "My child, we are select people."[34]

Elba Cabrera remembers trying to find an apartment when she was newly married:

> When my husband and I tried to get an apartment in the same area where my mother and sister lived, they wouldn't rent to us because they didn't want Puerto Ricans. My mother was very light skinned and Evelina looked Italian and I think that is why they could rent in that area. We had to live with my husband's parents for a year.[35]

Michael Seltzer, a leader in the field of human services and a Distinguished Lecturer at Baruch College, did not follow in his father's real estate footsteps. His father and uncle owned two apartment buildings in the Bronx. Michael explains that he found out his father was discriminating:

> In my teenage years, I learned about some of the uglier aspects of the Bronx real estate industry. My father and uncle used brokers to screen out any nonwhite renters. In retrospect, the practice was akin to an unspoken form of apartheid. There was an unwritten and unspoken conspiracy in the Bronx among landlords to keep out blacks and Hispanics.
>
> With the white migration to Co-op City from 1968 to 1973, the introduction of Section 8 housing in 1974, and the ensuing white flight from the south and central Bronx, fewer whites were interested in renting apartments in the central Bronx. As a result, the Seltzer brothers partially relented from their race ban and started to rent to black policemen.[36]

Entry-Level Jobs Disappear

From 1947 to 1976, at the height of the Puerto Rican and African American migrations to New York, the city lost five hundred thousand factory jobs, jobs that the relatively unskilled residents desperately needed.[37] Factories automated and moved to the southern states, where the lack of unions allowed the companies to pay lower wages and earn higher profits. Sometimes people were able to transition to other jobs. Others had to go on welfare.

Women I spoke with at senior centers also talked about the factory work and the factory closings:

> I made belts on 22nd Street for twenty years until the factory closed.
>
> I worked making garter belts at a factory on Fifth Avenue and 33rd Street for thirty-three years. I lost the job when the factory closed.
>
> I worked for a short while on 28th Street sewing colored stones onto clothing. Then the factory closed. I got divorced and had to go on welfare for a while.[38]

Isabel Butos, now an active senior citizen, talked more in depth about the factory closings and the potentially deadly health risks workers had to take if they were to keep their jobs:

> My husband worked in a metal factory in Queens. Many of the people who worked there died of cancer. He worked there another two years after people started getting sick. He was very sick for two years after they closed the factory. He got cancer from asbestos. He died in 1990 at age fifty-nine. We didn't know anything and never got anything, insurance, anything.[39]

Plumbers, electricians, and masons can earn a good living without a college degree. But prized union membership in high-paying construction and other trades, a key to a middle-class income for many white ethnic groups, was generally closed to minorities. Over the years at CAB, as we helped people find employment, we could never figure out how to get people into the trade unions.

One of the important career paths that was open to people of color was civil service. Historically, these government jobs, with stable employment and good benefits, offered an important path out of poverty for many African Americans and Latinos, as well as for immigrants before them. Carmen Cordova found that the civil service route worked well for her:

> I worked for the City of New York for thirty-seven years in various departments. Civil service jobs were a good career choice. In my family, the highest education anyone had was third grade. Graduating high school was the equivalent of you getting a PhD. There was never any discussion when I was young of my going to college; that was beyond people's expectations. Working for the city government gave me a steady job with benefits, health insurance, and vacation and sick leave.[40]

However, the City's fiscal crisis of the mid-1970s caused painful layoffs of thousands of newly hired and provisional civil service workers. The layoffs hit minority workers particularly hard. Half of the Hispanic, a third of the African American, and 22 percent of the white City workers lost their jobs.[41] Kathryn Speller was among those affected:

> I found a job at the Bureau of Pest Control. However, I was provisional and was laid off when the City was in fiscal crisis under Mayor Lindsay. I collected unemployment benefits for a while.[42]

For many reasons, residents of the South Bronx could not get access to the higher-paying uniformed jobs—the union jobs in police and fire departments. The passage of the Civil Rights Act of 1964 outlawed discrimination in employment based on race, nationality, sex, and creed, but it was not until 1990 that black New Yorkers were represented in higher-paying civil service jobs in proportions approaching their share of the population.[43] Indeed, claims and lawsuits for discrimination against the fire department continue as recently as 2017.

Other work disappeared through outsourcing. I remember an upsetting conversation with a friend who held a high-level management position with a bank. She was very concerned that the bank was contracting out the cleaning of its branches and had just fired its cleaning staff, people who were long-term employees, paid a salary with health insurance, vacation, and sick-leave benefits. The company that won the contract to clean the banks was offering to hire the laid-off staff as hourly employees who would have no benefits and earn a fraction of what they had been making. Outsourcing caused many low-wage earners to fall into poverty.

The lack of sufficient employment opportunities was devastating. When I came to the South Bronx in the late 1960s, one-quarter of the residents were on welfare. In another ten years, it was close to 40 percent.[44] Ms. Speller recalls:

> Once Eric was born, my mother found a room in someone else's apartment for me and the two children. I had to go on home relief. All the investigators were white and they were horrible to me. But that isn't where you were for the rest of your life. I got a job. I was on welfare for only a few years.[45]

Carmen Cordova similarly describes a difficult period of her life:

> My family had never been on public assistance or food stamps or any gov-
> ernment supplement. When I divorced from my first husband, I couldn't
> manage financially. It was very humbling to apply for public assistance. I
> was embarrassed to use the food stamps, and I never told any of the family
> members I was on public assistance. I was only on public assistance for a
> short time. I was working for welfare and was receiving welfare at the same
> time.[46]

And Divina Rivera, an outspoken senior citizen, remembers the impact of
job loss, having to go on welfare, and how she felt forced to make less-
than-ideal arrangements with her children:

> I worked in a factory making dolls but was laid off when the factory closed.
> I was able to live on the $50 a week that I collected from unemployment.
> When that ran out, I had to go on welfare but I didn't want to stay on wel-
> fare. I enlisted my daughters' help, gave them keys and made them promise
> to come home straight after school, lock the door and not open it for anyone.
> I took a job in Manhattan where I worked for twenty-six years. People there
> looked down on me because I was Puerto Rican and from the Bronx. Both
> of these things were held against me.[47]

Almost every other block in the South Bronx hosts a bodega. They
replaced the Jewish-, Italian-, and Irish-owned neighborhood butchers,
fish markets, groceries, bakeries, and delis. The owners worked very long
hours and employed relatives, as is often the case in small businesses.
Carmen describes the work ethic:

> My uncles owned bodegas. They worked seven days a week and very long
> hours from 7 A.M. to 10 P.M. They usually hired their family members to help
> out at the store. My father had a full-time job in New Jersey, and after he got
> home from work and had dinner, he would work in my aunt's bodega in the
> evening and on weekends.[48]

Low Expectations

Getting a good education was (and still is) a challenge. An excellent public
school system that had helped so many immigrants and their children—

people like Gene Oliva and Stan Freilich (introduced in chapter 1)—frequently failed black and Latino students. Research has repeatedly shown the effects that teachers' expectations have on children. Called the Pygmalion effect, a teacher believing certain students are particularly bright will raise the achievement levels of those students, even if, in fact, the students are average.[49] A teacher expecting that black students, for instance, will do poorly or have behavior problems will act differently toward those students and can cause them to be expelled more frequently and have lower rates of graduation.[50]

Jean Smith, an African American woman, broke many glass ceilings during her fifty-year career at Chase Bank. She is a longtime board member of BronxWorks. Because of her own teenage experiences, she retains a passion for helping youths become educated:

> I was in a school for gifted children when we lived in Manhattan. [When we were moving to the Bronx] the guidance counselor said I should go to Grace Dodge High School, which was a vocational school, and become a cosmetologist. This despite the fact I was in accelerated classes. It was never suggested that I take the exam for Bronx High School of Science and we had no way of knowing about these options. This is an example of low expectations for African Americans. Luckily, we didn't do what she said.[51]

Carmen Cordova's sister, like so many other children of color, was incorrectly labeled and placed in special education:

> If you were behind academically, the child was put in special education. My sister was incorrectly classified and was put in a special education class where she slept all day. My sister graduated high school with a commercial diploma despite being in special education. She struggled and was able to overcome being in special education. She never aspired to go to college. It hurts me because I know this type of stereotyping and prejudice still goes on today.[52]

A lifelong Bronx resident, Vivian Vázquez has devoted her career to helping young people succeed. She worked for CAB during its formative years and initiated many of CAB's children and youth programs. She now works for New Settlement Apartments. Vivian produced a documentary, *Decade of Fire*, about the Bronx of her childhood. She states:

The only services our family received were from our school except for emergency health care from Lincoln Hospital. My parents received their GED degrees at the local school. However, school was the first place I smoked pot, at age eleven. No one on our block spoke English but we were punished in school for speaking Spanish. Probably the worst thing was that there were no high expectations for the students. There was not even a language of expectations.[53]

For seventeen years, Eileen Torres worked with me at BronxWorks, rising to the position of general counsel and then succeeding me as executive director. She attended Pace University, a local college, on a merit scholarship and then Northeastern Law School, where she earned her law degree. She discusses one aspect of low expectations:

> I enjoyed the years I spent at Cardinal Spellman High School and do think I received an excellent education. However, I do feel that—at that time— perhaps without any mal-intent, they did not encourage me to attend, or even apply, to an Ivy League school. And, yes, the discussion centered on where I would feel most comfortable or would do well—and obviously the counselor felt that I shouldn't apply for an Ivy League school. I had already experienced what it meant to be an "outsider," having been raised in what was originally a predominantly working-class white neighborhood. Having the counselor essentially confirm my fear was enough for me.[54]

And not all the Puerto Ricans who came to New York City during that period were poor. Eric Soto was born in the South Bronx. His father, a bilingual teacher for the NYC Board of Education, had earned his college degree in Puerto Rico, but the teaching jobs in New York paid several times what those on the island paid. Eric was able to attend Immaculate Conception Catholic School, which at the time was very diverse, with Irish, Italian, black, and Puerto Rican students. Eric says, "We played together, fought together, and were friends. There was no tension." But as many other middle-income Bronx families of all backgrounds had done before them, Eric's family moved out of the Bronx when they were able to do so. They bought a house in Mount Vernon, a suburb of New York City, when Eric was in seventh grade. Eric came back to the Bronx to attend Cardinal Spellman High School (where Supreme Court Justice Sonia Sotomayor and my colleague Eileen Torres also graduated).[55]

Drugs, AIDS, and Prison

In addition to the loss of entry-level jobs, racial discrimination, poor housing, middle-class flight, and disintegrating schools, other issues lined up to afflict the people of the Bronx. Illegal drugs and the Rockefeller Drug Laws joined a perfect storm of factors that caused much poverty and suffering.

Heroin, marijuana, and later crack cocaine were the three main drugs that bedeviled the people of the Bronx. In 1898, Bayer started selling heroin as an over-the-counter cough suppressant, and by 1900 it was being used to treat morphine addiction. Heroin did not become illegal until the 1920s, when approximately two hundred thousand people were already addicted. Use of the drug grew through the '30s into the '50s, especially in cities. As many as 10–15 percent of the U.S. military serving in Vietnam returned addicted. Use continued to grow through the '80s and '90s as availability and quality increased. Popular entertainers Janis Joplin, Jim Morrison, and John Belushi all died of heroin overdoses. Inner-city young people were at particular risk as drugs flooded into their neighborhoods.[56]

Joan Canada (introduced in chapter 1) recalls the rapid change to her once stable, child-friendly neighborhood:

> People's apartments were regularly being robbed, televisions reported stolen, Christmas gifts stolen. The junkies were daring, and driven. Some would let their partners down on a rope from the roof to get into a window. The most demoralizing part was that it was being done by people I knew from elementary school, individuals I grew up with, my extended brothers. So many young people were lost (either died or trapped in addiction and crime) as a result of drugs and incarceration. Many came out of prison with a new belief system. They came back to the neighborhood as "Black Muslims" [Nation of Islam], which brought in another dynamic, a dynamic that affected not only religious, but social and political thought.[57]

Allen Jones, a professional basketball player who grew up in the Patterson Houses in the South Bronx, was hooked on heroin in ninth grade. He writes from his experience:

> You start to see people, once clean and happy, staggering around the neighborhood run down, dirty, with no pride left at all. All that concerns them is

finding the Queen. Once you are hooked on heroin, you would kill our own mother if she stood between you and your drugs. Queen Bitch Heroin can make a man murder, steal, cheat, and do all sorts of ungodly things to prove his love for Her. And the more you give Her, the more She wants.[58]

Marijuana became popular in the 1960s. Although it can be argued whether or not the drug itself is harmful, certainly the jail sentences that resulted from marijuana possession and sales had devastating consequences.

The plague of crack cocaine—a cheap, quick, and very addictive high— arrived in the mid-1980s, and for ten years families and neighborhoods gravely suffered. For the first time, significant numbers of women as well as men became addicted. Children were neglected. Health experts and the media speculated about the long-term effects on children born addicted— the "crack babies." We saw crack vials among the litter of paper, bottles, and chicken bones on the sidewalks and in the doorways and halls of apartment buildings. Crime rates continued to climb.

Ricky Flores is a professional photojournalist who started document- ing life in the South Bronx at a young age. He freelanced for the *Daily News*, the *New York Times*, and the *Village Voice*. Ricky now works as a staff photographer for the *Journal News*. He describes what it was like to grow up in a period dominated by drugs and destruction:

> I think you had to have a certain amount of narcissism to survive, a strong sense of self. You could have a good friend or a family member, then they would completely change and turn on you because of drug abuse. You had to be wary of people and be a good judge of them. People would change in a matter of weeks. Your good friend would be begging you for money that he said he owed someone, otherwise he would be killed. The amount that he would ask for was not the sum of someone in debt but of someone looking to score some crack. You had to turn hard and push them away because you knew the money was for drugs. You wanted to help people but how could you, there was no drug treatment, no help.[59]

Joyce Davis served as president of NWBCCC and then as executive director of Mount Hope Housing Company. She is a congregational leader at Walker Memorial Baptist Church and has supported many other Bronx organizations. Currently she works for Mid-Bronx Senior Citizens Council. She recalls the rapid changes on her block after she purchased a house she loved:

> The block was nice for a while. Then all of a sudden, the Bronx started to change. It was like we were sleeping and woke up. People selling drugs on corners. Certain people owned the corners. There were lines of people waiting to buy drugs. They would stand there with ten garbage cans with fires to keep warm. The Bronx was the first to know crack. We were the people to tell others crack was happening in our community and affecting the quality of our lives, our young people. It blew up.[60]

Crack interacted with another plague of the mid-1980s, the AIDS epidemic. The hysteria associated with AIDS was initially focused on Haitians. Next gay men were blamed and ostracized for spreading the disease. In the Bronx, however, AIDS was primarily a disease of drug users and their partners. Intravenous drug users shared needles to inject heroin, and the disease spread to other users and then to their wives and girlfriends. As women became addicted to crack, some turned to prostitution to get money for the drug, spreading the disease further. Very quickly the South Bronx became an epicenter of the AIDS plague. Child neglect increased with the rise of addiction, and the numbers of children placed in foster care skyrocketed. For the first time, significant numbers of women joined the ranks of men who were labeled "street homeless," people who lived on the streets and in the parks. Kathryn Speller describes the influence of crack on families:

> When I was coming up, I lost a lot of my friends to heroin from overdosing. However, to me, the heroin epidemic was not as bad as the crack epidemic. If a person was on heroin, often they could still function. Crack destroyed the whole family. The woman is the foundation of the family. Crack was a female drug that tore the family down. I remember hearing babies crying, looking out the window, and seeing mothers pushing the stroller to the crack house to get high. It was a sad thing to watch.[61]

In 1973, New York State decided that long prison sentences were the solution to the problem of drugs. The New York State Legislature, with the urging of many citizens who were concerned about crime, passed the Rockefeller Drug Laws. Penalties for drug involvement were fifteen years to life. The prison population soared with nonviolent offenders. In a report, the New York Civil Liberties Union referred to the drug laws as "New York's Jim Crow Laws." The report states that 90 percent of the people confined were black or Hispanic although the majority of drug users were white.[62]

President Reagan responded to the drug problem with the slogan "Just say no to drugs." Under his leadership, the U.S. Congress passed the Anti-Drug Abuse Act of 1986, which set harsh penalties for users and dealers of crack, far harsher than for the powdered form of cocaine used mainly by white people. In the following ten years, the number of Americans involved with the criminal justice system doubled.[63]

The Racketeer Influenced and Corrupt Organizations Act (commonly known as RICO), enacted in 1970 for the purpose of prosecuting organized crime, was now used to prosecute crime associated with gangs and illegal drugs. Paul Lipson, cofounder of the Point Community Development Corporation, former chief of staff for Congressman José Serrano, and a consultant on issues of economic development, youth empowerment, and environmental justice, describes the law's impact:

> RICO resulted in a form of collective punishment, causing the incarceration for long stretches of many young people on the periphery of drug dealing. It hollowed out entire neighborhoods, sending many employment-eligible young men to prison and removing them from the cohort of eligible partners, husbands, fathers, voters, business owners, homeowners, and taxpayers. I knew a young man who was in a gang. One of the gang members murdered a rival drug dealer. The young man refused to take a deal for a lighter sentence after the actual murderer was tried and convicted. The young man went to trail and was convicted of conspiracy. He is now serving a life sentence in a federal penitentiary.[64]

Upon release from prison, many found it almost impossible to get a job. The incarceration of so many people broke up families and destabilized poor neighborhoods. Now that a significant number of white, middle-class young people are dying from drug overdoses, politicians of both parties are calling for treatment, not punishment, for drug use. How many black and Latino youths were sent to jail for possession of marijuana, a drug that is now legal in ten states and the District of Columbia, and approved for medical use in twenty-three states?

Severe Service Cuts by a City Close to Bankruptcy

The fiscal crisis of the mid-1970s and the resulting severe budget cuts made NYC a less desirable place to live for all New Yorkers, but the City's distress affected low-income New Yorkers disproportionately. Vivian Vázquez's experience was typical:

> In 1975, I attended IS 52 as a sixth-grader. I remember taking home economics and choral classes. My older brother played guitar in school and my older sister took art classes. These were eliminated by the time I was in eighth grade.
>
> No after-school programs were offered. We would go home after school, put our books down and go outside to play. By 1975, there were plenty of abandoned buildings to engage in risky activities and hide in. There were burned-out, abandoned buildings everywhere. While dangerous, the streets were our playground.[65]

Federal policies contributed to the City's budget woes, including the construction of highways and tax incentives for home mortgages, which encouraged the middle class to move to the suburbs. As the middle class left, so did the money they paid in taxes. President Nixon's cuts to the War on Poverty funding—money that helped pay for services—contributed to the City's budget deficit.[66] Unable to pay its bills, NYC came very close to declaring bankruptcy. The City, led by Mayor Abraham Beame, looked to municipal unions, the banks, the state, and the federal government for help. President Ford's initial response to the City's request for help was captured in a famous *Daily News* headline of October 29, 1975: "Ford to City: Drop Dead."[67] But the other parties chipped in—the state, the unions with their pension funds, and the banks by loaning the City money and (as the federal government would later) buying municipal bonds. A Financial Control Board was appointed to run the City.[68]

The City was saved from bankruptcy, but the cuts to balance the budget and reduce the debt caused much hardship, escalating the poverty of the Bronx. In the next few years, around six thousand teachers (plus crossing guards, school secretaries, guidance counselors, and school security guards), six thousand cops, and twenty-five hundred firefighters were laid off. The fire department had recently suffered other significant cuts.

Thirty-five fire companies, most of them in poor areas, were closed or relocated. With cuts to the sanitation department, garbage piled up on city sidewalks. All of the City's fifty neighborhood health clinics were closed, and the health department lost a third of its staff. Funds for methadone treatment were cut. There is evidence that these cuts led to a lack of preparedness for the HIV and crack epidemics. The City University of New York also lost a third of its staff and started charging tuition for the first time. The parks department cut about fourteen hundred jobs, and the maintenance of neighborhood parks ceased. Subway and bus fares were raised. People in the South Bronx paid a huge price for the City's disinvestment in poor areas.[69]

Almost all music teachers, like the one who had inspired Stan Freilich (see chapter 1), were laid off. Children would no longer have the opportunity to learn to play musical instruments in school or sing in choruses. The cuts to the parks department eliminated the sports teams, like the baseball and football teams that played such an important role in Gene Oliva's childhood. After-school programs closed. Libraries, another refuge for children, were cut to three or four days a week. Children could sit bored in apartments or hang out in the street, where they were likely to be tempted by drugs and easy money. Even when the City's finances boomed years later, many of the services earlier generations had benefited from were not fully restored.

Weak Social Infrastructure

Social service and religious organizations, which provide structure for community life, lagged in adjusting to the new populations and were unable to provide significant support to the newer residents. Most of the established organizations were in flux. The predominant social service agencies were Jewish. They either closed, focused on the shrinking elderly population, or adapted over time to serve a broader population. The three YMHA facilities in the South Bronx closed or changed hands. A senior center I had worked in when I finished graduate school in 1973, the Mt. Eden Center, was in a synagogue. It closed when the synagogue closed, as did the Burnside Senior Center. As synagogues closed, some were bought by African American churches, but it took a few years before the congregations expanded to fill their new homes. Small Latino churches were established and, with time, flourished. The Catholic churches remained strong but underwent a change of parishioners, from primarily Irish and Italian to Puerto Rican and African American.

It was obvious to me when I started working that there were very few social service agencies, few places people could go for help. Some health centers opened to replace hospitals that had closed, and a few day-care centers existed. The handful of small programs for children and youth were far from adequate given the size of the population.

The blackout of July 13, 1977, symbolized the despair: stores were looted, fires were set, people were arrested. Although the whole city was affected, the South Bronx and parts of Brooklyn suffered the most. Entire blocks of stores were looted and destroyed.

The years 1970–85 were the hardest time for the people of the South Bronx. Jack Doyle, who was born, raised, and educated in the Bronx, has an organizer's skills and is the executive director of a large, successful Bronx housing and social service agency, New Settlement Apartments. In a conversation with me, Jack summed it up this way:

> You remember what it was like in the '80s. Stripped cars, dogs wandering around. There were areas where buses were rerouted out of neighborhoods. Street signs were missing. Mt. Eden Avenue had many vacant storefronts. Absence of resources, of opportunities, of services, not just abandonment of buildings but of everything.[70]

BUT PEOPLE HAVE STRENGTHS AND FAMILIES

With so much against them—the lack of jobs, poor education, discrimination, drugs flooding into neighborhoods—the people of the South Bronx had it hard. But these problems are only part of the picture. Bronxites also had strengths and resources. Particularly important were generosity and the strengths of family and community.

Supreme Court Justice Sonia Sotomayor grew up in the Bronxdale public housing project, which is now named after her. After her father died, the family moved to Co-op City. She graduated from Cardinal

Spellman High School, Princeton, and Yale Law School. She returns frequently to the Bronx to speak to groups, has warmly greeted children for seven years at the Dream Big event sponsored by the Bronx Children's Museum, and has canoed the Bronx River. She continues to demonstrate the strong family and community ties she valued growing up in the Bronx, which are described in her book *My Beloved World*.[71] These values are shared by many other current and former Bronxites.

Julie Belizaire Spitzer, a senior staff member of BronxWorks, has been promoted many times during her twenty-five-year career. Julie, who has a master's degree in social work, is an expert in tenants' rights and housing court. She grew up in the South Bronx:

> When I was young, we had so many extended family members from Haiti living in one building. My family made it a great experience. We could play in the hallways. I have very nice memories running from floor to floor. It was safe because the members of the community looked out for each other. We played with our neighbors in the streets, running though the fire hydrants and participating in block parties. There were other groups of extended families from different backgrounds and we were friends with some of them.
>
> I never realized I was poor because I didn't know how other people lived. We always had toys to play with, my father never wanted us to feel deprived, so he made toys for us from wood, like knock hockey. We played games like kick-the-can. We played jump rope and double Dutch, things that didn't cost much money. [My father] knew we were poor but he didn't allow me to feel it.[72]

Carmen Cordova's memories are similar:

> The extended family and friends alternated apartments and got together on Saturday nights and partied. I remember all the fun we had, dancing and listening to music. My sister and I learned how to dance salsa and merengue and to this day, I enjoy dancing.
>
> In our culture, we always want to help someone out. There is a saying, "Ay bendito"—"Poor thing" in English. If someone is hungry, "Ay bendito," give them some food. If someone is homeless, "Ay bendito," take them in. It is not just towards Puerto Ricans; we helped other nationalities too. The family is very important, the extended family. It was not about obtaining material stuff.[73]

And Eileen Torres recalls:

We had a neighbor who had three children, we only had two. The daughter
came to eat a lot with us. My mom would always buy extra groceries knowing the girl's mom would need to "borrow" from us prior to her husband's
pay day.[74]

Jacqueline Smith Bonneau, who grew up in Morrisania, told the Bronx
African American History Project:

We had three bedrooms and there were nine of us. When we took in
Thelonious [Monk] and his family, that made thirteen. We didn't have bunk
beds, and no one had their own bed except my mother and father. We just
doubled up as best as we could. . . . My family took in a lot of people over the
years.[75]

Nicolas Cruz retired after helping thousands of people in his work as an
information specialist and case manager for over twenty years at
BronxWorks. His decision to buy a house in the Bronx has been a tremendous asset to his extended family:

We had a desire to buy a house so we started saving money. We wanted a
place for my wife's parents, who had been very good to us. We bought a two-
family house so they could live with us and pay low rent. Then my mother
didn't want to be alone and she asked if she could live with us. We constructed an apartment for her in the basement. Now we have a brother-in-
law who is disabled living here and our daughters are almost grown and can
stay here in the future.[76]

Gladys Carrión is an attorney whose career focused on child welfare
issues. I first met her when she worked for Bronx Legal Services. She
served as a trustee for City University, as the commissioner for NYC's
antipoverty agency, as the executive director of two nonprofits concerned
with children's problems, and as child welfare commissioner at both the
city and state levels. She grew up in the South Bronx a few years before the
fires:

I grew up on Kelly and Longwood. It was a very close-knit neighborhood. I
never realized I was poor until I went to high school. I went to school with
Italians, Irish, Asians, African Americans. The Bronx burning was not the

experience I lived. I felt supported by my family and neighborhood. Most of my friends had intact families. My parents came from Puerto Rico. My father had a third-grade education. He was an elevator operator; my mother worked in a factory. They struggled and worked hard like everyone else. I remember coming home, having a boyfriend, three blocks away from home he gave me a kiss. By the time I got home, my mother knew. You had to respect everyone even if that person wasn't your aunt.

I went to PS 130. You were tracked. If you were smart, you had lots of advantages. I got to read the *New York Times* in third grade. We were taught how to fold up the paper while you were reading it, like people do on the subways so as not to bother the people sitting beside them. In high school, I learned that my culture was not valued—that is when I became conscious of having been raised in a marginalized community.[77]

3 Why the South Bronx Burned

The buildings started to get abandoned between Fox and
Simpson. From my window, I would see the buildings burning, a total of five buildings across the street. The next day
you would hear that a fireman got killed. We didn't have a
camera, didn't see it through TV but out my window.
Hearing on the news that all these people passed away,
suffocation.

Sotero Ortiz, known as BG183, street artist and founding
member of Tats Cru

People died during that time. People's buildings were
burned down. Our photography is evidence of the crime
done to us. We suffered.

Ricky Flores, professional photojournalist

During the fall of 1977, when sportscaster Howard Cosell supposedly
announced that "the Bronx is burning" during the World Series and
President Carter visited Charlotte Street to see the burned-out buildings
and vacant lots, the South Bronx instantly became a notorious and feared
place. To many people, it became the symbol of all that was wrong with
urban America. More than in other cities in the Northeast and Midwest
that lost factories, population, and land value, the devastation in the South
Bronx was seen as a failing by the people who lived there, not as a conse-
quence of broad economic factors. For the residents of the South Bronx, it
was a time of severe hardship and a daily fight for survival.

From 1970 to 1981, 108,000 apartment units were lost to abandonment and/or fires.[1] Often buildings were abandoned by the owners

This fire at Macy Place on March 9, 1980, was just one of thousands of fires during this tough period in the South Bronx. Joe Conzo Jr., then seventeen, witnessed the fire near his grandmother's day-care center and took several photographs of it. Children were traumatized from growing up in such dangerous situations. Photo credit: The Archive of Joe Conzo Jr. at Cornell University Library.

before they burned. During several of these years, the Bronx had as many as twelve thousand structural fires a year, the majority of these in the South Bronx. The destruction of so many buildings caused a huge loss in population. The number of people living in the South Bronx went from 768,837 in 1970 to 453,798 in 1980—a decrease of over 310,600, or 40 percent of the population, in just ten years![2] To put that figure in context, 310,000 is close to the total population of St. Louis, and greater than the total population of Pittsburgh, Cincinnati, or Newark.

New York City is divided into community districts. The South Bronx comprises six of the twelve districts in the Bronx (see Table 1). Some areas in the South Bronx suffered more than others. Public housing was not affected by fires, and areas with very high concentrations of "the projects" lost less population. District 2 lost 66 percent of its population, or sixty-five thousand people, in ten years. District 3 lost a hundred thousand

Population Decline and Regrowth in the Six Districts of the South Bronx, 1970–2010

Community district	Total population				
	1970	1980	1990	2000	2010
1. Melrose, Mott Haven, Port Morris	137,557	78,441	77,214	82,159	91,497
2. Hunts Point, Longwood	99,493	34,399	39,443	46,824	52,246
3. Morrisania, Crotona Park East	150,636	53,635	57,162	68,574	79,762
4. Highbridge, Concourse Village	144,207	114,312	119,962	139,563	146,441
5. University Heights, Fordham, Mount Hope	121,807	107,995	118,435	128,313	128,200
6. East Tremont, Belmont	114,137	65,016	68,061	75,688	83,268
All six districts	*767,837*	*453,798*	*480,277*	*541,121*	*581,414*

SOURCE: Data from NYC Department of City Planning.

in those same ten years. Districts 4 and 5, comprising the West Bronx, had a less dramatic population loss, although some buildings were abandoned in the early '80s and rebuilt in the late '80s. Other districts lost half of the apartment buildings, and a few census tracts lost 90 percent.[3]

My husband's cousin, Danny Gainey, was a fireman in Engine Company 82/Ladder Company 31, which for years was the busiest firehouse in the world. They responded to an average of thirty calls a day, about half of which were false alarms. A member of the company died responding to a false alarm, falling off the truck. Other fires were in abandoned buildings and still had to be extinguished so they would not spread to adjacent buildings. Two or three fires a day they called "real fires"—fires in occupied buildings.

Danny received the Mayor LaGuardia Medal for a rescue, along with other medals and citations. He was doing a routine inspection by himself and noticed smoke coming out of a building. He pulled the fire alarm.

Neighbors told him the building was occupied. He ran in, without any gear, and up the smoke-filled stairs. He tripped on an unconscious woman and child and dragged them out. People told him there was a woman in the apartment above the fire. He ran back inside and up the stairs, broke open her door, and carried her out.[4]

The extent of the fires was vast, as was the suffering. In one year, 1974, there were over thirty-three thousand fires of all types in the Bronx—structural, content, chimney, vehicle, and outdoor.[5] That year, 140 residents and three firemen were killed and fifteen hundred people were injured in fires in the South Bronx.[6]

Other areas of the city also suffered from fires, particularly Harlem and parts of Brooklyn. Carolyn Pelzer, who was rehoused in the Bronx after becoming homeless from a fire in Brooklyn and living in a shelter for three years, describes what it was like:

It was a real horrific event for me and the kids. The fire occurred in 1985 at around 5:30 P.M. when I was coming home from work. I noticed smoke coming from the building as I had stopped to speak with a neighbor. We lived in a two-family walk-up on the third floor. On the first floor was a Pentecostal church.

As me and my sons were about to head up the stairs, my late husband came running from the other direction exclaiming, "The building is on fire!" He ran up the stairs telling me to stay downstairs. However, I glanced up at the window and saw my daughters looking out the window crying and scared. I became fearful of losing them and ran into the building to help my husband get our girls out of the apartment.

As I fought through flames to get to them, we became trapped inside the apartment. As the fire completely consumed our entrance and means of getting out, we moved into the front bedroom with the fire moving towards us very fast. My husband had gotten the attention of some Con Edison workers and other people who had gathered in front of the building. We threw our daughters out the window and jumped ourselves. The people on the street helped catch my daughters, myself, and my husband. The girls suffered with fractured ribs, scrapes, and scratches. I ended up in the hospital having my head hit the concrete. My husband suffered a fractured arm. Thank God, we were all very lucky to come out of this fire with no life-threatening injuries. We had a rough time for a while afterwards. However, we had some good supports during that time.[7]

CHANGING ECONOMICS OF RESIDENTIAL
REAL ESTATE

The physical destruction of so much of the South Bronx, the fires and the building abandonment, occurred in the context of a widespread change in population from predominantly middle-class white to middle- and lower-income Puerto Rican and African American. But popular opinion to the contrary, no evidence exists that the low-income people of the Bronx deserve the blame for the collapse of the South Bronx. Rather, they were victims of unanticipated economic forces, political decisions, disinvestment, and racial fear—a confluence of factors they could not control.

In the years leading up to World War II and during the housing shortage in the following ten years, multiple-dwelling building ownership was a reliable source of income for many relatively new immigrants. Many first- and second-generation Jewish immigrants, as well as people from other backgrounds, learned about building management, saved some money, and entered the field of real estate. Although their tenants often moved and shorted them a few months' rent, the buildings made enough money to cover those kinds of losses.

From a landlord's point of view, changes in the economics of building ownership in the 1960s and '70s caused many of the problems that led to the decline of the South Bronx. Operating costs increased. The City required buildings to use low-sulfur fuel, which was more expensive, in order to cut down on air pollution. The City also required that heat be provided all night, increasing fuel costs. Property taxes increased, as did water and sewer charges. Rent control limited income from rent increases (unless the owner could increase the number of units by dividing them into smaller ones; then they could rent these small units at high prices to African Americans, who had few housing options).[8] Oil shortages caused fuel costs to skyrocket, with a 700 percent increase in the cost of oil from 1967 to 1981.[9]

The value of the landlords' investment in their buildings plummeted. Historically, a building was valued at four or five times the annual income it earned for the owner, known as the rent-roll. On the Grand Concourse, buildings sold for six or seven times the annual rent-roll. In some areas of the South Bronx, the price of apartment buildings plummeted to as low as one-quarter of the annual rent-roll.[10] The economics of owning apartment buildings was changing. So was the racial composition of the tenants.

In 1967, the American Jewish Congress, in conjunction with the Protestant Council of the Bronx, the Catholic Interracial Council of the Bronx, and the Planners for Equal Opportunity, undertook an exhaustive study of a 260-block area encompassing the Grand Concourse and its side streets, arguably the nicest area of what later became known as the South Bronx. The report raised concerns about the future of the area. It stated that although the area was still a very good place to live, newspaper articles about neighborhood population changes were fueling anxiety among the white residents that could cause them to flee the area. Black and Latino families were moving into the lower part of the Grand Concourse while the northern part was still mostly white. The report documented that the income level of the black and Puerto Rican families in the area, who still comprised less than 25 percent of the population, was similar to that of the white population. The area was becoming integrated and, at that time, was not becoming poorer. Family size was also comparable, without signs of overcrowding in apartments or public facilities such as schools. Crime had gone up somewhat, but crime had increased nationwide, and it had actually risen less in that area than in the city as a whole. Juvenile crime was also lower than in the rest of the city. Nevertheless, an overblown fear of crime was keeping senior citizens from going out at night. The YMHA (which occupied the building on the Concourse that CAB would later own) had canceled evening programs for seniors because so few came.

The report stated that vacancy rates in all the buildings were exceptionally low, demonstrating that apartments were still in demand, even fifth-floor walk-ups in buildings on the side streets off the Concourse.[11] Landlords were having no trouble renting out their apartments, and their buildings were still at maximum rent-paying capacity. What had changed was the real estate market: the value of the apartment buildings had significantly decreased, apparently in anticipation that the area would become a "slum." The report detailed worries that owners might quit investing in their building maintenance, thus causing deterioration. Some landlords might increase profits in the short run by turning over apartments in their buildings quickly as a way to increase rents while decreasing necessary expenses. The report made five recommendations

for steps that could help stabilize the area, including community organizing and relieving intergroup tensions.[12] Sadly, the situation the report
tried to prevent came to pass.

MANY OWNERS QUIT INVESTING IN THEIR BUILDINGS

The age of the buildings also mattered. Most of the apartment buildings in
the West Bronx, where I worked, were built in the 1920s and '30s. By the '60s
and '70s, those buildings were in need of renovation—upgraded electrical,
plumbing, roofs, windows, pointing, and so on. With the very rapid change
in their tenant composition—from Jews, Italians, and Irish to blacks and
Puerto Ricans—many owners were less inclined to invest significant sums in
their buildings. Many buildings quickly deteriorated. As they did, many of
the remaining middle-class tenants, those who hadn't already moved to the
suburbs or Co-op City, left and were replaced by lower-income families.

For a while, the NYC Human Resources Administration (the department that administers welfare, food stamps, and Medicaid) was paying
higher-than-market rent, and welfare recipients could thus afford rents in
many Bronx buildings. Taking advantage of this, some landlords decreased
services such as heat and hot water, causing long-term tenants to leave, so
they could increase the rent as the apartment turned over. They reached
out specifically to people on welfare, causing a rapid influx of very poor
families. This, in turn, caused more long-term tenants to flee, allowing
more apartments to turn over.[13] However, for a period of nine years, 1975–
84, there were no increases in rent payments for public assistance recipients. Landlords were entitled to modest rent increases each year, but people's welfare grants did not go up to cover those increases. By 1983,
two-thirds of the families on welfare were paying, or trying to pay, rent in
excess of what was provided by welfare. The other, non-rent, part of the
welfare grant (referred to as "food and other") was extremely limited, so
even if a family was very frugal, it was not enough to cover the excess rent
charges. Families frequently fell behind in their rent payments, causing
loss of rent income for the landlords. It was a relief, at least for a few years,
when Governor Mario Cuomo raised the rent levels, effective in 1984.[14]

At CAB when I was helping people with their housing issues, I noticed a change in the management of buildings. When I first started at CAB and there was a problem in a building, I could often pick up the phone, call the landlord or his agent, discuss the problem, and reach a conclusion. After a few years, leases and rent bills listed the owners as the (XYZ) Corporation— the address was a post office box, and if a phone number was provided, no one could be reached who could resolve the issue. Many owners no longer wanted to be engaged directly with their tenants. Tenants found this very frustrating, became angry, and often responded by withholding their rent until their complaint was addressed. These disputes ended up in housing court, not an ideal solution for either party.

Vivian Vázquez (introduced in chapter 2) grew up amid the fires. She tells me:

> Our landlord was a Holocaust survivor. He lived in the building and did all the work himself—he shoveled the coal, fixed plumbing problems, took care of the halls. When he died, the new owners didn't care and the building fell apart.[15]

Irma Rodríguez, who would later become executive director of the non-profit Queens Community House, worked at the Southeast Bronx Neighborhood Stabilization office from 1977 to 1983. Her job was to prevent problems in the deteriorating areas from expanding into more stable ones. She recalls:

> Many of the buildings in earlier years had been family owned. I was friendly with a woman who was the super of a building and she would talk about the previous owners of the building, an Irish couple, who really cared and took care of the building. But older folks eventually sell, and generally sell to the group that offers them the most money. Especially if the sale was not done with a bank mortgage, it could be to anyone no matter how ill equipped they were to run the building properly. We saw buildings where Con Ed turned off the power or the City turned off the water, and the owner would jerry rig the stuff to stay afloat a while longer. Some of it was dangerous.
>
> Many of the landlords were particularly difficult to deal with. There was a kind of lawlessness about some landlords regardless of their ethnicity. They openly disregarded leases, warranty of habitability, and attempted to bribe everyone.[16]

A downward spiral commenced, not always in the same order: new tenants, often a new landlord, lack of costly repairs and day-to-day upkeep, fewer tenants paying full rent, perhaps a problem tenant, more withdrawal of services, building not profitable. Some landlords clearly "milked" their buildings—providing little or no services such as heat and hot water, making few or no repairs, but collecting rent from some tenants and still making a profit. Many buildings were allowed to run down to the point that they were uninhabitable and had to be abandoned.

REDLINING AND MORTGAGE CHURNING

Redlining, initially a purposely discriminatory policy of the federal government, played a major role in the changing economics of South Bronx real estate. Redlining started in the 1930s with the Federal Housing Administration's decision to refuse to provide mortgages in areas that were predominantly black (or Jewish), stating that those areas were poor credit risks. Neighborhoods would be circled in red on a map, and no lending would be made, despite evidence of a person's creditworthiness. This denied opportunities for home ownership to African Americans and, with it, the ability to build up equity and wealth through owning a home. The practice was picked up by private lenders throughout the United States. Although it was outlawed in 1968, the practice continued quietly in the Bronx and elsewhere through the '70s, '80s, and '90s and continues today in many places.[17]

Banks redlined large areas of the South Bronx, as did insurance companies, making it difficult or impossible for owners to get loans and sometimes insurance. The redlining affected owners of multiple dwellings as well as private houses. Owners deferred maintenance, patching the roof instead of replacing it, neglecting to paint window frames or fire escapes. As buildings deteriorated, vandalism increased. Many experienced landlords gave up and sold their buildings.[18]

Housing experts who worked as housing organizers during this period discuss the disastrous effects of factors such as redlining, banks bundling and selling off mortgages, over-leveraged buildings, and mortgage churning. Bill Frey, then an organizer for the Northwest Bronx Community and

Clergy Coalition, talks about trying to explain the destructiveness of redlining when he was doing tenant organizing:

> Redlining was identified as a key issue but it was hard for tenants to see how it directly affected them. The financial model that landlords had used for years was to buy a building with a mortgage, partially pay down the mortgage, and then refinance, using the money from the refinancing for repairs and profit. We looked at various problem buildings and discovered that even if the owner had had a mortgage and had paid on it, the bank was unwilling to renew it. Redlining meant that the owners did not have the money to make repairs. Some sold their buildings; others quit making repairs and "milked" the buildings, collecting rent for as long as they could but putting nothing into the building.[19]

Irma Rodríguez details the role of the banks in these machinations:

> There were problems with the banks. Redlining played a critical role in the demise of buildings. Redlining occurred both with mortgages and also with insurance. Redlining was complicated. Sometimes it was lack of lending that allowed unscrupulous lenders to be the only credit choice. Sometimes the banks did not provide oversight of buildings and allowed the buildings to deteriorate. The banks started packaging the mortgages and selling them off to subprime dealers. Since they didn't hold the mortgage themselves, they didn't really care if it was paid.[20]

Some landlords were more actively devious. They sold the buildings back and forth to themselves through various corporations, each time increasing the price. They also insured the building for the highest possible price. Then, when they hired an arsonist and had the building burned down, they collected an inflated insurance payment, much higher than the actual value of the building. It was more profitable for them to destroy their buildings than to continue to operate them. Harry DeRienzo is the founder and, for many years, the executive director of the Banana Kelly Community Improvement Association. Banana Kelly was one of the first groups that fought to bring back buildings in their section of the Bronx and sponsored the rehabilitation of two thousand units of housing. Harry has written about the landlords' shady practices:

> Owners often engaged in "mortgage churning", a practice whereby the owner would "sell" a property on paper for an inflated amount, receiving

what was seen as the market value in cash, and taking the balance above the market value in paper (as a purchase money mortgage). With this "paper", the new owner could extract as much rental income as possible, but would also have a huge "basis" for depreciating the property and claiming the tax deduction. For example, a $1,000,000 purchase depreciated over 27.5 years, could allow an owner to shelter over $35,000 in income per year (at that time, about three times the nation's 1975 median income).[21]

Again, Irma provides further details:

> In the '70s, some landlords were overleveraging their buildings. Buildings were sold over and over again at a profit, sometimes selling to people who wanted to get into the market but didn't know what they were doing. Families would get together and pool their money and buy a building but then they couldn't manage it. The insurance was worth more than the building. So sometimes they torched the building. An organizer who worked for me and lived in the area, who also happened to be a functional heroin addict, told me that the going rate to hire someone to take down a building was $150.[22]

WAS IT ARSON?

It is impossible to know what percentage of the fires were caused by arson. However, in Harry DeRienzo's opinion:

> 90 percent of the arson was caused by landlords. But most buildings burned for other reasons. The buildings were getting old. There were electrical fires. The fire stopping material between the floors decomposes over time. Fires would start in the basement and travel up through the walls and catch the roof on fire. The firemen would put out the roof fire, but hours or days later the fire would start up again from the basement because it was never fully extinguished.
>
> My community board lost 70 percent of its population within five years. I started working in this area in 1972. The worst was from 1975 to 1981.[23]

Vivian Vázquez states:

> My uncle told me what started the fires. They were electrical, caused by old wiring.[24]

And Irma Rodríguez agrees with Harry in attributing blame for the intentionally set fires:

> There was lots of arson, definitely done by landlords, not tenants. The arson
> occurred in buildings that were over-leveraged. The buildings were flipped
> over and over again by speculators until the insurance was worth more than
> the buildings.[25]

At the height of the fires, city fire marshals attributed 7 percent of the fires to arson.[26] Many people think this number was an understatement because the number of fire marshals was cut and all fires were not investigated. However, it is clear that the vast majority of fires were not caused by arson. Most started in the ways that fires start everywhere: from faulty or jerry-rigged wiring, space heaters, dropped cigarettes, kitchen fires, candles, malfunctioning furnaces, children playing with matches. Clearly, the poor condition of many buildings and the overcrowding in apartments heightened the likelihood of fires. With the dire state of the City's finances, the sanitation department's removal of garbage had declined and piles of trash lined many streets. Many buildings were already abandoned when they caught fire. In those situations, it was likely that the building was torched by an agent of the owner for insurance proceeds, accidentally by squatters living in the building, or by alienated young people looking for excitement.

Owners faced little risk but significant rewards if their buildings burned. It is puzzling that insurance companies did not investigate claims more aggressively. Perhaps it was just easier to pay out claims than face likely lawsuits for not paying. Similarly, the banks that had initiated the mortgages often sold them to other financial institutions.[27] Additionally, as rehab money became available, it was more readily available for vacant buildings. An owner could collect insurance money and then apply for funds to rehab the building.[28]

A small percentage of the arson-initiated fires may have been set by tenants, perhaps poorly housed tenants on welfare hoping to be rehoused to a better situation. The city at that time had a dual system of sheltering homeless families. Families that were homeless because of fires were moved into better shelters and had more priority for placement into permanent housing. They would not be placed in the infamous "welfare hotels" like the Martinique and the Holland, where families were provided one room, filthy mattresses, insufficient beds, no cooking facilities, and no window bars even if young children were in the household. Neither would they be placed into the Roberto Clemente Tier 1 shelter, where families— men, women, and children—were tightly packed on cots on a gym floor. Rather, the fire victims were placed into shelters where they had a small apartment set up with basic amenities and were given priority for public housing. However, there is no evidence that arson by tenants was widespread. When arrests were made for arson, those arrested were landlords and individuals paid by landlords to set fires. For example, in June 1975, eight landlords and their associates were indicted for arson in the South Bronx.[29]

During the whole decade of the 1970s, arson was widespread in cities throughout the United States. In 1979, the U.S. Senate held hearings on "arson for profit," examining its impact on insurance rates. Recommendations from the hearings included categorizing arson as a federal offense and urging the insurance industry to take more active steps to combat it.[30]

One reason that so many buildings were destroyed in New York City was lack of sufficient capacity within the fire department. In 1971, after Mayor John Lindsay requested that he reduce costs, Fire Chief John O'Hagan hired the Rand Corporation to recommend cuts to his department. On the basis of various assumptions, Rand recommended closing fire stations primarily in low-income areas like the South Bronx. Seven fire companies were closed, including one of the busiest in the Bronx. When the fiscal crisis of the mid-1970s hit, additional cuts had to be made. Higher-income areas like the Upper East Side had the political clout to prevent fire company closings in their neighborhoods, so cuts were made in low-income areas. With so many fires in the South Bronx, it was not unusual for several companies to be busy with one fire when another call came in. With insufficient capacity to respond quickly or adequately, minor fires could become major losses.

Making matters worse, the City also changed the fire department's alarm boxes in poor neighborhoods. The older ones were pull-lever boxes that everyone knew how to work. The new boxes, called Emergency Reporting System, required voice communication with an operator. However, many people did not know how to use them correctly, and the

Ralph Acevedo, a teenager at the time, standing on a pile of rubble from a demolished building on 167th Street and West Farms Road in March 1989. Paul Lipson had organized a training program sponsored by Bronx Frontier called "A Day in the Life of the Bronx," in which guest photographers worked with teens to take pictures of their neighborhood. Note the abandoned building in the background. Photo credit: Mark Rosenthal.

areas where they were installed had significant increases in what were deemed false alarms but were likely failed attempts to use the boxes. The supposed high incidence of false alarms was seen as further evidence that the people of the South Bronx were causing the downfall of the area. With the new alarm boxes, when voice contact was made, it was often hard to hear and understand the other party. As another cost-saving step, the City cut the number of engines responding to many alarms. And the difficulty of effectively fighting the fires was made worse because many fire hydrants were in disrepair.[31]

The effect on children was immense. Two people have told me they feel like they suffer from post-traumatic stress disorder from growing up among the fires, drugs, and gangs. Families moved frequently as their buildings or neighboring buildings were damaged by fire. Children were traumatized. Ricky Flores remembers what it was like:

> I grew up in the South Bronx during the years of the fires and drugs. When you are young, you just know your immediate world, that is your entire world. Even with all that was going on around us, we did what children always do, we went outside and played. The South Bronx was systematically targeted for destruction. Whole blocks were razed. We were the recipients of [Senator] Moynihan's policy of benign neglect. People were scattered during one of the worst times in the history of New York City [and that had] a profound effect on the city and state.[32]

Deon Shaw's childhood memories are much the same. She has lived in the Bronx all her life, and problems with housing have affected her all her life. When she was growing up, the fires had a great impact on her family:

> One day my sister and I went to school and when we came home, there was an electrical fire and the building burned down. The apartment was burned, all the other buildings were already burned down, it was kind of scary. My mother sent us to stay with a cousin on Stebbins Avenue while she looked for better housing. It was horrible. We used to go into the abandoned buildings, and jump from the second floor onto the mattresses. It was a fun thing. They didn't have playgrounds, or after-school programs, not much else for kids to do. We played skellies, with bottle tops and wax. I remember staying at our cousin's house for maybe five years.[33]

And in the words of BG183 (Sotero Ortiz):

> People died, but it was just another day for us. No electronic games. A lot of your time was outside, from early morning. Handball, Johnny-on-the-pony. In the summer, you had the free lunches, frozen juice, frozen baloney sandwiches, little packages of mayonnaise. As I grew up, that was my entertainment. A little bit of argument, fights, parents would put us together again, then you become friends again.
>
> My father was working in a factory, mother was home taking care of us. I asked why are we still living here, no building in front of my building, always looking at abandoned buildings. I would walk through a pile of bricks, a rusty nail or needle would go through my sneakers. I was scared. Several times, I would take my socks off and squeeze the blood out and keep going.[34]

The fires and the desolation had an immense effect on the entire community, as well as on individual families. Trust and hope were destroyed as people lived in fear. With frequent moves, it was impossible to keep extended families together, and some nuclear families were torn apart too. Attendance at community institutions such as churches and schools plummeted and some closed. Many felt they had to flee.

Once a building was abandoned, junkies and other scavengers would strip it of any material that had value, such as plumbing and wiring. Sometimes the stripping would start when the buildings were still partially occupied, leading to very dangerous conditions. Stripped buildings had less value and were more likely to be demolished.

City leaders and community groups debated the fate of abandoned buildings. Should they be torn down to prevent more fires, or should they be boarded up with the hope that, in the future, resources would be available to rehab them? Were empty buildings a danger, likely to catch fire and destroy other buildings, injure people, become drug dens? Some thought the South Bronx a lost cause. Should the City just write off the South Bronx and let the population decline further? Some officials advocated planned shrinkage.[35] Could the land be reclaimed and used for urban farming? Would anyone want to live in the South Bronx in the future? Was government ownership the answer?

With regard to buildings that were boarded or bricked up, a smaller debate raged. Was it worth the money to put decals on the boarded-up windows, mostly pictures of window curtains and flowers in small pots, to make the appearance more benign, or was this deceptive and a waste of money? An attorney I knew, Bruce Gould, who worked for the NYC Department of Housing Preservation and Development, made an argument that is similar to the "broken windows" philosophy of policing—that appearances matter, that broken windows on a block make the whole block look like a slum, and that people will then act accordingly. Thus, the argument went, making these empty, boarded-up buildings look a bit better was a worthwhile minor investment.

By the end of 1986, the City owned about ten thousand multiple-dwelling buildings, comprising close to a hundred thousand apartments throughout the city, taken because of unpaid taxes. Referred to as "in-rem" buildings, about half of them had tenants.[36] These were some of the most substandard buildings in the city, and the government did not have the resources to manage, let alone rehabilitate, such a huge stock of housing.

Although the in-rem buildings were scattered throughout New York City, a disproportionate number were in the South Bronx. In areas of the South Bronx, either vacant, rubble-filled lots or in-rem buildings occupied most of the land.

The physical deterioration of so much of the South Bronx affected almost everything, even the famous landmarks on the Grand Concourse in the West Bronx. By 1970, the once impressive Concourse Plaza Hotel, which had hosted Franklin Roosevelt, the Yankees, and so many extravagant parties, was a welfare hotel. In the early 1980s, the YMHA building, which had been built as a children's shelter, was sold to the Girls Club of New York. The building was still used as a youth center but was quite dilapidated, with the front steps crumbling and closed off, paint peeling off the walls inside, and the swimming pool and locker rooms old, corroded, and seldom used. The Andrew Freedman Home, once a residence for genteel elderly people, was closing. The old Family Court building, next to the Girls Club, was closed and demolition was forthcoming. Loew's Paradise Theatre, where Gene Oliva had proudly worked as an usher (see chapter 1), had been changed into four theaters, obliterating the beautiful architecture, including the domed roof that had shown the stars in the heavens. In a few years, the Paradise closed. The Ascot Theatre, just down the block from Loew's Paradise, had quit showing avant-garde movies and was showing porn. Most of the synagogues were closed, some converted to other uses and some vacant.[37] The gym at Roberto Clemente State Park along the Harlem River was used to house homeless families. It provided no privacy, no dignity. I was shocked the first time I visited it.

So, there was a confluence of factors that caused the destruction—an upwardly mobile middle class moving out of the Bronx, increased numbers of low-income people moving in, accelerated middle-class flight caused by fear of crime and the opening of Co-op City, increased building operating costs, aging buildings, the dramatic devaluation of real estate, landlord disinvestment, severe government cuts to services, a near bankrupt city.

It is still customary to blame people living in devastated communities for the conditions in their area. That has the effect of absolving the rest of society from dealing with the complex issues that cause such destruction. How much easier it is to blame the victim than to deal with disinvestment in poor communities, complex economic issues, racism, structural unemployment, and inequality.

It is important to remember that it wasn't just the South Bronx that burned. Other areas of New York City had fires and significant loss of housing, such as Harlem in Manhattan, and Bedford-Stuyvesant and Brownsville in Brooklyn. The difference was one of scale. In the Bronx, half the borough was affected, home to 750,000 people. Some districts lost two-thirds of their population. In the other boroughs, the losses were less severe in their proportions.

4 People Fight Back

1960S AND 1970S

The 1.7-mile walk from Clay Avenue to Bronx Community College is twenty-four blocks and takes forty-five minutes. Most people, if they didn't have a car to drive, would take a gypsy cab or, if that was too expensive, a bus up the Grand Concourse and then a crosstown bus to travel to the college. Rosalina Luongo was poor and had no carfare. Her only option was to walk the whole way, despite being pregnant and despite the heat of summer, intensified by the miles of concrete. As she walked she noticed the drug dealing and the burned-out stores on Burnside. But like so many people, she was absolutely determined to improve her situation. With tremendous resilience, some residents advanced through education, some through hard work, some through advocacy, and some by starting organizations. Rosalina earned an associate degree, then a bachelor's, and then a master's degree in social work.[1]

As devastation spread, life for the people who remained in the South Bronx became increasingly difficult. The schools no longer served the needs of many children. Hospitals closed. Religious institutions were just starting to adapt to new populations. Many nonprofits closed. In the mid-

1970s, when the South Bronx was at its lowest point and New York City was in the throes of its most serious fiscal crisis, the City's housing director, Roger Starr, proposed the radical idea of planned shrinkage. New York City could solve the problem of what to do about its decaying poor areas by simply withdrawing City services. Resources could then be moved to more affluent areas that were worth the investment. Without police, fire stations, hospitals, and schools, the people remaining in the areas designated for shrinkage would have to leave. The land would become vacant and could be reused in future years, for industry or housing, as the economy improved.[2]

However, the people of the South Bronx, supported by elected officials, were having none of that. Residents, acting singly and in groups, had started taking steps to turn around the South Bronx at least ten years earlier, in the 1960s, and were certainly not going to give up. The '60s were a time of social activism and upheaval, much of it positive, like the increasing awareness of racial and gender inequality, and some of it destructive, particularly the growing use of highly addictive drugs.

MOTHERS FIGHT FOR QUALITY EDUCATION

Evelina López Antonetty epitomizes effective Bronx activism during the '60s and '70s. Born in Puerto Rico, she lived all her adult life in the Bronx. Her early jobs in New York were with government-funded antipoverty programs, including Head Start. She became the president of the PTA at her children's school. She complained to the principal that children were punished for speaking Spanish in school, that parents were not welcome in the school—and the principal threw her out of the school, despite her being the head of the PTA. In response, she went on to organize United Bronx Parents (UBP) with a mission to make schools responsive to the community and to provide needed services. UBP grew quickly, and by 1967 it had nine funded programs and satellite offices in four South Bronx neighborhoods. It offered help with housing and welfare problems. For children and youth, UBP offered child care, dance classes, drug prevention, ESL, and other educational programs. Some of those programs,

This photo was taken in 1978 during the ribbon cutting when ownership of the school annex site was officially transferred to United Bronx Parents (UBP) from New York City for one dollar and the site became known as "La Escuelita." From left to right: Lillian López, UBP board member Miguel Rosario, Lorraine Montenegro (Evelina's daughter and her successor at UBP's reins) with her daughter Stacy, Elba Cabrera, news reporter Melinda Nix, and UBP executive director and founder Evelina López Antonetty. Photo credit: Francisco Molina Reyes II.

as well as office space, were located at La Escuelita, the building that Evelina had convinced the city to give to UBP. After Evelina's death, UBP continued to use the building until Lorraine Montenegro, Evelina's daughter who succeeded her, retired.[3] Vivian Vázquez (introduced in chapter 2) was one of those who benefited from UBP's children's programs, which provided an alternative to playing unsupervised on the streets and in abandoned buildings:

> Eventually, my sister and I became involved with UBP and participated in its summer camp program. Through the efforts of the older youth at UBP and 52 Park, a softball league was established for both boys and girls. The

league had about four girl teams and four boy teams. We fund-raised for our own t-shirts and played all summer long.[4]

But organizing was arguably the most significant aspect of Evelina's work and had the most impact. Elba Cabrera, Evelina's sister, spent most of her career working in the arts and is called by friends and admirers "La Madrina de las Artes." Early in her career, Elba worked with Evelina and is rightly proud of her sister's accomplishments:

> People were really interested in their children, that they should do well in school. We tried to make the schools understand that the children should be taught on par with everyone else. The teachers were not prepared. The children were not getting the same education. She managed to get the district superintendent, Bernard Donovan, removed. She would take parents downtown to picket. She took up causes like bilingual education. Evelina brought in teachers who spoke both languages, who could relate to the kids.
>
> During the teachers' strike of 1968, she actually broke the lock to open the school with the help of the principal, and opened the school, to show that the community wanted the schools open. She was arrested. During that time, the police chief for the Bronx named Evelina "the hell lady."[5]

Kathy Goldman, who later founded a food advocacy organization, Community Food Resource Exchange, and was one of the founders of Food Bank For New York City, worked for Evelina in the early years. She recalls:

> One big focus at UBP was a series of parent trainings that turned into monumental events. We did simultaneous translation. What to do if you have to see the principal? Never go alone. What to do if your child is suspended, etc. Parents were terrified of the school administrators who wielded a great deal of power over their children. The main Hispanic elected officials were speakers at these sessions. Sometimes six hundred people came.[6]

Evelina is credited with being a moving force behind bilingual education in the Bronx, in New York City, and nationally. PS 25 in the Bronx was NYC's first bilingual school, transformed because of Evelina's advocacy. Fernando (Freddy) Ferrer, who was the Bronx borough president from 1987 to 2001, remembers Evelina from NYC Board of Education meetings, years before he was borough president:

We were giving John Doar [president of the Board of Education in 1968]
a hard time. Evelina had an umbrella and she would bang it on the glass
table top. One day she cracked it. I adored her. She was extraordinarily
tough but was also kind.[7]

Evelina organized protests against the movie *Fort Apache the Bronx*.[8]
Her grandson, Joe Conzo Jr., a noted photographer, remembers that
campaign:

The film company making the movie *Fort Apache* approached my grandmother . . . to use her day-care center as a place for Paul Newman, the star
of the movie, to rest during the shooting. She wanted to see the script first.
After reading it, she said hell no, this portrays people as drug addicts and
pimps. My grandmother liked to have younger people take the lead, and
Richie Pérez, who had been a Young Lord, became the face of the opposition. They formed CAFA, Committee Against Fort Apache, to rally community opposition. Richie argued that the movie would have a negative impact
on our children and how the world viewed us. We followed the film crew all
over the Bronx and New York City, protesting every chance we got. I was a
teenager with a camera and took photos of the protests. In the end, the
movie added a disclaimer that it did not portray the real, hardworking people of the Bronx.

This was just one episode in my childhood, which was influenced by my
grandmother, an affectionate, feisty, "hell lady of the Bronx," and my mother,
Lorraine Montenegro, who was just like her. My playgrounds as a young
child were City Hall, the Board of Education, Columbia University,
Washington, D.C.—watching as the adults advocated and demonstrated for
a wide range of important local and national issues.[9]

Farther west in the Bronx, Aurelia Greene—who would later serve as
an assemblywoman for twenty-seven years and as deputy borough
president—was getting an education in educational issues. Aurelia
Greene, whose family was from the West Indies, grew up in the Bronx. She
remembers attending her first parents' association (PA) meeting:

My neighbors nominated me for president of the PA. I had no idea what
they were getting me involved in. The big issue was decentralization. I
wanted community control of schools, not decentralization. Decentralization
gave the community no input.

I became a community activist. I became active in Morrisania Education
Council; it was an outgrowth of President Johnson's War on Poverty. We

opposed the teachers' strike of 1968, kept the schools open, got teachers to cross the picket line, told the lunchroom staff to cross the picket line, and told the parents to send the kids to school and they did.

At the end, we had a celebration for the teachers who had crossed the picket line. It was so successful we had the event for years to raise money for scholarships for students to go to college. We decided to make an appeal to colleges throughout the country to give scholarships to students here. Many did. My husband, Jerome Greene, was the author of the Public School Paraprofessional Program. So, we were able to get housewives and mothers to go back to school. Many became teachers, paraprofessionals, and leaders in the schools. Those were the glory days for me in the '70s.[10]

WAR ON POVERTY

In the 1960s, the federal War on Poverty brought some needed financial resources to the Bronx. The passage of the Economic Opportunity Act and the Food Stamp Act in 1964 provided poor Americans with income and assistance. Medicaid pledged comprehensive health care to very low-income families. Medicare promised health insurance to retirees, but it also covered disabled workers. The Older Americans Act funded nutritional programs and other health-related needs for the elderly.[11] The Immigration Act of 1965 ended quotas that favored immigrants from Europe and, as a result, allowed immigration of people from Africa, the Caribbean, and Asia, many of whom would come to the Bronx.

People mobilized to take advantage of the funding opportunities that the War on Poverty offered. The legislation called for the maximum participation of the people it was intended to help. Leaders arose. One was Ramón Vélez, a controversial leader who, by registering thousands of new voters, had significant political influence. He brought money, programs, and housing into the community. He was investigated repeatedly, but no charges were ever brought against him for misusing government funds.[12]

Fighting for Edible Food

In 1968, War on Poverty legislation provided funding for summer lunches for low-income children. Getting those summer meals instituted in NYC was a battle, though—as was getting the City to improve the quality of food served in the schools. Kathy Goldman describes how Evelina led the fight:

> A group of about a dozen parents from PS 25 came to see Evelina, complaining about the food at the school. Their children really needed that meal but the food was horrible. The mothers felt comfortable complaining about food because food was something they knew about.
>
> Evelina invited every elected official to come to lunch. Rather than giving them lunch at UBP, she took them to PS 25. Seymour Posner, an assemblyman, ate the food and got really sick. Congressman James Scheuer went crazy because it was federal money paying for the food.
>
> We collected the garbage at a number of schools, the food the children were not eating, and took it to Federal Plaza. We wanted them to see the amount of waste. We had called all the newspapers and got a lot of publicity.

The lunches improved. Kathy describes the next important battle:

> UBP was involved in getting more meals for the children, school breakfast and summer lunch. Despite available funding, the Board of Education refused to have the summer meals, saying we are not going to get into this. Evelina pressured the state education commissioner to make the City do it. The state commissioner called her up and said we will give UBP the money directly to do summer meals in NYC. It ended up to this day to be an important program: a thousand locations in the five boroughs, 250,000 meals a day. UBP did everything, found the place where the meals were put together, got the refrigerators, freezers, hired the four hundred people who got jobs. It is not easy scaling up that size [of a] food program.[13]

UBP provided the meals for the entire city for two years, then local providers were selected for each borough. Fifty years later, studies show what Evelina and the parents knew: that healthful school lunches actually improve children's performance. Students given healthful meals showed a 4 percent gain on standardized exams.[14]

Evelina was not afraid to challenge the status quo in order to give the children in her community a chance to succeed. Parents needed to be seen by teachers and principals as important partners in decisions affecting the schools. Children could not learn on an empty stomach. Teachers needed to learn new skills to work with students who did not speak English, and the schools needed to diversify their staff, to hire teachers who were of similar backgrounds as the children.

Evelina understood that communities can have power if they organize and demand it. She knew how to involve elected officials strategically. By starting UBP as a social service organization as well as an advocacy vehicle, she offered important supportive services to families, providing a model for other organizations that came later. Unfortunately, Evelina Antonetty died in 1984, when she was sixty-two years old.

Seniors Gotta Eat, Too

Recognizing that malnutrition and isolation were serious problems among the elderly, the Older Americans Act, part of the War on Poverty legislation, provided funds for nutrition centers for low-income senior citizens. Colleagues of mine, Jeanette Puryear and Larry McFarland, wrote proposals to establish seven senior citizen centers in the West Bronx. Other groups started centers too. The centers were particularly important because so many seniors were isolated from their families who had moved to more affluent areas. Because of this foresight and hard work, the West Bronx was not shortchanged in senior centers, unlike most other types of human services funding. Over the years, some of the centers closed as the City moved funding to other areas, but the centers that were left continue to play an important role in the lives of thousands of low-income seniors.

Linda Zehnder, a gerontologist, was the first director of the Burnside Concourse Senior Center, located in a basement of a synagogue near the CAB office. She remembers her years there:

> Because of the large number of Jewish seniors, our center served kosher meals. A rabbi would come by unannounced to make sure we were observing dietary laws properly. There were two other centers providing kosher meals very nearby.
>
> All the young Jewish people had moved out to Co-op City and other places. The Jews who were left were elderly. Many were Holocaust survivors. Most were very poor and often did not have the benefits they were entitled to. I spent a lot of time helping them apply for benefits such as food stamps and SSI. Because many had long lived without adequate food, the meals were very important to the seniors. When I got there early at 7:30 A.M. to

catch up on paperwork, they would be outside waiting, even on bad days. The center was their whole life.

Gertrude Landau (the first director of the William Hodson Center in the Bronx, the first senior center in the United States) was a friend and mentor of mine. I remember her saying to me when I became overly anxious about some of the seniors, "Just remember they managed before you came into their lives. They are survivors, they got through concentration camps."[15]

FIGHTING FOR A DECENT HOSPITAL

Another sign of the community's power was the battle for a new Lincoln Hospital. The public hospital for the South Bronx, Lincoln was widely known as "the butcher shop." Elba Cabrera recalls her sister's role in this battle:

> When you said Lincoln Hospital, you said, "I don't want to go there, I would rather die than go there." Evelina got involved in Lincoln, the old Lincoln. They weren't doing what they needed to do for the community and she got very involved.[16]

Housed in a huge, deteriorated building that was condemned, Lincoln was clearly the worst hospital in NYC. It had open wards, peeling paint that could poison hospitalized children with lead, and rats in the emergency room. People sometimes waited days to be seen in the latter. Money to build a new hospital had been in the City's budget for twenty-five years but was always used for something else. The Young Lords, a Puerto Rican activist group loosely linked with the Black Panthers, took over the hospital by seizing the administrative office with the help of doctors and nurses on July 14, 1970. Police in riot gear surrounded the building. Mayor Lindsay sent Sid Davidoff, his assistant, to negotiate with the Young Lords. Davidoff later affirmed that he thought their demands were reasonable and that he was sympathetic to them. The Young Lords, thinking they had been heard, were able to leave the hospital, many wearing white lab coats, without being arrested.[17]

While a college student, Miguel (Mickey) Melendez traveled to Chicago with five others in a cramped Volkswagen "bug" to learn about the new Young Lords organization. He became one of the original founders of the

NYC Young Lords Party. Now an educator, he remembers some of the highlights from their work:

> There were two takeovers at Lincoln Hospital. Lincoln was not providing adequate care to the community. The building was condemned four or five times. Condemned for rich people but OK for poor people of the South Bronx. We [Young Lords and the Health Revolutionary Unity Movement] organized doctors, patients, and hospital staff. There was no patient's bill of rights. We put up a complaint table. The first takeover was about the poor quality of care being provided and to demand the building of the new hospital.

Through this action, the Young Lords won their demand for a new hospital, which was opened in 1976, six years after the seizure of the hospital. This represented a huge victory for the community. Mickey continues:

> During that time [late '60s and early '70s], there was a severe heroin epidemic in NYC. There was one hospital in NYC, Morris Bernstein in Manhattan, that provided in/outpatient detoxification programs. Most patients came from 104 zip codes, the Bronx zip codes. At Lincoln, there was no in/outpatient detox. We thought the theories of how methadone worked justified Lilly Pharmaceuticals, the sole producer of methadone; at the end of its trail was a lot of dollar signs.
>
> November 10, 1970, was the second occupation. We went in and established a detox program in the nurses' auditorium. People worked without salaries for months. The best we could negotiate was breakfast, lunch, and dinner for people. We kept it going until funding came through.[18]

Dr. Peter Moyer joined the staff of Lincoln as a young internal-medicine resident shortly after the takeover. He spent six years at Lincoln, most of that time in the old hospital. In his later career, he became medical director of Boston EMS, Fire and Police, and chairman of emergency medicine at Boston University School of Medicine. At Lincoln, he treated the illnesses of a very poor population:

> Medically I saw hypertension, asthma, diabetes, alcoholism, heroin overdoses, and endocarditis and hepatitis from IV drug use, diseases from Puerto Rico like schistosomiasis (a parasite found in freshwater snails in Puerto Rico's rivers) and rheumatic heart disease (not seen now except in the developing world).

Dr. Moyer remembers the Young Lords at Lincoln:

> The Young Lords were active and had an information table in the lobby. They had an educational program, and a meal program for youth. They had a ten-point program about health reform in the South Bronx.
>
> In July '71, a group of mostly white young doctors and nurses emerged from the health wing of Students for a Democratic Society. They decided Lincoln would be a good place to concentrate their efforts so they all went to work at Lincoln. They called themselves the Lincoln Collective. It made Lincoln fairly chaotic but many were good docs. They worked in parallel with the Young Lords. A renowned senior faculty member, Helen Rodríguez, became the new Chair of Pediatrics—a boon to the program's stability.[19]

The Lincoln Collective is credited with pioneering two significant initiatives: improvements in outpatient care delivery and using acupuncture to treat drug addiction. I remember many of CAB's clients going to Lincoln for acupuncture. Pablo Guzmán, now a senior reporter for CBS News, was a Young Lords leader and active in the Lincoln Hospital struggle. Juan González, a founder of the Young Lords, was a columnist for the *Daily News* for thirty years and a noted journalist. The Young Lords and the hospital medical staff demonstrated that concerted organized action can make a huge difference in the quality of health care provided to a community.

FIGHTING FOR COMMUNITY COLLEGE

Residents were increasingly unwilling to accept the lack of adequate institutions. Evelina Antonetty, Ramón Vélez, Herman Badillo (then Bronx borough president and later a congressman) and other leaders fought for the establishment of a community college in the South Bronx that would serve the dominant Puerto Rican as well as the African American population. To properly serve the Puerto Rican population, they wanted the college to be bilingual. Elba Cabrera remembers:

> I remember all the meetings with the City working to found Hostos. It was a big fight to get Hostos, they didn't want to give it to us.[20]

The passage of the Higher Education Act in 1965 made financial aid available to low-income students, providing financial support for the

rapid growth of community colleges nationally. The City was experimenting with open admissions, a policy that allowed any NYC high school
graduate to attend a City University of New York (CUNY) four-year or
two-year college, depending on the student's grades. The goal was to
increase African American and Latino enrollment. The CUNY colleges
were tuition free at the time.

Hostos Community College opened in the fall of 1970 in rented space
that had been a tire factory on 149th Street and the Grand Concourse.
Hostos was chartered to address the health needs of the area, particularly
the critical need for bilingual health workers. Low-skill manufacturing
jobs were disappearing, and the newly emerging service economy needed
educated workers. Unlike most other colleges started around that time,
Hostos was rooted in the neighborhood, both geographically and cultur-
ally. Even though the community surrounding it was crumbling, Hostos
was a symbol of the growing influence of the Puerto Rican population, a
sign of hope for upward mobility for the people of the South Bronx, and a
guardian of Puerto Rican culture.[21]

After her husband died, Supreme Court Justice Sonia Sotomayor's
mother, Celina, started attending Hostos Community College to become a
registered nurse. It was a challenge being a student at the age of forty-
four. She graduated in 1973.[22] Hostos Community College's president, Dr.
David Gómez, comments:

> Sonia Sotomayor's mother's story could be anyone's story, either our current
> students or their parents. Most of our students work and go to school. Many
> have children. They stay up late at night, at the kitchen table, studying. They
> struggle hard to get an education. Even for those who drop out, their expo-
> sure to college may help build the expectation that their children will go to
> college.[23]

Hostos's physical plant was very inadequate, the worst in the City's system. There was no library, no auditorium, no cafeteria, no child-care
center, no elevator. Classes were very overcrowded. And just as bad, the
Board of Higher Education had only signed a ten-year lease for the space.
Unlike other colleges, Hostos owned no property and thus could easily be
eliminated. Students and faculty advocated and publicly demonstrated for
more space. In 1974 the State Legislature provided funds to purchase a

Rally to Save Hostos Community College, in front of Chase Manhattan Bank at
149th Street near Third Avenue in the Bronx. This large rally on November 19, 1975,
was the first major activity of the Community Coalition to Save Hostos led by Ramón
Jiménez. Photo credit: Gerald J. Meyer Collection, Wallace Edgecombe photographer,
Hostos Community College Archives and Special Collections/The City University of
New York.

large building directly across the Grand Concourse. Hostos was now
accredited and the student body was rapidly growing. But disaster was
brewing as the City's finances worsened.

Dr. Gómez arrived at Hostos in 1974 at the age of twenty-two as a
research associate, just a few months before the City's fiscal crisis. CUNY's
budget had grown tremendously because of the increasing student population in all the colleges. The City was on the verge of bankruptcy. The
Emergency Financial Control Board, effectively in charge of the City's
finances in 1975, was demanding huge cuts in order to balance the City's
budget and unfreeze the bond market. Describing the reaction of the

faculty and students to the realization that the City was likely to close Hostos or merge it with Bronx Community College, Dr. Gómez recalls:

> There was an outpouring of frustration, coupled with resolve. It won't be our college that closes. I didn't lead the charge, others did. The movement was partly inspirational and partly chaotic. Ramón Jiménez was one of the charismatic leaders. Others involved were José Rivera, José Serrano, Carmen Arroyo [all either elected officials or future elected officials]. It didn't start out as a movement but coalesced into a movement. It started out with frustrated people.[24]

Students, faculty, and community residents organized letter-writing campaigns, mass demonstrations, and the takeovers of buildings. They were led by Ramón Jiménez, a Harvard Law School graduate and adjunct faculty member; Gerald Meyers, a professor; Nilsa Saniel, a student and mother of three; Wally Edgecombe, in the development office; Efrain Quintana, of an ex-prisoners association; Petri Byrd, then a student and now on the TV show *Judge Judy;* and many others. They demanded that Hostos stay open. One day, faculty and students took chairs onto the Grand Concourse and taught in the middle of the street, causing a major traffic jam for puzzled motorists. People marched on symbols of power, including the offices of the *New York Times.*

The seizure of the college's main building on March 24, 1976, lasted twenty days—the longest takeover in the history of colleges in the United States. During that time, a day-care center was set up in the president's office. Classes were taught. UBP helped provide food and support. Thousands of supporters were involved, including religious leaders Father John Flynn and Reverend Paul Moore. On the eleventh day of the takeover, the Board of Higher Education voted to close Hostos.

To end the occupation, Ramón Jiménez and forty others agreed to be arrested, risking having a criminal record to save this important institution. They were led out of the building in chains to the cheers of hundreds of their supporters. Ultimately, Bronx legislators, including Robert Garcia and Jóse Serrano, were able to add a provision while voting on the state budget that Hostos stay open. The college was saved. Ramón went on to open a law office in the area that provided legal help to residents for the next forty years. What a difference this major victory has made in the lives of thousands of people over the years, as Dr. Gómez explains:

> A community college degree is now equivalent to what a high school degree was in the 1940s. The high school degree was the great differentiator, now it is the community college degree. When Hostos students get a degree, possibilities open up for them that were not there before. The degree is life-changing for them.[25]

Marion Streater Johnson, my dental hygienist, earned her dental hygiene degree at Hostos in 1983. She grew up in the Forest public housing project and had a happy childhood, shopping at Alexander's Department Store, eating hamburgers at White Castle, and going to the Whitestone Drive-In movie theater:

> I attended a vocational high school and became a dental office assistant. I worked in that position for sixteen years, working for many different dentists, some on the Grand Concourse. My husband wanted me to go to college. The courses at Hostos were hard. Each semester I had to take between nineteen and twenty-one credits. It took two years and a summer. The tests kicked my butt. They weren't like the multiple choice that I had in high school, where you chose A, B, C, or D for your answer. Instead the choices were A and B, B only, A and C, etc.
>
> Hostos's dental hygiene program is highly accredited, as is the x-ray technician degree. Getting the degree was life-changing for me. It doubled or tripled my earning potential. I am my own boss, no one is standing over me telling me what to do. I still love going to work. I am sixty-eight. I have lived in the Bronx since I was seven. I still love the Bronx.[26]

Hostos now enrolls over seven thousand students annually and has a graduation rate above the national average for community colleges. Its allied health programs remain strong, and other specialties have been added.[27] The efforts of community leaders to start Hostos and the struggle of students, faculty, and residents to save it resulted in a stable and growing institution that provides a path to upward mobility for tens of thousands of South Bronx residents.

The South Bronx has another important community college, Bronx Community College, which occupies a forty-five-acre campus that used to be New York University Uptown. It has thirty academic programs and enrolls 11,500 students from a hundred countries, including a thousand students from twenty-seven African nations. Dr. Thomas A. Isekenegbe, who is from Nigeria, is president of Bronx Community College. (A little-known fact is that the Young Lords, prior to taking over Lincoln Hospital, also took over Bronx Community College to demand the establishment of Latino and black studies departments.)[28]

FIGHTING FOR A COMMUNITY, FOR REAL JOBS, FOR A FUTURE

Hetty Fox's parents were the first African American homeowners on Lyman Place in the Morrisania section of the Bronx, very near where Joan Canada lived.[29] After graduating from college, moving to California, earning two master's degrees, and teaching at the college level, Hetty felt compelled to return to her childhood neighborhood in 1970. The neighborhood was deteriorating and she wanted to do what she could to help bring it back.

She bought a house, renovated it, and turned it into an arts and education community center, including running an after-school program for children. She sponsored holiday parties for children, making sure all those twelve and under received a present. For forty years, Hetty ran a summer play street, often for twelve hours a day. Understanding the importance of community, she wanted neighbors to know each other, and she wanted to hear the sound of children having fun. Lyman Place and the area around it are now renovated and rebuilt. It's clear that Hetty made a difference in the lives of many children.[30] Her life demonstrates the impact a determined person can have.

The same year Hetty Fox moved back to Lyman Place, Astin Jacobo, a union organizer, had to flee the Dominican Republic. He settled in the Crotona area of the Bronx and took a job as a custodian at a Catholic school. Knowing the impact sports can have in young people's lives, he persuaded the school to allow neighborhood children to use the gym after school hours. He organized sports teams and, over a number of years, got the City to create two ball fields in vacant lots in the area, one of which is named after him.

Astin helped found the Crotona Community Coalition and served as its president for twenty-five years. The group worked on issues of crime, arson, and housing; created community gardens; stopped the City from tearing down six blocks of partially occupied buildings; and organized tenants' associations. He was delighted with the eventual renaissance of his area, when all the abandoned buildings and vacant lots were rebuilt. Thanks to his hard work, in 1998 the Mary Mitchell Family and Youth Center opened. A street near the Bronx Zoo was co-named Astin Jacobo Way.[31]

Many other people with a strong sense of social justice found their own ways to fight for fairness. Community activist Kathryn Speller tells why she got involved fighting for men who were paid a stipend, not a real salary, for doing hard, dangerous work:

> The Bureau of Pest Control was cleaning out abandoned buildings and empty lots, filled with all kinds of garbage and debris, causing rat infestation. The men who worked in the field came from a training program and were mainly ex-convicts and ex-addicts. It was hard for them to get jobs. They were not paid on a par with City workers. They worked in their own clothes, with just sneakers, no protective overalls or boots. I became an organizer for the union because the men were being taken advantage of. We got them recognized as City provisional workers with benefits. Some received three to four years' back pay. This changed their lives. They became City workers, not slave labor. They were better able to support their families and become part of society.[32]

STREET GANGS' PEACE TREATY

Vivian Vázquez reflects on the youth gangs of her childhood:

> My mom sold Avon to the gang members' girlfriends. The gang members were young, naive, stupid, not paid attention to. There was a lack of social structure, and the gangs filled that void in the lives of the young people. The gangs were scary but the members were also our neighbors. There are still gangs. Maybe there are fewer kids in the gangs, but now they have guns.[33]

Since the 1940s or even earlier, like much of New York City, the Bronx had youth gangs, prone to fighting and illegal activity. With the terrible and deteriorating conditions in the South Bronx in the late '60s and '70s, violent gangs flourished. Over forty gangs were active in the Mott Haven-Hunts Point area. One of the larger gangs, the Ghetto Brothers, was starting to morph into a positive force, influenced by the Black Panthers, Evelina Antonetty, and Evelina's daughter Lorraine Montenegro of UBP. But the beating and killing of twenty-five-year-old Cornel "Black Benjy" Benjamin, the "peace ambassador" for the Ghetto Brothers, had the potential to start a round of retaliatory killings.

Benjamin Melendez, the leader of the Ghetto Brothers, wanted to avoid more violence. He called a peace meeting in December 1971 at the Hoe Avenue Boys Club. Over two hundred gang leaders attended and agreed to the peace treaty. The treaty helped reduce street violence. Gang members could often walk safely through other gangs' territories and attend other gangs' street parties. Many credit the peace meeting with allowing hip hop to develop as cross-fertilization of musical ideas and styles developed in the street parties. Hip hop allowed young people to have fun, express themselves, and compete without violence.[34]

Another example of a gang member who turned his life around to help his community is Fernando Laspina, the leader of the Savage Skulls. After serving time in prison, he attended Hostos Community College, participated in the fight to save Hostos, then went on to earn a bachelor's and a master's degree. He taught at Hostos for ten years, became a youth counselor, and opened a boxing organization, El Maestro, for youth in the area. His gym also serves as a cultural center.[35]

CHURCHES AND COMMUNITY-BASED AGENCIES SLOWLY START FILLING THE VOID

New community institutions such as churches and nonprofit human services agencies slowly started to take root and grow as the population changed. In the late 1950s and '60s, a handful of youth-serving agencies moved to the Bronx from Manhattan. Madison Square Boys Club opened a clubhouse in the Crotona Park section in 1958, which later became the Hoe Avenue Club House. The Police Athletic League's Lynch Center, started earlier in the '40s, had a tremendous influence on the development of the arts. East Side House Settlement bought a brownstone in the Mott

Haven section of the South Bronx in 1963. It offered youth programs to residents of New York City Housing Authority projects. Kips Bay Boys Club moved to the Bronx in 1969. Casita Maria moved from East Harlem to an unused synagogue in Longwood in 1961. Many people who grew up in the area credit Casita Maria for providing a haven where they could pursue their interests and talents. BG183 (Sotero Ortiz) remembers it well:

> I was born in 1963. We moved to 923 Simpson Street in 1968. Casita Maria was right across the street. Everyone went there, all the neighborhood kids went there, table tennis, basketball court, summer youth program. Casita took kids different places, on trips out of the city. We also had a softball team. In the winter, you got a card that gave you activities from 6 to 8 P.M. There really was nothing else around. Fortunate that it was right across the street. If kids lived further than four to five blocks away, you couldn't really travel there.[36]

Most of the institutions that served the white population closed or changed hands, leaving a significant void for many years. Three large YMHA facilities in the South Bronx closed, as did other Jewish agencies. These established agencies had been comparatively well funded, through member donations and the United Jewish Appeal and Federation of Jewish Philanthropies. For new, upstart organizations in very poor areas there is no obvious philanthropic base of support. Some Jewish organizations had the foresight to identify local groups to take over their work. For example, the Forest Neighborhood House, founded in 1945 by the National Council of Jewish Women, transferred its operations to a newly incorporated African American organization, the Southeast Bronx Neighborhood Centers, in 1971.[37]

A few agencies were founded in the '60s to serve the newer population. ASPIRA, a Puerto Rican youth development agency founded in 1961, worked with young people in Manhattan and the Bronx, several of whom became well-known leaders, including Fernando Ferrer and Gladys Carrión. Claremont Neighborhood Centers was founded in 1965, serving residents of public housing in Morrisania. Davidson Community Center was started in 1965 in the West Bronx. Bronx River Houses (home to

Afrika Bambaataa) and its community center provided a stage for early hip-hop musicians. Bronx Frontier, founded in 1978 by Irma Fleck, experimented with creating community gardens using compost material from the Hunts Point Produce Market and later from the Bronx Zoo. Seneca Neighborhood Center, with director Edd Lee, provided youth activities in Hunts Point. Bronx 2000, founded by David Muchnick in 1979, experimented with economic development plans, including salvaging wood from shipping pallets for use in making furniture and flooring. Bronx Frontier, Bronx 2000, and Seneca Center are no longer operational.

Federal antipoverty funds provided a base for community corporations and multiservice centers, such as the Hunts Point Community Corporation, the Hunts Point Multiservice Corporation, and the South Bronx Community Housing Corporation.[38]

The West Bronx Jewish Community Council was started in 1972 to give support to the poor, frail, elderly Jewish population still living in the area and later expanded its mission to serve a broader population. South Bronx Action Group provided assistance similar to CAB's but was much farther south. Its executive director, Carmen Allende, served as a board member for CAB for many years. Some small agencies that were started around the same time lasted a few years and then closed. Remember that the South Bronx is a large area and was home to over 750,000 people, so these nonprofits could serve only a small fraction of the population.

Several African American churches bought large synagogue buildings, allowing them to expand as the African American population in the Bronx grew. First Union Baptist Church bought the Tremont Temple Gate of Mercy on the Grand Concourse in 1974. Walker Memorial Church moved from Harlem to the mid-Bronx area in 1975 and purchased the Sephardic Center on East 169th Street.

Outside of government, the Catholic Church, with its many parishes and multitude of churches, arguably had the most capacity to assist. Most of the Catholic schools remained open during this period. Most priests in the Bronx did not see themselves as social activists. However, those who did had great impact. In 1973, Paul Brant, a doctoral student at Fordham University, and Father Jason McCarthy of Holy Spirit Church raised money from local banks and started the Morris Heights Neighborhood

Improvement Program to work on local housing issues. Morris Heights provided the model for what became the Northwest Bronx Community and Clergy Coalition (NWBCCC).[39]

The Morris Heights Neighborhood Improvement Program closed after a few years. But it spawned the Morris Heights Health Center, now a large facility in the West Bronx serving the health needs of forty-eight thousand low-income Bronx residents annually. With funding from the Economic Opportunity Act of 1964, it was part of the national movement to establish community health centers in underserved, poor areas. Community health centers in the Bronx now have thirty-seven primary care sites and a total of 117 sites (including school-based, mental health, and other specialized services). Nearly half of the Bronx's low-income residents are patients of a community health center.[40]

Another well-known network of community health centers in the South Bronx is the Urban Health Plan, founded in 1974 by Dr. Richard Izquierdo, who had been treating patients in his office and saw the huge unmet need for high-quality health care. He bought an abandoned building and created the San Juan Health Center, which became the Urban Health Plan. Dr. Izquierdo, a highly respected leader in many community activities as well as the driving force behind the health center, received the Surgeon General's Medallion in 2007. His daughter, Paloma Izquierdo-Hernandez, succeeded him as CEO and oversaw the expansion of Urban Health Plan from a one-site facility to a network of nine federally qualified community health centers, plus school health centers and several other programs. Urban Health Plan is an acknowledged leader in the treatment of pediatric asthma and pioneered the extensive use of community health workers. They have developed a model of upward career mobility for staff from the community and have won numerous awards.[41]

STARTING THE CITIZENS ADVICE BUREAU

Kathryn Speller describes the situation of the West Bronx in 1970:

> There was very little formal help for people in the area. The Jewish agencies had closed or were just serving elderly Jews. The Catholics had a large hospital for the terminally ill, Calvary Hospital, which later moved to

the North Bronx. The building became Project Return, a residential drug treatment program. There were some small senior citizen centers. Youth were very underserved.[42]

Mildred Zucker, a social worker for the Federation of Protestant Welfare Agencies, was the driving force behind the establishment of a CAB in the Bronx. During and after World War II, Great Britain had developed a network of several hundred easily accessible offices, also called Citizens Advice Bureaus, where residents could get information and/or referrals on virtually any problem they were facing. Mildred thought that people in the Bronx, especially low-income people, could benefit from this type of very practical assistance—someone they could meet with easily who would help them resolve the problems they were having, no matter what the problems were.

At a conference in 1964 in Washington, D.C., on "Extension of Legal Services for the Poor," Mildred presented a paper arguing that the British CAB model should be transplanted to the United States. The social service system, fueled by War on Poverty funding, was developing in America to help the poor, but it was bureaucratic and could be hard to navigate.

In April 1972, a CAB office was opened in the Bronx. The Federation of Protestant Welfare Agencies and the West Bronx Council rented a store-front at 2103 Grand Concourse. Ed Kaufman, who had a master's degree in social work, was hired as the first director of CAB in May 1972.

The opening of the office was a community effort. The Bronx Council on the Arts helped design the center. Most of the furniture was donated, and other agencies provided transportation to pick it up. Young people from a drug treatment program painted the center, a local tailor made the curtains, and community residents donated plants.

The need for the service was confirmed within its first three months as community residents made more than eight hundred visits to the office. Word-of-mouth was always the most effective outreach. About half of the people who sought help were seniors, primarily white seniors. However, CAB always had bilingual (English- and Spanish-speaking) staff and helped large numbers of younger Puerto Ricans and African Americans.

From the very beginning, the main issue people of all backgrounds needed help with was housing. The second area that residents requested help with was public benefits, primarily food stamps and welfare. Employment ranked third. Some days the center, staffed only by the director, his assistant, and a youth corps worker, stayed open until midnight to meet the demand. They filled out forms, made phone calls, and wrote letters.

The office had clearly established itself as a vital community resource at the end of its first year, having handled 8,380 visits by 4,787 different people. The racial and ethnic mix in the neighborhood was rapidly changing. Toni Downes, a graduate social work student placed at CAB who later became its second executive director, noted that by 1974, the population was becoming younger as more families with children moved in. A study showed that 20 percent of the population of the neighborhood was black, 29 percent Puerto Rican, 17 percent Jewish, 12 percent Irish, and the remainder from other backgrounds; 17 percent of the population received some sort of cash assistance, and 20 percent received Social Security.

Ed Kaufman also worked to improve systems that affected people's lives. In his reports, Ed documented the more than doubling of cases handled at the Fordham Welfare Center with no increase in staff. He stated that people were being denied their rights. He also discussed the need for a psychiatric counseling service for senior citizens and noted the opening of the first senior citizen center in the area. Ed understood the problems senior citizens were having. In terms of the changing neighborhood and an increase in crime, he wrote in a report that although many, but by no means all, senior citizens may have wanted to move, many could not because of their low income:

> The infirmities of age and fear of moving to new neighborhoods where they will have no friends and not know the area are reasons hindering the elderly from moving. Many elderly do not feel they have the strength to pack and otherwise prepare for a major move. Also, the elderly, unable to travel, are dependent on local physicians and merchants who make special arrangements with the senior citizens.[43]

Ed worked closely with Community Board 5 to bring attention to these problems, by cosponsoring public hearings and writing letters. He initiated a large annual Thanksgiving Day dinner for senior citizens, run by volunteers, and it continued for more than fifteen years. Seniors in the area needed small jobs done, such as fixing the pulleys on windows so they could be opened and closed, changing lightbulbs in ceiling fixtures, fixing leaking faucets, and caulking windows—all tasks that could be very difficult or impossible for many elderly people to do for themselves and ones that many landlords were unwilling to do. With support from the congressman and the borough president, Ed started the city's first minor-repairs program for the elderly.

For many years, a key supporter was Sister Gemma Hessian, the administrator of Calvary Hospital. She became the first executive director of Fordham Tremont Community Mental Health Center, which she helped start along with Father Robert Benome and Brother Patrick Lochrane. Gemma chaired CAB's management committee and later the board of directors.

The staff in the early years consisted of the executive director and an assistant. Myrna Pérez worked at CAB over twenty-five years, was promoted many times, and later became the director of an office. She was a very caring person who was greatly respected by everyone who knew her.

By the time Ed Kaufman left CAB in 1977 and Toni Downes was hired as the next executive director, the service was entrenched in the community. As always, more than 40 percent of the problems were housing related. Toni describes the work:

> Folks from the neighborhood who couldn't read due to illiteracy, language barriers, or declining eyesight would bring in official correspondence to ask what it meant. Or they brought in notices that food stamps or financial assistance were being cut. People didn't know what was expected of them to retain benefits. Housing-related issues were a significant part of weekly volume: eviction notices which required immediate attention and considerable staff time on the phone, senior-citizen rent-increase exemption recertifications, notices of rent increases that were improperly calculated, and always, residents struggling to get apartment repairs completed.[44]

CAB received good publicity from the start. A long article in the *New York Post* described the founding of the office and the important role it was playing in the community. An article in a Sunday edition of the *New York Times*, titled "Bringing Help to Neighborhoods," had a photo and described several people who were helped.[45] *El Diario-La Prensa* published an article titled "Soluciones para la Comunidad."

In 1977, Jerry Shroder, a senior staff member of the Community Council of Greater New York, and Toni Downes were able to convince the NYC HRA to fund CAB with a $50,000 grant from the recently passed Title XX of the Social Security Act. This was a very significant accomplishment because it provided a stable source of funding for a good many years.

I started as executive director of CAB in 1979. Toni had just moved the agency to 2050 Grand Concourse, the "old Elks Club building." The location was perfect, right on a busy corner of the Grand Concourse, very accessible to thousands of people. Clearly, the large stone building had once been as grand as the Concourse. The beautiful brass door weighed a ton—so heavy it was hard for the seniors to open. Downstairs was one of the largest oak bars I have ever seen. CAB rented one large room on the street level, with lots of windows looking out on the Concourse. The front end of the room was used as a waiting area, with donated, mismatched chairs. In the back was the photocopy machine that seldom worked as it should, an electric typewriter with bottles of Wite-Out, and many file cabinets filled with case records. By the end of the day, a cloud of smoke clung to the ceiling. Most people smoked in that era, and it was viewed as an infringement to ask someone to stop. In the middle of the room were an assortment of donated wooden desks, each with a chair for the worker and a chair for the client. Privacy was lacking, but that didn't seem to bother people much. Everyone there had problems.

Fittingly, we shared many of our neighbors' and clients' building problems. Heat in our office was sporadic and never adequate in winter. We learned how hard it is to write case notes with gloves and winter coats on. Roaches lived in desk drawers and (later, when one was purchased) the water cooler. I brought in boric acid to sprinkle along the edges of the drawers.

I understood early in my career at CAB why most of our clients needed an advocate. Staff members had advantages and tools that our clients didn't. We had phones. Unable to afford home phones, most residents had to use pay phones on the street and tried to reach the welfare worker or landlord until their dimes or their quarters ran out. Staff, when we called on behalf of a client, could leave a callback number. Unlike so many of our clients, we were literate—we could read, understand, and fill out often complicated government questionnaires. We spoke English. We had some clout—we were calling from an agency, keeping records of whom we spoke to, and could make official complaints if necessary. We had typewriters and photocopy machines. We could parse out and describe complicated problems in such a way that the other party, government or landlord, could more easily understand and act on them.

Over the years, we also developed connections: a lawyer at Legal Aid who would give us advice or take a case, a friendly landlord who would rehouse someone in an emergency, a contact at the central office of the Human Resources Administration that oversees welfare and food stamps who would intervene in egregious cases, a food pantry that could give out emergency food to a family in dire straits.

In the early years of CAB, the '70s and '80s, we were the only agency offering this kind of help in our Grand Concourse area of the South Bronx. The line outside of the office would form well before nine o'clock each morning. The small staff struggled to see everyone who was waiting. Meanwhile, the Lower East Side of Manhattan, an area of similar size to ours, had six large, well-established settlement houses. West Bronx residents needed help and we were pretty much it.

HOSPITALS CLOSING, JOB LOSS, BLACKOUT

The Bronx was hit hard during NYC's close brush with bankruptcy in the mid-1970s. Residents mobilized to fight the threat of hospital closings. Like many others, including Kathryn Speller and her friends, I marched in those demonstrations. However, unlike the battle to save Hostos Community College, these fights were lost. Two large, important hospitals, Fordham and Morrisania, were closed in 1976. The loss of Fordham, the Bronx's first public hospital, was a huge blow to the community, which had mobilized strongly, staging sit-ins and other demonstrations to keep it open.[46] To fill the gap, Bronx Lebanon Hospital expanded its capacity over the years and Montefiore Hospital, located in the North Bronx, opened clinics in the South Bronx. Another public hospital, North Central Bronx, was built adjacent to Montefiore. In low-income areas, hospitals are especially important, as emergency rooms are too often a primary source of care when people are ill.

Despite the efforts of nascent housing groups, the housing crisis worsened during the '70s, with thousands of middle-class people leaving (along with their tax money), accelerating the abandonment of buildings by landlords. The rise of heroin and the decline of municipal services during the fiscal crisis, including garbage collection, fire coverage, and adequate funding for education and parks added to the growing despair. Half of Hispanic civil service workers and one-third of African Americans working for the City lost their jobs.[47] Crime was up throughout the country, especially in the cities, including New York and certainly the Bronx.

The impact of the NYC blackout of 1977, which occurred in the heat of summer, was particularly harsh in poor areas. Many of those areas exploded. Looting was widespread. A friend told me that his teenage brother brought home a television; their father was so outraged that he beat him severely. Fifty new cars were stolen from a dealership in the Bronx. The fire department struggled to deal with hundreds of fires. Thousands were arrested.[48] Many local businesses closed permanently as a result. Some credit the blackout for the rapid development of hip hop, as musicians were able to procure equipment that night that was otherwise unaffordable to them.[49]

Joseph Reyes was twenty-two years old and working in his family's dry-cleaning business on the corner of Burnside, one block east of the Grand Concourse. He now owns the business. Joseph recalls:

> We were driving home from the store when we heard there was a blackout. We heard later that evening that stores were being vandalized. We didn't expect anything since the neighborhood where we lived was quiet. Driving down the Grand Concourse the next morning, we could see all the vandalism. We could see the gates pulled off the stores, both the roll-down gates and the accordion gates were pulled off and the stores were vandalized. The smoke was still coming out some of them. It was kind of scary. We arrived at East Burnside, corner of Anthony, and everything was intact. Quite a few of the storekeepers who lived in the area came in and protected their property and our block. The stores on the west side of the Grand Concourse were heavily damaged.[50]

Years later, some of our senior citizens believed that our local business street was called Burnside because so many stores had been burned. Deputy Borough President Aurelia Greene describes the aftermath:

The blackout changed everything, it was the downfall of the Bronx. That was when people really started running from the Bronx. They didn't want to stay here. It was everyone. You couldn't find anything. I shopped in Albany, I stopped shopping here because the stores weren't here.[51]

Sallie Smith, who still lives in the area, agrees:

Burnside and Tremont were very viable business districts before the blackout of 1977. There was a very nice supermarket with a butcher to cut the meat you wanted. There were jewelry stores and restaurants. The stores weren't just the cheap stores you see today. After the blackout, many of the stores didn't come back. The real estate market never really recovered.[52]

Joe Conzo Jr.'s family prioritized the community's needs in their response to the blackout:

I remember a unique experience of the blackout of '77. My mother took me and the other kids to a warehouse in Hunts Point where the food for summer meals was stored. We moved all the food to refrigerated trucks so it would not be spoiled. Children depended on the school meals during the school year but would go hungry during the summer without the summer lunch meals.[53]

DON'T MOVE, IMPROVE

Even during this time of extreme hardship, more pockets of resistance to the destruction arose. As apartment buildings became abandoned, the City did one of only two things—either demolished them or sealed them up, neither of which improved the neighborhoods. Community groups started resisting the demolition of buildings.[54] Some people took matters into their own hands. Squatters moved into a few abandoned buildings and started repairing them themselves. Their claim to ownership, their equity, was not money but their hard labor. The "sweat equity" concept was born.

Residents of a portion of Kelly Street that was curved like a banana formed an organization they called Banana Kelly Community Improvement Association, Inc. It was started by Leon Potts, the son of a man who owned four buildings on the block, and activist Harry DeRienzo, who became the executive director. Along with thirty neighborhood residents, they took over three abandoned buildings in order to prevent their demolition. Although there was really no government or private funding available at that time for housing renovation, they were able to cobble together two grants to get started and eventually closed on a sweat equity construction loan in 1979.[55] Banana Kelly grew more rapidly when funding became available for building renovation in the late 1980s. By the mid-1990s, it had rehabbed more than two thousand units of housing and was actively managing a thousand units.[56] Harry DeRienzo talks about the importance of community in this success:

> Government, the private sector, and society as a whole wrote off the South Bronx, as they did so many other so-called inner-city neighborhoods. But, as we aptly demonstrated, within these neighborhoods were communities of people who had formed strong social networks over years of government and private neglect. These are the people who preserved and rebuilt the Bronx.[57]

The pastor of St. Athanasius Church, Father Louis Gigante, along with Sister Miriam Thomas, started reclaiming a section of Longwood in the late '60s, forming the South East Bronx Community Organization (SEBCO). Father G, as he was known, was fluent in Spanish from his time as a young priest stationed in Puerto Rico and had a background working with young people. An outspoken and aggressive advocate for his community, he was not opposed to taking direct action, including disrupting a City Council hearing and setting a huge bonfire in his area to draw attention to the deplorable conditions in the neighborhood. He ran for Congress unsuccessfully in 1970 but was elected to the City Council in 1973.

By 1976, Father G was able to acquire resources to rehabilitate 360 units of housing, using funding from tax shelters and Section 8. By the mid-1980s, SEBCO managed over two thousand apartments, including some in Hunts Point. Father G retired as an active priest in 2002 but stayed on as head of SEBCO for another five years. By the time he fully retired, SEBCO was responsible for building or rehabbing six thousand units of housing. His area of the South Bronx was one of the first reclaimed, and the results were extremely impressive. His name can still be seen from the Bruckner Expressway, in huge letters on the sides of buildings.[58]

Sister Thomas was the administrator of the Simpson Street Development Association for thirty-two years. Greatly beloved by the community because of the depth of her involvement in many community organizations and activities, she had an apartment building and a street named after her.

Other community development groups formed shortly after SEBCO: South Bronx Overall Economic Development Corporation with John Patterson in 1972; Mid-Bronx Senior Citizens Council with Jeanette Puryear and Dennis Terry in 1973; the Mid Bronx Desperados with Genevieve Brooks and Father William Smith in 1974; the Longwood Community Association with Thomas Bess and Marilyn Smith, which led to the Longwood Historic District, in 1980;[59] Bronx Shepherds with Bronx pastors and Ted Jefferson in 1980; and Highbridge CDC with Father Donald Sakano and Jorge Batista in 1984. Genevieve Brooks, prior to starting the Mid Bronx Desperados, was one of the first community leaders to try to draw attention to the fires and the arson.[60] As more and more pockets of good buildings formed and spread, hope started gaining over desperation. Many of these groups now manage thousands of units of housing.

Farther north in the Bronx, residents had great concern that the abandonment, crime, and fires that had destroyed so much of the South Bronx would overtake their neighborhoods. Based on the success of the newly formed Morris Heights Neighborhood Improvement Association, Paul Brant raised funds to hire organizers for parishes. NWBCCC was formed in 1974 as the umbrella group for the newly formed associations. The neighborhood associations worked on issues related to housing, crime, drugs, and quality of city services.

One key to successful organizing is to have some early victories. Bill Frey, one of the first organizers when NWBCCC was being formed, describes one of its first successes:

> One of the early issues was with a block of private homes on Valentine Avenue that the Lindsay administration was going to condemn in order to build a school. The white homeowners heard about it and sold. Latinos and African Americans bought the houses, not knowing the homes were going to be condemned. It was my first experience working with people who were able to change their conditions through organizing. They actually beat City Hall and saved their homes.

Redlining by banks was a huge issue. Redlining served as a death warrant to areas. Families could not buy homes and owners of multiple dwellings could not borrow funds to make needed repairs. Bill describes how NWBCCC tackled this:

> We had to gather the information about who the local banks were actually lending to. Teams of people, perhaps a mailman, a worker in a luncheonette, a teacher, and a clergyman would go to the bank and ask for the information. The banks were required to provide it because of the Home Mortgage Disclosure Act. What we found was that the banks were not making loans in the Bronx, except maybe a few in Riverdale, and that the money was going to the sun belt, to Florida. The deposits were from the Bronx but the money was being invested far away.[61]

Members of the coalition used that information to confront the banks. If the banks would not meet with them, they would picket the banks' offices or the homes of the banks' directors in wealthy suburbs like Scarsdale. They demanded that the bankers and insurance company executives attend public meetings where they were asked to commit to specific corrective actions in front of large numbers of community residents. Joyce Davis, then of Mount Hope Housing and NWBCCC, thinks back on the battles:

> We didn't get all the drugs out but things got better. There was no way for people who owned homes to get insurance, we were redlined. The [NWBCCC] dealt with all those issues, insurance, drugs, crime, housing. They made me understand that people power equals change. Coming together we make things happen.[62]

Individuals also did what they could in their own immediate neighborhoods. Concerned neighborhood activists like Loretta Roderick Smith, a founding member of Mount Hope Housing who had a street named after her, organized play streets so the children would have a place to play in the summer. She was one of the many people who understood the importance of giving back, a phrase one often hears in the Bronx. Kathryn Speller describes efforts on her block:

> With Rick Cordero, I formed a neighborhood block association and tried to start tenants' associations in all the buildings in our neighborhood. We put on block parties and hired buses for outings to Rye Playland. People from all back-

grounds got along and banded together for the good of the neighborhood. We advocated to get the empty buildings closed up with cinder blocks. Because I am black and he was Hispanic we were able to unite people better.[63]

CITY SEIZES DERELICT APARTMENTS

The passage of Local Law 45 of 1976, also known as the quick vesting law, had tremendous impact. The law changed the length of time the City waited to take ownership of tax-delinquent properties from ten years to two years. Very rapidly, the City found itself owning a hundred thousand units of housing, a great many of which were in the South Bronx.[64] A new City agency, the Department of Housing Preservation and Development (HPD), was charged with handling this inventory.

Nicole Levin, who had studied art and architecture, was working for Ramón Vélez at the time. She later worked for HPD for many years, creating new programs promoting collaboration with community organizations and overseeing CAB's and other nonprofits' contracts that focused on stabilizing this housing portfolio. She describes the daunting task HPD faced:

> There was mass confusion. This was before technology, so cataloguing which buildings were occupied, which were safe, which had heat, who was paying rent, what repairs were needed was pretty much impossible.[65]

Despite the confusion, the City had to move ahead quickly to stabilize as many buildings as possible. The City's initial response was the creation of two resident-driven programs, sweat equity and Tenant Interim Lease (TIL). The volume of buildings was so massive that within a few years, three programs were settled upon to handle the majority of the huge inventory of buildings: TIL, Community Management, and Private Ownership Management Program (POMP). Community Management allowed local nonprofit housing groups to manage the buildings, with the City funding some essential rehab. Under POMP, for-profit landlords could manage the building for a year, make major repairs, and then buy the building for a nominal amount. Nonprofit advocates felt that POMP was a giveaway to for-profit landlords and used the slogan "Don't Pimp with POMP" to state their opposition to this windfall for owners who may have previously neglected or even abandoned buildings. Banana Kelly had provided a workable model for sweat equity, but the program was phased out in 1980.[66]

TIL allowed tenant associations to work toward turning their buildings into low-income co-ops where tenants would own their apartments, with the government footing the cost of major rehabilitation. Nicole Levin describes the process:

> With TIL, HPD's working motto for tenants in the buildings was "If you can do it, we will let you." For example, they told tenants if the tenants could collect rent and invest that money in the building, the City would also invest, maybe by putting them on automatic oil delivery, or by repairing the roof or buying a new boiler. Classes training tenants in building management maintenance and governance were created. Once basic repairs were completed and tenants were competent in management, they could buy their apartments for $250 each.[67]

Since many of the buildings were in very poor condition when ownership was transferred to the City, there were no easy fixes because what was needed was a lot of money, which did not appear until about ten years later. But these programs provided tools for the tenants to take self-help steps with some assistance from the City. In the South Bronx, more and more pockets of housing improved. Anchors of stability appeared here and there.

Public housing was not affected by the fires and abandonment and remained occupied throughout the period. This is not to say there were not significant problems in public housing, with crime, drugs, and increasingly deferred maintenance. But for many residents, public housing was a stable place to live, with low rents, if one could ever get through the long applicant waiting lists.

MUSIC: BRONX CULTURE TAKES OFF

Music was an important part of the lives of African Americans and Puerto Ricans living in South Bronx neighborhoods before the fires. During the hard years, music changed but continued to play a major role in the survival and revival of the South Bronx. One thing was constant: the many musical traditions influenced and enriched each other. African American music was influenced by West Indian and Puerto Rican music. Puerto Rican music, in turn, was influenced by Cuban, Mexican, African American, and Caribbean music. Music, dance, visual art, spoken word, and theater were created by people who saw themselves as artists, but also by teens, by elders in the park, by families inside their homes. Historian Mark Naison remembers:

> Everyone living in the South Bronx had black music as well as Latin music as the sound track of their lives. Even when buildings were burning, the middle class was leaving, school music programs were shutting down, and the rest of the city and the nation were writing off the Bronx, the people of the Bronx were not only listening to music, they were creating music that would sweep the world.[68]

The Hunts Point Palace, a huge dance hall that closed in the 1980s, illustrates the trends in music reflecting the Bronx's history and culture. (It has a place in my family's history because my mother-in-law, Loretta Hamilton, told stories about singing at Hunts Point Palace as a young woman with her sister, Edna. They called themselves the Apple Sisters, Corey and Seedy. Clearly, they were amateurs.) The website Place Matters traces those trends:

> The Palace was host to nearly a century's worth of American popular music; swing music in the 1920s–1930s, big band jazz dance bands in the 1940s, Latin music in the 1940s–1970s, and hip hop in the 1970s and 1980s. During the heyday of Latin music in the Bronx, the Hunts Point Palace rivaled Manhattan's Palladium. All the best dancers went there. With ornate architecture and beautiful balconies, it had glamour. The "big three"—Tito Puente, Tito Rodríguez, and Machito—often played here, as did stars like Arsenio Rodríguez, and jazz greats like Stan Getz and Dizzy Gillespie.[69]

Mambo, Salsa, Jazz, and More

Although mambo and salsa were nurtured in East Harlem, many of the musicians lived and performed in the Bronx. Near the Hunts Point Palace was the Tropicana, a Latin music club that attracted the best talent. Gene

Norman, of Afro-Caribbean background, recalls the influence that Latin music from the Tropicana Club in the 1940s and '50s had on him:

> I remember as a kid twelve years old or so, on a summer night, hearing the trumpet riffs of the mambo band floating through the air like a pied piper's tale . . . as the neighborhood became more and more Hispanic, music took on a greater and more engulfing place in your life. Music seemed to be everywhere.[70]

Arthur Crier, who became a doo-wop singer with the Halos and the Mellows and later a songwriter for Motown, remembers the clubs in Morrisania that hosted so many famous jazz musicians in his neighborhood:

> Morrisania was a tremendous place for music. We had Freddy's, the Blue Morocco, and the Apollo Bar, about three blocks from each other on Boston Road. People came to these places from all over. As a kid, I thought they would always last.[71]

Mark Naison writes:

> Among the famous jazz musicians who lived in Morrisania—all of whom visited the Boston Road Clubs—were Donald Byrd, Herbie Hancock, Elmo Hope, Bertha Hope, Thelonious Monk, Henry "Red" Allen, Lou Donaldson, Tina Brooks, Oliver Beener, and singer Maxine Sullivan, while the famous doo wop artists from Morrisania included the Chords, the Chantals, the Clickettes, the Mellows, and Arthur Crier.[72]

The Chords, which formed in Morris High School, had a 1954 hit song, "Sh-Boom," that sold a million records, the first urban harmonic song to do so. The young women in the Chantels, who started singing together in the choir of St. Anthony of Padua, had a million-record hit in 1957 called "Maybe."

Club 845 on 161st Street and Prospect Avenue was an important center of bebop and frequently featured Charlie Parker, Sonny Rollins, and Dexter Gordon. The singer Sylvia Vanderpool opened her club Blue Morocco in 1956, where the singer Nancy Wilson was discovered and where Jimmy Castor played in the house band. A Castor song from the '70s, "It's Only Just Begun," was used heavily by the early hip-hop DJs.[73]

Eddie Palmieri is one of the longest-performing musicians from the Bronx. A pianist, composer, and bandleader, he was born in 1936 and has performed for close to seventy years. He learned to play the piano when he was very young.[74] At thirteen, he switched to the timbales and played in his uncle's band. He returned to the piano shortly thereafter. Throughout his career, he was encouraged and influenced by his older brother, Charlie, who was a musician of note. As a bandleader, he became known for blending American jazz into Afro-Caribbean music and for using trombones and a flute in place of trumpets, creating a unique sound. He has been awarded ten Grammys, including the first-ever Grammy for Best Latin Recording, and is a National Endowment for the Arts Jazz Master.

Theaters also played a role in the development of Bronx music. One of the most significant was the two-thousand-seat Teatro Puerto Rico, where performers from all over Latin America entertained audiences. It also showed Mexican movies, giving Bronx Puerto Ricans a taste of mariachi music.[75]

Music was also in the streets as people sat outside on hot summer nights. Puerto Rican groups played music on the sidewalks and in the parks, often with conga drums. Talibah Roberts, who grew up near Crotona Park East and became a school teacher, remembers the amplified music:

> Whoever would have the best equipment or good stereo, they would bring their radio right from the living room and bring it outside and play it. Or sometimes, people would put speakers in the window, with the DJ working the system, and we're standing outside in front of the building and we would dance.[76]

Bobby Sanabria, a Latin jazz percussionist and drummer, grew up in the Melrose projects in the '60s and '70s. He describes the importance of Latin music, particularly salsa, in the life of his community:

> I always say I grew up in the worst of times and the best of times. The South Bronx was burning on all cylinders, both literally and figuratively. NYC was exploding with creativity in music, theater, and art—the last great period for all of that happening simultaneously.
> Salsa, forget it. Salsa was the music, the gospel of the masses. It would be coming out of speakers from a bodega. People on the corner would be doing

air trombone to a Willie Colon record like white boys doing air guitar to a Led Zeppelin record. Junkies mimicking Eddie Palmieri with his grunts playing piano. In terms of the mainstream culture of the streets, it was just that.

Bobby started playing professionally while still in high school:

> The lucky thing for me was that music saved my life. By the time I was in high school I was already playing timbales in some low-level salsa groups doing some gigs. Back then I got on the subway at all hours carrying those things in a big narrow fiber case with wheels. You'd have your sticks in a stick bag and the cymbal and bells and put them in a cymbal bag you carried on your back. I remember carrying those things through the rain and snow just to get to a gig.

Perhaps the high point in the history of salsa was a concert put together by a Latin record company, Fania. It was a risky enterprise. The old Yankee Stadium had a capacity of fifty-seven thousand. Would that many people come out for a salsa concert? Bobby describes the scene:

> The Fania All Stars played at Yankee Stadium on August 24, 1973, for a crowd of over forty thousand mostly Puerto Rican people. The top bandleaders from the label and their sidemen and vocalists performed that night in a supergroup format: Johnny Pacheco, Ray Barretto, Willie Colon, Larry Harlow, Roberto Roena, Cheo Feliciano, Barry Rogers, Lewis Khan, Bobby Valentin, Nicky Marrero, and many more. The only thing bigger was the Beatles at Shea Stadium.
>
>   If you look at the newspapers at that time, the three major TV networks, no one covered it. Someone told me there was a one-line mention in the *New York Times*. That tells you one thing, they didn't give two shits about us.[77]

Miguel (Mike) Amadeo is widely credited as a key person who promoted and preserved Latin music. A composer and musician, he purchased a Latin music store in 1969 that developed into an important Bronx asset for distributing and promoting Latin music. Renamed Casa Amadeo, it is the longest continuously run Latin music store in New York City and the first Puerto Rican–owned site on the mainland to be listed in the National Register of Historic Places. The store, with mementos in the window, displayed guitars and maracas for sale along with hundreds of well-organized CDs. At age eighty-two, Mike is very charming and welcoming. He remembers his earlier days in the Bronx:

> My family moved to the Bronx in 1948 when I was thirteen. The neighborhood was beautiful. You could walk the streets at 2 and 3 A.M., which I did when I came back from performing. It was very safe. I started composing music at a young age, age fourteen. I got two cents for each record sold. I would get checks from the record company for $1.80, $3.52. When I went in the army, I got a check for $35 before I left.[78]

Mike stayed during the rough years of the '70s and '80s, although the building that housed his store was virtually abandoned. He had to get water from the fire hydrant. His building is now owned by Banana Kelly and is in an area of other well-maintained buildings. In 2009, CAB honored Mike Amadeo as a Living Legend. The artwork we gave him is hanging in his living room at home. New York City, in recognition of Mike's significant contributions to Latin music and preserving Latin culture, renamed the section of Prospect Avenue near his store "Miguel Amadeo Way" in 2014. Hundreds of his friends, fellow musicians, and elected officials helped him celebrate the honor.

Hip Hop

Hip-hop culture, the art form for which the Bronx is most famous, sprung up in the South Bronx in the '70s. In his family's apartment at 1520 Sedgwick Avenue in the West Bronx, DJ Kool Herc (born Clive Campbell) experimented with new sounds, building on Jamaican music traditions. His sister held a party in the building's community room on August 11, 1973, during which he used two turntables to extend the drum beats or "break beats" in the records. This innovation in the music led to b-boying and b-girling, also called breakdancing. Three of the breakdancing greats were Crazy Legs, Trac2, and Mr. Wiggles. Four categories of amazing moves were incorporated in fiercely competitive breakdancing contests.

DJ Kool Herc started appearing at the Club Hevalo on Jerome Avenue near Tremont Avenue. He asked Coke La Rock to add his poetry to the music, and thus MCing started.[79] Although the term *hip hop* was not coined until years later, he is credited with starting a new form of music.

DJs Tony Tone and Kool Herc at the T Connection, White
Plains Road and Gun Hill Road, circa 1978. The street near 1520
Sedgwick Avenue where DJ Kool Herc threw the first hip-hop
party in 1973 has been co-named Hip Hop Boulevard and is
considered hip hop's place of origin. Joe Conzo Jr. documented
hip hop's early days with his photography. Photo credit: The
Archive of Joe Conzo Jr. at Cornell University Library.

His apartment building has been recognized as the birthplace of hip hop
by the NYS Department of Parks, Recreation, and Historic Preservation.

DJ Afrika Bambaataa (born Kevin Donovan), a former gang leader,
founded a youth-oriented group called the Zulu Nation.[80] Performing in
the community center and on the grounds of the Bronx River Houses, he
attracted large numbers of young people to his performances and spread
the popularity of hip hop.[81]

A third major originator of hip hop was Grandmaster Flash (Joseph
Saddler). Initially he played in abandoned buildings and in school yards,
such as PS 63 in Morrisania. If necessary, DJs would hook up turntables
to power from streetlights or utility poles. A manager arranged for
Grandmaster Flash to play at clubs in the Bronx and then in Manhattan.
Sylvia Vanderpool (who had owned the club Blue Morocco) and her husband Bobby Robinson had started Sugar Hill Records and produced several albums and singles of Grandmaster Flash and the Furious Five. Their

hit single "The Message" in 1982, with the rap performed by Melle Mel, was one of the first socially conscious hip-hop songs. It described the impossibly hard life for young people in areas like the South Bronx and had tremendous impact. Grandmaster Flash was also featured in the 1983 film *Wild Side* along with another well-known Bronx group, the Cold Crush Brothers.[82] Members of the Cold Crush Brothers included Charlie Chase, Tony Tone, Grandmaster Caz, Almighty KG, and others.[83]

Elena Martínez is a folklorist at City Lore and co–artistic director of the Bronx Music Heritage Center. She has coproduced several documentaries, including *From Mambo to Hip Hop: A South Bronx Tale.* She places the emergence of this new culture in the context of the time:

> By the time of hip hop, kids didn't have music teachers. Young kids, out of nothing, used devastation to create. They didn't have instruments. Grandmaster Flash used turntables as instruments. They used abandoned buildings to perform. Amidst all this destruction, they were able to create out of that sadness and decay.[84]

These creations—like the music of the Caribbean and the Mississippi Delta blues—drew on African oral traditions. Hip-hop culture provided an alternative to street life and drugs for many teenagers by allowing them to express the reality of their lives as well as dreams for material wealth. Some claim it helped bring down the crime rate. Rather than violent fighting, rivals battled with words, dance, and music. This new art form also provided an important source of income for many young people; they could earn cash by being an MC, hosting parties, winning prizes in dance contests and talent shows, and writing lyrics.

Young hip-hop pioneers received some support from established Bronx musicians and from community centers that let them practice and perform. Arthur Crier, the doo-wop star, organized talent shows at the Murphy Houses where the Cold Crush Brothers performed. He took them to Rikers Island to perform for the young people jailed there. The Webster Avenue Police Athletic League hosted many hip-hop jams, as did some of the community centers in public housing.[85]

Hip hop focused attention on the South Bronx. The four original elements of hip-hop—MC (rapper), DJ (disc jockey), b-boy (breakdancer), and graffiti expanded to include fashion, social commentary, and other expressive forms. It made the South Bronx a cool place to be from. People who had leadership skills and a business mindset could become wealthy and famous. By the late 1980s, hip hop had moved into the mainstream of American music.

Fitzroy Christian migrated to this country in 1971 from the island nation of Antigua and Barbuda. He moved to the West Bronx in 1975, where he is a community leader working to prevent displacement of low-income people. He is also an amateur musician who loves the interplay of various cultural traditions in music:

> A large percentage of the people involved originally in hip hop were West Indian. These included Grandmaster Flash (Barbados), DJ Kool Herc (Jamaica), Africa Bambaataa (Jamaican and Barbadian parents), and Doug E. Fresh (Barbados). Apart from block parties, park events, and community center affairs, these artists also performed at clubs and musical venues in the Bronx. Hip hop, jazz, Latin jazz, in the same clubs, different weekends. It was from this heady mash-up of musical genres—a potpourri, as it were—that the Bronx became the birthplace of such a unique cross- and inter-ethnic mixture of music. I remember going to some of these clubs, both as a performer with my steel band and a partygoer.[86]

OTHER ARTS AND GATHERING PLACES

During the tough times of the 1970s, except for the sidewalk, a roof in the evenings, or an occasional community center, there were not many places people could go to escape the heat of the apartments in the summer and to hang out with friends. Instinctively realizing that people, including his family, need public spaces to gather and have fun in, Chema Soto eyed the vacant lot near his daughter's school for a casita. The Place Matters website explains:

> Casitas are small houses surrounded by gardens created to recall the look and feel of the Puerto Rican countryside. One of the city's oldest and largest, Casita Rincón Criollo was built in the late 1970s, when José "Chema" Soto and his neighbors reclaimed an abandoned, garbage-filled lot. He plunged in and began clearing debris. Other residents joined him, and soon around fifty people found themselves taking care of land they did not own. Together they created a little home of their own and called it Rincón Criollo

Master plenero Benny Ayala gave plena lessons in the 1990s at the original site of Casita Rincón Criollo, which has since moved to Brook Avenue and 157th Street. In the 1970s, José "Chema" Soto had led the effort to clean a vacant lot and construct the casita. Plena is a traditional form of Puerto Rican folk music played on the *pandereta*, a type of hand drum. Photo credit: Martha Cooper/City Lore.

("Downhome Corner"). Casita members used this corner to gather, garden, hold community events, and pass down musical and cultural traditions.[87]

Chema Soto went on to help start many other casitas in the Melrose section of the Bronx. Although Chema Soto died a few years ago, Rincón Criollo continues with widespread support. Besides the casita and another small structure, there are trees, vines, and small gardens, several Puerto Rican flags, and lots of inviting places to sit and chat. Several well-fed cats also call it home.

Bronx arts took a big step forward with the establishment of the Bronx Council on the Arts in 1962, followed by the Bronx Museum of Art in 1971. Housed originally in the rotunda of the Court House, the museum gained its own home in 1982, in a building that—like so many others—had been a synagogue, the Temple Emmanuel. It significantly expanded its space in

2006 by erecting a new wing.[88] Admission to the exhibits is free. The museum hosts special events each month, as well as ongoing programs for children and families.

The Pregones Theater was founded in 1979 by Rosalba Rolón to create and perform original musical theater and plays rooted in Puerto Rican/ Latino cultures. In 2005, it acquired its own permanent theater space that has 130 seats. It was a delight to attend an original short play performed by members of CAB's senior centers under the excellent direction of Pregones professionals.

Other forms of art, such as photography, played and continue to play an important role in the life of the Bronx. Ricky Flores discusses how he got his start as a photographer while growing up in Hunts Point without access to funds to buy needed equipment:

> When you eliminate jobs in a community, people still have to eat. There was a local marijuana dealer who was also a pawnbroker. People would sell hot goods to him. I turned to him to get photographic equipment. It was the only way I could afford what I needed. If it wasn't for him, I would not have been able to become a professional photographer. If you destroy people's economy, they have to try to find a way to make do. I don't condone it but I understand it. It made a big difference in my life.[89]

Joe Conzo Jr. also got his start in photography as a teenager:

> The *New York Times* called me "the man who took hip hop's baby pictures." I got my first camera when I was a teenager, it gave me something to do and made me more popular with the other kids. Film was hard to get but I found ways. I mainly shot in black and white because it was cheaper. I took photos of demonstrations my family took me to. My father was Tito Puente's manager and producer, so I took photos of Latin music. Then photos of the early Bronx hip-hop artists. My archives of over ten thousand images are stored at Cornell University.[90]

As early as 1979, some saw the value of art in outdoor public places, even in an empty lot in a desolate section. Bronx Venture, an economic development group headed by Mike Nunez and affiliated with Ramón Vélez, raised funds for a major sculpture to be placed in a vacant lot as a sign of hope for the community. Nicole Levin, who spearheaded the project, recalls:

The artist who was selected and conceptualized the piece, *Puerto Rican Sun*, was Rafael Ferrer. . . . Early one morning on a giant flatbed truck, thirty feet high and twelve thousand pounds of steel, the sculpture rolled into Fox Street. It was unveiled in October 1979 at a celebration where Tito Puente, the famous Latin jazz musician, and friends played. The community celebrated. It's still there today.[91]

The lot on which the sculpture sits is now a pleasant park with a playground. The sculpture was repaired and, in consultation with Rafael Ferrer, repainted several years ago. The park is surrounded by both renovated and recently constructed apartment buildings and a few infill houses. High on a wall of one of the buildings adjacent to the park are embedded fiberglass sculptures of five residents of the community by artists John Ahern and Rigoberto Torres. The Bronx Council on the Arts facilitated funding for the sculptures, titled *Live on Dawson Street*, in 1982.

In 1979, the Bronx Museum held a photography exhibit called *Devastation/Resurrection: The South Bronx*, picturing the South Bronx's varying neighborhoods. The exhibit primarily comprised photographs of various areas of the South Bronx, some neighborhoods healthier than others, some showing reclaimed buildings. The progress that community groups were making was emphasized. The 116-page accompanying catalogue included a history of the Bronx and histories of families. The exhibit and catalogue helped people realize that the South Bronx might actually come back.[92]

Carmen Vega-Rivera, an educator, arts advocate, and community activist, is a leader with the anti-displacement movement in the West Bronx. Many years ago, Carmen worked on the *Devastation/Resurrection* exhibit:

> To me the exhibit meant that amidst all the rubble, redlining, oppression, lack of resources and services, all the devastation, there is life. Culture, families, a sense of community, the arts, the celebration of similarities and differences among the various cultures and ethnicities in the South Bronx helped us survive, build, and maintain the Bronx, when "others" turned their backs on us. The exhibition was the first cultural blueprint of who was in our community and what were the many resources that helped sustain the Bronx.[93]

Bill Aguado was the executive director of the Bronx Council on the Arts for many years and a longtime CAB board member. Bill, still an influential leader in the Bronx, knows who deserves the credit for the revitalization:

> I think the crucial factor that brought the Bronx back was the people who stayed, people who maintained their commitment with their families. The unknown members who went to work at 6 A.M. in menial jobs, they are the heroes. We had personalities like Freddy Ferrer, the borough president, who played a major role, but I have to give the credit to the people and their institutions, including informal institutions.[94]

5 Progress, but Plagues Descend on the South Bronx

1980s

Guillerma Velázquez escaped what she feared would be a lifetime of poverty in the Dominican Republic by fleeing to New York in the 1970s. Like many immigrants, she had to make an enormous sacrifice to do so, leaving her two young sons behind until she could afford to bring them to the Bronx years later. She says, "My biggest difficulty was living with a broken heart because I had left my two boys, and my youngest was just three months old." By 1981, while working in a factory, she had taken English classes, earned her GED, and started taking classes at Bronx Community College, where she eventually earned an associate degree. Next was a bachelor's in accounting at Lehman College, another Bronx institution. In 1989, she moved with her sons into a beautiful apartment managed by a nonprofit, in a renovated building that had been a hulking shell for most of the '80s. Using what educational and housing resources were available, Guillerma changed her economic situation dramatically, in parallel with the improving South Bronx.[1]

FIRES EXTINGUISHED

By the early 1980s, two signs of hope appeared—the City's finances improved and the fires started to subside. The City could afford to start investing, even if slowly, in poor areas such as the South Bronx. With regard to the fires, perhaps most of the distressed buildings had already burned. In addition, the city had initiated the Red Cap program: fire marshals (wearing red baseball caps) worked in teams of fifty, assigned to a specific area of the South Bronx, and investigated every fire immediately. They started making arson arrests. Additionally, as part of the arson task force, teams of fire marshals and police investigated fires in the rest of the Bronx. The number of fires dropped significantly.[2]

Many of the housing and social service nonprofits that had been created in the past two decades were able to start expanding during the '80s. Important partnerships between government and housing groups formed. Legal services agencies, providing representation in civil matters and through class-action lawsuits, won key rights for people who were homeless. Politicians were elected who reflected the growing black and Latino majorities in South Bronx districts.

IMPORTANT BUILDINGS SAVED
FOR FUTURE GENERATIONS

Although building abandonment continued in sections of the West Bronx, other significant signs of the resurrection were emerging. Mid-Bronx Senior Citizens Council ("Mid-Bronx" for short), on whose board I sat for twenty years, acquired partial ownership of the ten-story Concourse Plaza Hotel. The residential hotel had been a famed institution: it was the place where the Yankees stayed when they were in town, where Bronx politicians closed their big deals, where the wealthy were married. Yankee players (most notably "The Babe," Babe Ruth) stayed there so often it was called the "Home of the Yankees." Stan Freilich's uncle, a prominent lawyer, lived there, and Gene Oliva's brother was married there (Stan and Gene were introduced in chapter 1). The hotel's significance is reflected in its size, its elegant architecture, and its location, two blocks up 161st Street from Yankee Stadium and across the street from the Bronx County Court House.

However, like the rest of the West Bronx, the Concourse Plaza suffered from deteriorating economic conditions and had been converted to a hotel housing homeless families. Some of the residents were victims of the fires in the South Bronx. In 1974, the City purchased it to use as housing for senior citizens. Because of the City's fiscal crisis, the hotel was not renovated until 1982, when it became home to 296 low-income senior citizens (a few of whom had been married there years earlier). Mid-Bronx used common space on the ground floor for meals and social services for the elderly and for its own headquarters. From such a prime location, the Concourse Plaza's new life set a hopeful tone for the rest of the area.[3]

Two years later, Mid-Bronx made another daring move, purchasing the Andrew Freedman Home, also on the Concourse near 166th Street. Both Jeanette Puryear, the executive director, and Dennis Terry, the board chair, were willing to take financial risks to save important resources for future generations of Bronx residents. The Andrew Freedman Home had been an elegant, landscaped, block-long residence for genteel elderly folks who had fallen on hard times and could no longer afford the lifestyle they were accustomed to.[4] This target population was vanishing and the place was virtually empty. Mid-Bronx's initial plan was to use the property and its huge, three-story building as a home for senior citizens. Over the years, Mid-Bronx also used it to house a large Head Start program, an art center, and other social services.

For years, I participated in Mid-Bronx board meetings held at the Concourse Plaza. The board was small—fewer than ten people. It dealt with issues around ending the partnership with the for-profit co-owner of the Concourse Plaza, the purchase and potential uses of the Andrew Freedman Home, the growing portfolio of renovated apartment buildings Mid-Bronx owned, the struggles to secure adequate funding for social services, and ongoing staffing and government contract issues.

CITIZENS ADVICE BUREAU

During the 1980s, I settled into my job as executive director of Citizens Advice Bureau (CAB). My motivation was a sense of social justice.

Children and families shouldn't have to deal with dysfunctional systems, poor schools, an often unhelpful welfare department, employment discrimination, and lousy housing. I thought systems should work for people, not make their lives miserable and even more difficult.

I was interested in expanding CAB's services to other districts, but I was too busy seeing clients all day. It was difficult just to hold on to the funding we had. It was impossible to get any proposal writing done in the office; we were all in one frenetic room. For a few years, I hoped the development office at the Community Council of Greater New York, our sponsoring agency, would get us some more funding, but we were not their priority. I stayed home a few days and was surprised at how much writing I could get done. I secured an antipoverty grant, expanded the funding base for our senior citizen services, and won a foundation grant to open an office farther north in the Bronx. As we grew, other staff helped write funding requests. Graduate students in social work did their required fieldwork with us and made invaluable, innovative contributions. They could also be asked to write funding proposals.

As noted in chapter 4, for more than fifteen years we held an annual Thanksgiving Day dinner for West Bronx senior citizens. CAB's board members and staff volunteered to help cook and wait tables before rushing home to have dinner with their families. My children manned the coat room while my husband stayed home and cooked dinner for our extended family. Professional entertainment, usually a musician who played dance music, added to the festivities. For several years, Mayor Ed Koch flew by helicopter to the campus of Bronx Community College and then took the short ride to the senior center with a police escort. The 150 to 200 seniors present, who had no family to visit on Thanksgiving, were thrilled to have a chance to mingle and talk to the mayor. (I always got a kick out of the photo of him with me—I had the impression that he would have preferred not to have to share the microphone.)

We celebrated our eighth and tenth anniversaries with open houses and workshops for the community. We were pleased that Congressman Jonathan Bingman and the Human Resources Administration commissioner, Jack Krauskopf, attended.

Other Bronx professionals joined the board of directors, including bankers, lawyers, a librarian, and community affairs reps from the police, utility,

Mayor Ed Koch, born in the Bronx, shares the microphone
with Carolyn McLaughlin at CAB's annual Thanksgiving
Day dinner for senior citizens in 1982. Photo credit: Jerry
Shroder.

and phone companies. The board met monthly, was dedicated, and was
always very smart and helpful. We held our first fund-raising event at the
Concourse Plaza, honoring our then chair, Joe Ithier, a wonderful supporter and spokesperson, and John Leonard, a banker committed to the
community. We raised $2,500. Moving into fund-raising felt like a big step.

CAB separately incorporated and broke off from the Community
Council in the mid-1980s. That meant we had to develop our own fiscal
and human resources functions. A big achievement was covering all our
growing staff, from handymen to professional staff, with a generous pension plan. Some city agencies were approving payments into a pension
plan as an allowable expense under their contracts with nonprofits.
Ironically, the NYC Department for the Aging, charged with improving
the well-being of the elderly, was not one of those. I knew that one assistant commissioner was sympathetic to the pension issue. When I heard he
was changing jobs, I jumped on the subway and found him packing in his
office. I was able to get him to sign off on the approval for our pension plan
on his last day of work. Our staff would not be left trying to live on just

Social Security when they retired. Eileen Torres, now executive director of BronxWorks, expresses the importance of this:

> One of our big contributions to the Bronx is being a good employer, hiring many people who live here or are from here, paying decent salaries and good benefits. You were always proud of the pension plans you set up. They are better now than on the for-profit side where people have to pay in first, and then the employer matches it.[5]

We did not contract out our security or maintenance services to save money, as many institutions did, but kept those positions as full-time, salaried staff lines with the same good benefits as social service staff. As the Latino population became the majority of the residents, we had Spanish-speaking staff in all our programs but did not require all applicants to be bilingual, allowing access to our jobs by African Americans and others who did not speak Spanish. For most of my tenure, about 85–90 percent of the staff were people of color and most were Bronx residents.

As we grew, I necessarily became more of a supervisor and administrator and less involved in directly delivering service and client advocacy, although the programs were always what interested me the most. I think (and hope) that I constantly pushed for program quality and for staff to act professionally. Funding and the demands of funders were a constant challenge, but our excellent reputation held us in good stead. Annual staff picnics, holiday parties, regular staff meetings where we shared information, and a biweekly staff newsletter helped create a sense of community within the agency. I cochaired the Association of Bronx Agencies to advocate for the needs of our clients and to facilitate interagency coordination. I also made a practice of inviting newly appointed city commissioners to speak to nonprofits in the Bronx at our site, as a way of getting to meet the commissioners, learning about their priorities, and giving them the opportunity to know CAB.

ALWAYS HOUSING PROBLEMS

In the early 1980s, we continued to help large numbers of residents on a one-by-one basis. We expanded our services for elderly crime victims to cover all six South Bronx community districts. Seniors had reason to be afraid; many were routinely victimized. Our Minor Repair Program could install locks or change cylinders if keys were stolen. We could perform security surveys and buy window gates and install them in apartments. We could partially replace stolen cash. For safety, we took seniors on group shopping trips. We helped vulnerable elderly residents move to safer buildings and neighborhoods.

Sallie Smith, a long-time homeowner, remembers CAB from the early years:

> I knew CAB through its Minor Repair Program. The senior citizen home-owners in the area couldn't afford to hire someone to do small jobs and many repair people didn't want to do small jobs. It was an excellent program. Awareness of it was spread through word of mouth through a large network of people. The repairmen would put air conditioners in windows, fix a lock, replace wall switches, put up window shades, change light bulbs, help hoarders throw things away. It was a great assistance to seniors.[6]

Ernesto, one of our minor-repairmen, clearly loved his job. He always arrived on time, did good-quality repairs, and interacted appropriately with the senior citizens; he was a great employee. But once, he was a "no show, no call" at work for two days in a row. When he came, he explained he had been arrested falsely on a gun charge. Staff rallied to his defense, only to realize over time that he had a second career as a loan shark. I sat with him and told him he had to make a choice, either our job or the loan shark business. With sincere sadness, he chose the one that would provide more financial support for his family and we said goodbye.

CAB rehoused frail senior citizens who were at high risk due to living in abandoned buildings. Many were very attached to the neighborhood and hated to leave. Housing for seniors was being built in the upscale Riverdale section of the Bronx, but often seniors refused to move there, declaring it was too hilly or cold. Some seniors talked about people walking through their walls, and until we made a home visit, we didn't know if they were hallucinating or if there were large holes in their walls. It was a really difficult time for so many people. The story of Mr. G. stays with me because it was seldom that I became that angry with a client.

Mr. G., a thin, very frail man in his early seventies, frequently came to the office because he was repeatedly victimized. He had lost the teeth on the left side of his mouth from being punched during a robbery. Now, as the last tenant remaining in his apartment building, it was urgent that he move to a safer place. He had never married and had no family.

Fearing he would be killed, I found him an apartment in a good building in the North Bronx. He came back to me a day or two later after seeing the apartment, saying, "Oh, Mrs. McLaughlin, I can't move there. It is in the back of the building and I always lived in the front." I responded angrily, "Mr. G., you are going to die in that apartment you're in, and it will not be my fault." A few weeks later, he told me that he had found an apartment—how I don't know, maybe one of the Jewish agencies helped him. He didn't hold my yelling at him against me because later he said, "Oh, Mrs. McLaughlin, Mr. McLaughlin is such a lucky man. If only I had met someone like you when I was younger." He continued to come in for help for years with comparatively easy issues.

Housing and welfare problems remained the two largest issues people asked us to help them with. As opportunities arose, we fed stories to the newspapers highlighting housing problems. Despite being in a low-income area, people on welfare could not afford the rents being charged and were at constant danger of eviction. New York State set the maximum amount welfare would pay for rent, and the amount was slipping further and further behind the actual rents landlords were charging.[7] We advocated for an increase, as did others. Welfare cases were often closed, leaving the family in crisis with no money for food or rent. It could take hours of work over the course of days to figure out why the case was closed and what was needed to reopen it. We filed thousands of Section 8 applications in hopes that people could get a rent subsidy to help them afford an apartment. For the elderly, we could file for a senior-citizen rent-increase exemption that would "freeze" their rent at the amount they were then paying. We also helped many apply for food stamps and Medicaid. All these income-support programs played an essential role in helping people—many of whom were working at low-paying jobs or were elderly—have the basic necessities of food, shelter, and medical care.

GREAT PARTNERSHIPS — SOCIAL SERVICES
AND LEGAL SERVICES

We developed close working relationships with Legal Services NYC and the Legal Aid Society, gaining crucial board support and staff expertise from both organizations. Richard Rivera, an attorney at Bronx Legal Services, was CAB's board chair for several years. He later became a Brooklyn Supreme Court judge. Sean Delany, whom I met when he worked for Bronx Legal Services, was counsel for our board of directors for twenty years and later became our board chair. He served as head of the New York State Charities Bureau and then as the executive director of Lawyers Alliance for New York. Sean provided invaluable guidance to me and the agency over the years.

Marshall Green became the attorney in charge of the Bronx Neighborhood Office of Legal Aid's Civil Division in 1987. As a graduate student in social work, his wife had been an intern with CAB in the early 1980s. With his help, a mutually beneficial relationship between Legal Aid and CAB developed, and Legal Aid began assisting our staff with housing court cases when a lawyer's skills were needed. Marshall comments:

> To a large degree, we serve the same people. We developed strong links. In fact, for a long time we out-stationed a lawyer at CAB/BronxWorks to provide legal representation to people BronxWorks identified as being in need. When BronxWorks more and more became involved in eviction prevention work, I shared my expertise to help fashion a very strong program. I became a board member of BronxWorks and then the board chair. Although no longer the board chair, I continue to be an active board member.[8]

We also identified clients who became members of class-action lawsuits brought by Legal Aid. One week in the winter of 1983, I realized that several families who came into our office had similar complaints. They had no heat or hot water—unacceptable living conditions but unfortunately not uncommon. The tenants also graphically described water flooding into apartments from broken pipes. What was very unusual was that there was no building superintendent and no one even asked them to pay rent. They all lived in the same building on Creston Avenue, near our office. The families had been rehoused there from "welfare hotels" in Manhattan, notorious run-down facilities that the city paid to house homeless families, rather than allowing families with children to live on the street or in cars. The welfare department had paid a month's rent, a security deposit, and a broker's fee to a local real estate company to secure the apartment. What the City or the prospective tenants didn't realize was that the building was already abandoned. The local real estate office was engaged in a horrific scam, taking the City's money and rehousing families in an abandoned building.

I tried calling public officials, but to no avail. Later that week, on a cold night, a baby died in the building. I never learned the cause of the death. Desperate to help, I called Marcella Silverman of Legal Aid, who was just starting the Homeless Family Rights Project. Marcella is now an assistant professor at Fordham Law School and remembers the situation vividly:

> In spring 1983, we were called by Carolyn McLaughlin from CAB to 2032 Creston Avenue in the Bronx. It was a big, sprawling apartment building. We walked in and had to search out the apartments. We found families with children in what could only be described as an abandoned building: broken windows, no electricity, no hot water, no gas, empty apartments, drug deal-ers, water cascading down. I didn't get how it could happen. It was beyond the pale.

I remember a TV crew filming the deplorable conditions. The situation was featured on the nightly news. Three of the families in that building became some of the first families to join the *McCain v. Koch* class-action lawsuit, which eventually granted homeless families the right to decent, safe shelter. The impact of this lawsuit on the lives of homeless children cannot be overstated. Marcella continues:

> The *McCain* case was started in March 1983. The goal was to establish that families with children who were homeless had the right to adequate, safe, and suitable emergency housing. It was brought following a similar case for single people. Some families with children had been denied any emergency housing at all (some sleeping out of doors), or were referred to hotels with shocking conditions: tiny cramped rooms, blood- and urine-soaked mat-tresses, no clean sheets, without safe cooking or eating accommodations.

When Legal Aid brought the conditions of the Creston Avenue building to light, the City closed the building and tore it down. The tenants were sent back to hotels. The property remained a parking lot for many decades but was developed into a eleven-story residential building in 2016.

As the number of families becoming homeless continued to grow, the City looked for other shelter options, including a gym in a state park in the South Bronx. CAB opposed the use of the gym at Roberto Clemente State Park as a congregate shelter with no separate living spaces for families. When it did open, the sight of rows of cots with men, women, and children all sleeping together on the gym floor was heartbreaking and shocking. Marcella worked with other Legal Aid attorneys to close Roberto Clemente Shelter:

> The lawsuit also challenged the conditions and long-term placement at Roberto Clemente shelter. I remember children getting ill. One kid would get sick and they would all get sick. There were only mass bathrooms, so everything spread around. It was not being used as true emergency space for a night but for longer-term housing.[9]

Dr. Hal Strelnick, now chief of the Division of Community Health, Department of Family and Social Medicine of Montefiore Medical Center and assistant professor at Albert Einstein College of Medicine, supplied some of the expert medical testimony for the lawsuit:

> It looked like a refugee shelter, an open space designed for other purposes. There were lots of electrical outlets, in the floor, on the columns, just waiting for a child to stick their finger in. There was no privacy, no sense of how to keep the families supported. The families were kicked out in the morning, and came back in the evening. The MO was they wanted people out looking for housing, working on their problems. It was very physically isolated. The families had a hard walk to the bus stop.[10]

In 1986, when New York State ordered Roberto Clemente closed, 190 people were living there, including 108 children. New York City is seen as a progressive city that tries to take care of people, but at that time, its safety net, although improving, was still inadequate.[11] Also in 1986, CAB published a study titled "Tenants of the West Bronx on the Way Out, but No Place to Go," documenting the rent affordability issue for low-income tenants. Half of the residents of the West Bronx were issued a "dispossess" notice each year, and four thousand of those resulted in evictions by city marshals. This number understates the extent of the problem, as many tenants move out ahead of the marshal's visit. The causes of this crisis were many. The welfare department had increased the amount it would pay for rent by only 25 percent in the past nine years, while median rents had increased by 93 percent. Low-wage jobs were not paying enough to keep up with the rising rents. The report cites the dearth of resources available to help tenants, while virtually all landlords hire lawyers to represent them in housing court.[12] Thinking that the West Bronx was on its way back up, speculators were buying apartment buildings for several times the amount the buildings had sold for just a few years prior, sometimes overloading the buildings with debt. They planned to raise rents to make their investments profitable.[13]

TWO STEPS FORWARD

Despite the affordability issues our clients faced, real progress was being made in improving the housing stock. Some private landlords used a different financial model than those whose buildings were failing. They found ways of making a profit on buildings while providing good housing to their tenants. Joseph Bodak, a Polish immigrant, bought up foreclosed buildings in the West Bronx comparatively cheaply and repaired them using his own, not borrowed, money. Because he did not have to pay a mortgage and because his tenants, satisfied with the conditions in their buildings, paid their rent, he made a profit—while providing decent, affordable housing for lower-income families. Whenever I called his office on behalf of a tenant, I received a quick, very satisfactory response. The Citizens Housing and Planning Council selected Joe Bodak to receive the Good Landlord of the Year Award in 1986.[14] He proved that owning well-kept buildings could be profitable.

Because of the presidential visits, Charlotte Street is often cited as a main example of both the extent of abandonment and the resurrection. Charlotte Street and the area around it had fifty-one apartment buildings. By the time of President Carter's visit in 1977, only nine remained and eight of those were damaged by fires.[15] Pictures of the president standing on an empty lot filled with rubble were seen around the world. Ronald

Reagan also visited the street, in 1980 while he was running for president, and the area looked much the same. Reagan criticized Carter for not rebuilding the area, but when he became president, he cut funds in half for public housing and for federal housing subsidy programs such as Section 8.[16]

But efforts were being made to rebuild the area. The City's South Bronx Development office, headed by Ed Logue, partnered with Mid Bronx Desperados, headed by Genevieve Brooks, to erect suburban-style, prefab ranch houses. It was believed that home ownership would stabilize the area, because homeowners invest in their properties.[17]

In 1981, after seeing a model home, the Acosta family applied to own one of the new eighty-nine prefab houses being built for Charlotte Gardens. José Acosta, a maintenance worked at Hunter College, had decided he wanted to own a home and had started to save. His wife, Leticia, was a phlebotomist at Lincoln Hospital. The apartment they were living in lacked adequate heat and their young son had been ill with pneumonia. They felt lucky to be selected for one of the houses, as a thousand people had applied. They chose their site, a nice corner lot. But they had to wait until 1987 to move in. Delays were caused partly by site conditions, rubble, and deep basements from the apartment buildings previously on the site, and also by issues with the developer. The price increased from the $50,000 they had planned to spend to $66,000. They decided to pay extra for the attractive bay window in the living room and for upgraded kitchen cabinets. It was worth the wait.

When they first moved in, they could see down the street for blocks, almost as far as Hook and Ladder 31/Engine Company 82 firehouse, which had been the busiest fire station in the world. No other buildings were left standing to block the view. Only once, early on, did they have a problem, when someone stole their garden hose and garbage can. They have now lived in their three-bedroom, two-bath home for thirty years. The two Japanese cherry trees in the yard have grown tall and beautiful. Their children have all grown up. They still like their house and neighborhood. Homes in Charlotte Gardens list for as much as $500,000.[18]

The symbolism of actually having homes on this infamous land was powerful. It started to feel like the South Bronx could be rebuilt. Families were eager to invest in houses. The Charlotte Street development was criticized as not being dense enough, and when private houses were built in later years, they were two- and three-family attached houses.

The community development corporations (CDCs), groups like Mid-Bronx, Banana Kelly, and SEBCO, were gaining more city-owned proper-ties to manage and eventually own through the City's Community Management Program. The City provided some limited funds to rehab the buildings. These properties, seized by the City for tax arrears, provided an important inventory for the rebuilding and repopulating of the Bronx. Nonprofit local development groups were the right groups to own and manage them, because their mission was to provide decent, affordable housing. They reinvested the rent money back into the buildings, rather than pulling profits out of the buildings.

MEDICAL CARE FOR THE HOMELESS

In 1984, Dr. Strelnick applied for funding that would eventually provide essential health care in CAB's four shelters:

> The Robert Wood Johnson Foundation announced its interest in funding health-care programs for the homeless. Major cities could submit only one application and the application would come from the City. The day the pro-posal was due, the Xerox machine broke. Then as I was delivering the pro-posal, my car overheated and I had to leave it. I was running down the street to HRA with the four copies of the proposal, got to the entrance, took an elevator to the office, I am half an hour late. I go into the office, there are piles of applications but no one is around. I just put ours in the pile and leave. [Ultimately] we got the nod to start the services in the Bronx. We called the program Care for the Homeless. It provided health services to homeless people in soup kitchens and shelters.[19]

His description brings back anxious memories of similar issues I had at CAB when submitting important proposals—except that if we were late, our proposals were rejected. Once I foolishly agreed to drive the staff member who wrote a refunding proposal for a youth employment pro-gram into Lower Manhattan to deliver it. After running a few red lights, we got stuck in traffic from a parade. When she realized we were not going to make it and her program would lose its funding, she burst into tears.

ELECTED OFFICIALS

In the mid-1980s, the Bronx was hit with a series of corruption scandals involving some of its highest elected officials, including Borough President Stanley Simon, Democratic Party Chairman Stanley Friedman, and congressmen Mario Biaggi and Robert Garcia.[20] All were tried, found guilty, and served jail time with the exception of Garcia, whose conviction was overturned on appeal.[21] Reflecting changes in the composition of the districts, more Puerto Rican and black individuals were elected in state and city races. Their sensitivity to the needs of their constituents likely added to the liberal tilt on the City Council. As corruption knows no racial or ethnic barriers, in ensuing years, several politicians from the Bronx at the state and city levels also found themselves in legal straits.

Over the years, generally I tried to keep a reasonable distance from elected officials, not wanting to be seen as supporting one over another. At times, we were asked by a few elected officials to do things you couldn't legally do as a nonprofit, such as carry petitions for them. When I received such requests, I either told them outright we wouldn't do it or just ignored the request. One time, a politician actually threatened to hold up our existing funding contracts unless I "did something for him"—he was propositioning me! I ignored him too. After that, I often took a staff member with me when meeting with certain electeds. Generally, I had a policy of not asking politicians for money or support, unless I had a long, positive history with them. If they wanted to support us because of the quality of our work, they could. If not, we were OK without their support.

Gladys Carrión grew up in the South Bronx and led many city, state, and nonprofit agencies. She tells me:

> I remember one of the downsides of running an agency was managing the politics. Your organization was never politicized, unlike so many. You managed to walk that line. It was not easy, to your credit and your organization's and board's credit, to create an organization that is respected and that was not in any politician's pocket.[22]

Some of the elected officials with whom we had good, long-term, working relationships and who never asked us for anything were Aurelia Greene, our assemblywoman and later deputy borough president;

Congressman José Serrano; and Fernando (Freddy) Ferrer, our City Council member who became borough president when Stanley Simon was forced to resign.

When she was elected to the New York State Assembly in 1982, Greene was one of the few African American women in the state legislature. She served as a role model during CAB's Take Your Daughter to Work events, loved and supported CAB's HIPPY (Home Instruction for Parents of Preschool Youngsters) program, and participated in a turkey distribution event with Senator Hillary Clinton one holiday season. She discusses breaking through the "glass ceiling":

> The then assemblyman resigned unexpectedly. I was his female district leader. I went to see the county leader. I said I was ready to run for the position. He said you should stay home and take care of your children. I said I will run and I will win. He supported my opponent who got indicted during the time I was running. In the end, he had to support me. I took over 90 percent of the vote, and that led to my twenty-seven years in the assembly. I was the nineteenth woman in the legislature in the history of the state. Two African American women from the Bronx were ahead of me, Estella Diggs and Gloria Davis.

Greene chaired major state committees, including the Commission on Adult Education and Skills Development, Consumer Affairs, and the Banks Committee:

> I was the first woman chair of the Banks Committee. I did that for eight years. The speaker wanted me to be speaker pro tem. That was the position I finished with. I oversaw the legislative sessions in his absence. I enjoyed it tremendously. The thing that stood out the most was the Banks Committee— I had twenty-nine men and one other woman. The men were very respectful. I always enjoyed talking about it. I couldn't believe they put so many men on my committee. In later years, we got up to fifty women in the legislature. I was chair of the Women's Caucus.[23]

Jóse Serrano's family moved from Puerto Rico to New York in 1950 when Serrano was seven. Educated in the Bronx, he served in the New York State Assembly for sixteen years before being elected to Congress in 1990. As a congressman, his priorities have included health, environment, and issues related to poverty, immigration, and Puerto Rico.[24]

Freddy Ferrer was raised in the South Bronx in what was then a stable, low-income neighborhood. He considered it a good place to grow up. Later the decline set in, gradually at first, then rapidly, as building conditions deteriorated. Ferrer was educated in Catholic schools, including Cardinal Spellman. He then attended New York University's uptown Bronx campus (now Bronx Community College). In 1982, at the age of thirty-two, he became the City Council member for CAB's area. He became borough president in 1987, serving in that position until 2001. He provided thoughtful leadership during the crucial period of rebuilding.

CITY GOVERNMENT STEPS UP IN A BIG WAY WITH REAL MONEY FOR HOUSING!

In 1985–6, the housing picture changed dramatically. Rather than the destructive disinvestment of the '70s, New York City started investing in low-income communities in an amazing way. With improved bond markets, the City could again borrow money. Mayor Koch issued a ten-year, $5.1 billion plan to repair City-owned occupied buildings, gut rehab the vacant buildings, and rebuild on vacant lots. About seventy-five thousand units were to be rebuilt in the Bronx. Finally, real money was available to do what was needed. It was like the Bronx hit the lottery! And a wise decision was made: much of the work would be done not by for-profit landlords and developers, but through the nonprofit housing groups (CDCs). These groups now had up to fifteen years of experience. With the nonprofit infrastructure in place and led by local experts, money and resources would be well used. Now buildings could be totally rehabbed, not just a patch job here and there. One frequently used model was for the City to arrange rebuilding and then turn over the ownership of the building to a qualified nonprofit, which selected the tenants and did the ongoing management.

Abandoned buildings, with and without flower-pot decals covering window openings, were visible from all the major highways, the subway lines, and the Grand Concourse. Freddy Ferrer argued that these buildings should be the first to be rehabbed, so that people would get a better impression of the Bronx and of New York City. He called it the Gateway Initiative. Thirty-one of those buildings were visible from the Cross Bronx

Expressway, with the potential to house fifteen hundred families.[25] Ferrer describes his approach to securing a good share of the $5.1 billion for the Bronx:

> In 1988, I hit Mayor Koch and Abe Biderman [chairman, NYC Housing and Development Corporation] with the Cross Bronx Expressway. It was part of what I called the Gateway Initiative. They always tried to minimize the projects that you brought to them but this time they couldn't.
>
> We put pictures of all the vacant buildings you could see from the Cross Bronx Expressway on thirteen easels. Our plan was featured in the Metro section of the *New York Times*. I remember I got a call from Abe Biderman. He said he never heard of the initiative before. That's because we just made it up. The test of their commitment was that they funded it. They knew it was a good idea.[26]

The New York City government, which played a significant role in the decline of the Bronx, deserves a lot of credit for financing much of the rebuilding of the South Bronx and other destroyed areas of the city. It also deserves credit for choosing to work with nonprofits. The Settlement Housing Fund (SHF), an organization CAB partnered with closely for over twenty-five years, was given title to fourteen rebuilt buildings in the West Bronx, named New Settlement Apartments (NSA). SHF asked CAB to be the service provider for tenants living in the area and provided us with an office and some funding. Jack Doyle, the executive director of NSA, describes how SHF obtained the buildings:

> SHF responded to a request for proposals from NYC to manage and own fourteen buildings on Townsend and Walton Avenues from 170th to 174th Street. SHF was selected prior to the buildings being renovated by the City and was given the opportunity to have involvement in the design and rehab process. However, at times Carol Lamberg, SHF's executive director, had to wait outside of the construction trailer in the cold while officials made decisions about confidential issues without her. The project, the largest site in Mayor Ed Koch's and Governor Mario Cuomo's ten-year Housing NY Plan, was funded by a quasi-government bond issue. The debt was repaid from receipts from Battery Park City. There is practically no debt on the buildings, which keeps the rents affordable.[27]

It was one of their apartments that Guillerma Velázquez was fortunate enough to move into:

I lived with my two boys in a one-bedroom apartment in Upper Manhattan. After applying, submitting the documentations, being visited by the NSA property manager, I was offered a two-bedroom apartment. The apartment was new and everything in it too. There was 24/7 security and good building maintenance. Having a nice apartment, my children attending school, and having a nice job, I felt like I was living a really independent life for the first time in my life.[28]

NSA illustrates the advantages of having nonprofits manage housing in lower-income areas. In addition to a commitment to keeping rents affordable, NSA has been successful in rehousing previously homeless families. Jack talks about that process:

Thirty percent of the units were (and still are) reserved for homeless families, including both people from the shelters as well as the "hidden homeless," families who live doubled up with other families. For the most part, the families who were previously homeless have been very good tenants. When we have examined our evictions and other reasons for move-outs, the rates are about the same for the previously homeless as for other families, including higher-income families.[29]

South Bronx Churches was formed in 1987 to work for social change, including improved housing. They sponsored the construction of over five hundred homes, including many two- and three-family houses. Partial financing came from loans from member churches.

By 1989, over 15,600 new apartments had been built in the South Bronx. Several CDCs requested that CAB provide services to their tenants on site, which we did, including NSA, Mount Hope Housing, and Highbridge CDC. The partnership with NSA, initiated by SHF's executive director, Carol Lamberg, was particularly successful and has continued for over twenty-five years.

TWO PLAGUES HIT: CRACK COCAINE AND HIV/AIDS

A major setback to all this progress happened in the mid-1980s with the introduction of highly addictive crack cocaine. Crack hit the South Bronx hard. The deteriorated state of neighborhoods and the high unemployment rates made the South Bronx particularly susceptible to this new, cheap drug. Initially most of the sales took place on the street. Then people would go to an abandoned building close by to get high. Since the drug was cheap to make and users required frequent fixes, the profits were huge. The crime rate, which had been falling, shot up again. New phrases entered the vocabulary—*crack head, crack house, crack baby*—and further stigmatized the South Bronx.

Community activist Kathryn Speller understood firsthand the problems young people were having with drugs:

> Some of my children had problems with drugs, as did so many young people in the Bronx. My daughter, who was a heroin addict and later had problems with crack, was in Bedford Hills prison for a year. A CAB staff person helped get my daughter into a halfway house when she was released. My daughter earned a college degree and is now a social worker, giving back to people in Ohio where she lives.[30]

CAB had opened a walk-in office for people who were homeless. Staff saw people struggling with problems of addiction, primarily to heroin and crack, and grew adept at helping them get treatment as resources became available. Options were detox, methadone maintenance, and/or residential treatment. As CAB's programmatic capacity increased, we ran harm reduction groups. These groups allowed people to discuss their drug use openly, share strategies for cutting back on their use, and minimize the associated health effects and risks. Some individuals are able to move from harm reduction to being drug free, through the help of programs or on their own. Although cutting-edge at the time, harm reduction is now an accepted treatment option for many struggling with addiction. Crack use started declining in the early 1990s. It was realized a few years later that babies born addicted to crack were not as permanently impacted as once thought. It was during this time that women, especially poor women, who tested positive for drugs in their system during pregnancy began to be seen as child abusers and criminals.

As we began to work with people who lived on the streets, we became aware of an unfamiliar, terrifying disease. Crack and heroin interacted with the newly arrived plague, AIDS, to a tragic degree. AIDS infected a great many women in the Bronx, as well as men. Intravenous drug users, mostly men, were infected with AIDS through sharing the needles they used for injecting heroin. Needle exchange programs hadn't even been suggested at that time and were later very controversial. Homosexuality was scorned in the Bronx, and any "on the down low" activities were kept hidden from wives and girlfriends, making them unaware that their partners could infect them. Additionally, with women becoming addicted to crack, the AIDS epidemic increased exponentially as some women turned to prostitution to support their addiction.

The hysteria in the country was intense. Ryan White, a teen from Indiana infected through a blood transfusion, was driven out of his school by fearful parents and teachers. In 1988, he testified before Congress. In 1990, the federal funding stream to provide medical care and support services to people with AIDS, the Ryan White Care Act, was created and named for him. (In 2011, CAB invited Ryan White's mother to speak at our annual AIDS conference. What a heartbreaking story of her son's death, but also what a tremendous advocate Ryan was and his mother became. Needless to say, we were all in tears during her talk.)

CAB opened our "Positive Living" program in 1988, one of the first such programs in the Bronx. Our staff was terrific, refusing to play into the hysteria and treating the clients in a respectful, compassionate manner. They helped people deal with their failing health. As medicines became available, staff helped patients get access to it. When necessary, our social workers helped dying parents make custody plans for their children. We helped families make burial arrangements and we attended funerals. As better medicines were developed, case managers helped people understand the "cocktail"—the complex mix of medicines they must take at various times of the day, with or without certain kinds of food. Staff started a harm reduction program so that clients could get a handle on their drug use. Our kitchen cooked nutritious meals. Housing specialists found apartments and other living arrangements. Case managers helped people keep their doctor's appointments and understand their illness.

This comprehensive approach in the Positive Living program developed over time, as resources became available and staff helped clients take advantage of medical advances. After years of sadness, with the new medicines, staff could help people think about and plan their futures. To this day, the Bronx remains an epicenter of new infections, but help is available to people with the HIV virus—at BronxWorks, hospitals, and other agencies. Thankfully, HIV infection changed from a death sentence to a chronic illness that people can live with. Scott Auwarter, an assistant executive director of BronxWorks, oversees the work with people who are homeless and those with HIV/AIDS. Scott joined BronxWorks as a staff member in 1988. He reflects on the change in prognosis since then:

> In the early years, seeing all the homeless people with AIDS in the hotels was very distressing, as every one of the guys died. A couple of the mothers of those guys stayed in touch with me for years. Now that is not the case. People don't generally die of AIDS any more.[31]

Norma Pérez, now sixty-nine, saw her son die. She worked for twenty-five years as an advocate for youths caught up in the criminal justice system. She worked despite being HIV positive herself, along with other serious health problems. She raised four children: her son who died, a daughter who graduated from Harvard Law School, and two nephews, both of whom were later imprisoned. Driven to contribute to her community, she keeps busy volunteering on the client advisory boards of several HIV/AIDS organizations, including BronxWorks. She advocates for people who need help. Norma tells me:

> I have been HIV positive since 1989. I was sending kids I counseled for testing and thought I should be tested myself. I got HIV from unprotected sex after my husband died. At first the medicines were too much, I was on fifteen different pills. I am down to one pill a day now. I also had hepatitis C. I got cured. I also had diabetes at the same time. I took care of myself. I had to support myself and keep the house.

She talks about her son's difficult life and how he died:

> My son came to me and told me he was sick, that he had AIDS. I held a family meeting. I told the family if anyone doesn't want to be near him, just get up and leave. They all stayed. My son passed in 2005. Our children are supposed to bury us. When I visited him in the hospital, everyone was covered with gowns. I said I don't need all that, he is my son. He fell down a flight of stairs and cracked his skull. He was homosexual and he also used drugs. He lived with a transgender woman who was in the hospital the same time as my son was. She asked me to get her clothes because she thought she would be discharged. She died before he did.[32]

A man named Washington has been involved with BronxWorks' Positive Living program for a number of years. He was introduced to drugs when he was just thirteen and has struggled with addiction over the years. He held jobs with significant responsibility and, at times, volunteered in the community. He was hired by BronxWorks as a peer educator, to help other people facing similar issues. He recalls:

> I found out I had HIV in 2000, when I was thirty-one. I was in recovery, trying to stay clean. I was all over the place, not knowing who I could trust. I thought I was going to die alone. That is when I went to BronxWorks and asked for help. I met with a team of people. They helped me get healthier, they helped me think more clearly.
>
> Tashika was my case manager. She came to my door, climbed up the five flights, and checked up on me. They helped me get benefits. I was behind on my rent and they helped save my apartment. She went with me to appointments, to make sure I went. I relapsed in 2004. I was between jobs.
>
> I found a doctor who specializes in HIV. I hit the jackpot with her. I did not start a medication regime until 2013. The doctors monitored me but I made the choice not to take medicines. I was afraid of the stigma of taking the medicines.
>
> BronxWorks helped me get my life together. I was in the harm reduction group. I was still struggling with issues from the past, from love I didn't receive from family. Things in my past are where the drugs came from. I became a peer educator recently. I was hired because they saw that I got clean through BronxWorks, that I shared stuff. They see that I am active in the community.[33]

Bibi Karim, an experienced licensed social worker and department director, has been with BronxWorks for over twenty-five years. She oversees Positive Living, foster care prevention, and other programs. She explains the dynamics she witnesses:

> There is often a tie-in of sexual, physical, and emotional abuse with drug use and AIDS. Most of the abuse happens as children. The pain of the abuse and the pain of the reminders of the abuse stays with the person. Many don't recognize that they have mental health needs. They don't recognize the link between what happened to them as children and their current problems. There is also an intergenerational component. The parent looks for comfort and security from their partner and looks away from the abuse.

Bibi tells us that her clients want what we all want—being treated as a respected member of the community:

> Many of the clients want to give back. They want to be part of society. They want to be accepted. They feel, yes, I used drugs but I am not a bad person. So many people still condemn drug users.[34]

It's an important message. Washington says:

> I would like to help my community. I want to be part of the solution. I want to say I have been there and helped. I want to educate people on healthier living and getting involved, do service—each one, teach one. Someone good to be remembered when I leave this world, not as a drug addict. I am doing my best to be a positive presence for my peers and neighbors.[35]

GRASSROOTS PROJECTS MAKE AN IMPACT

Grassroots projects sprung up in many areas. In the early 1980s, Al Quinones and his friends organized a group they called 52 People for Progress, named after the local public school that's so famous in Bronx Latin music circles. Elena Martínez of the Bronx Music Heritage Center describes PS 52's influence on music:

> A lot of great musicians had gone to PS 52, including Eddie Palmieri, Ray Barreto, Orlando Marin, Manny Oquendo, Joe Quijano. That was when schools had music programs. They had a band of fourteen-year-old boys. The guys who grew up in that area had incredible exposure to music.[36]

Volunteers from 52 People for Progress cleaned up a nearby park, including picking up a bucket full of crack vials. They painted the benches with donated paint. For close to forty years, 52 People for Progress have taken care of the park and sponsored hundreds of salsa concerts with salsa greats such as Johnny Pacheco, Eddie Palmieri, and Tito Nieves. Even though many of the original volunteers now live in other places, they still come back to help—the park is such an important part of their lives.[37] Elena Martínez talks about the concerts and the park:

They charge a dollar for a performance. They hustle, hobble together a series of performances from July to September. They are a perfect example of community activism, of bringing the arts in. The parks department was going to put in handball courts. People fought this, demanded and got the amphitheater.[38]

The park, called Playground 52, recently underwent a $9 million renovation and reopened in 2018.

In 1988, my son, Kamau Karanja, while a student at Brown University, had the opportunity to be one of ten college students working in Hunts Point, the area hardest hit by the devastation. Being from the Bronx, Kamau was eager to participate. The project was designed by Paul Lipson. Maria Torres was another college student participant at the time, who went on to create the Point CDC, a youth and economic development center with an environmental focus, along with Paul and two others. Kamau describes the project:

> The idea was to provide mentorship to local teens, while also creating green space in the community. This was a time when crack cocaine and the HIV epidemic was devastating communities like Hunts Point. At every street corner people were lined up to buy drugs, prostitutes were actively soliciting business all around us, and the police were rarely, if ever, present. Very young children played in the street, unsupervised and often hungry.
>
> In spite of all of this, every day fifteen to twenty teens would show up to work alongside of us removing garbage, constructing garden beds, shoveling soil and planting vegetables. We ran a play street for the younger children. We were able to pay the teens a small hourly salary and ended up building wonderful gardens for the community.[39]

Ralph Acevedo, who grew up in Hunts Point with all this chaos, was a teen participant in the community garden project for six years. He clearly feels the summer project gave him support he needed at that key time in his life. He then took a part-time job as a teen counselor with a CAB after-school program. Upon graduating from college, he went to work full time at CAB as a case manager for homeless people. After many promotions, he became director of CAB's Homeless Outreach Team. He recalls:

> The Brownies [Brown University students] gave me a broader perspective, that there was more to life than I was seeing in my neighborhood. I was

growing up in a neighborhood where there were more abandoned buildings than occupied buildings. It was very violent growing up. I saw people die on the streets. There were a lot of temptations. Many of my friends were heavy into drug dealing.

I did the project every summer. I needed to do it, it was one of the things I looked forward to. It kept me from illegal activity. I realized if I applied myself there was a way out.

Here we were trying to grow vegetables. People see these mostly white people coming around and asked if we were being abused. After a while, they realized the Brown students were no threat to them. But we had to watch out for the Brownies, to make sure they were OK. They exposed us to this whole other element outside of Hunts Point. We went tent camping, bowling, swimming at Fire Island, spent time at Fordham University. But not all of us made it. One got killed, one committed suicide.[40]

Maria Torres, now CEO of the Point, while discussing the gardening project, also mentions the importance of the summer lunch program that Evelina Antonetty fought so hard to bring to the children:

We took the children to the local school for the summer lunch program. Many of the children, including young ones, were on the street the whole day. No parents checking on them. Summer lunch is still very important.[41]

IMMIGRANTS SETTLE IN THE BRONX

Immigrants had been moving into the Bronx throughout the twentieth century. To a large degree, since the 1970s, immigrants have been readily accepted by their neighbors in the South Bronx, perhaps because they didn't look markedly different or perhaps because their neighbors could understand what they were going through. However, as people of color, they would have to face ongoing challenges of discrimination in the broader society.

Over six hundred thousand West Indians migrated to New York City, the pace increasing after 1965 with the passage of the Immigration Reform Act and improved travel options. The largest percentage of these are from Jamaica. Colin Powell, a four-star general of Jamaican heritage, grew up in the South Bronx. Many of the early Jamaican immigrants moved to middle-income areas with home-ownership opportunities as their family incomes increased. Large concentrations of Jamaicans now live in the northeast Bronx.[42]

Dominicans saw the Bronx as an alternative to the overcrowding of the Washington Heights area of Manhattan and moved across the Harlem River to the improving housing there. By 1990, over eighty-eight thousand Dominicans were living in the Bronx.[43]

Domitilo came to the United States from the Dominican Republic when he was in his thirties. He struggled for many years, worked various jobs off and on the books, and finally settled in the Bronx. He tells his story:

> I went to the American Consulate in the Dominican Republic to ask for a visa twice and I was denied twice. I came illegally through Panama, Mexico, and Texas. Immigration put me in jail in Texas for sixteen days, three different jails. After six long, difficult years, I was able to get my green card.
>
> I worked at bodegas. I worked at a factory that made auto parts, that was a legitimate job. I drove taxis. It was worth it because I came to better myself and my family. Even though I wasn't able to bring the kids right away, I sent money and supported them.

Like most immigrants, Domitilo feels that his family contributes to America while benefiting from being here:

> I love all my children, they are great kids. I am proud of them. My son has been the light of his family. He has his own fast-food truck. My younger son is a translator in a college. My children can make a contribution to this country. It is a great country.[44]

Nigerians and Ghanians were the first groups to arrive in the Bronx in significant numbers from West Africa. By 1990, there were over twelve thousand Sub-Saharan Africans in the Bronx.[45] Ata Aduna came as a young man, attended Bronx Community College for two years, and then settled into physically taxing work as an attendant at nursing homes. Describing his adjustment to living in the Bronx and the hard work he did, he states:

> I never had trouble with finding jobs or housing. Most of the people in the area were Puerto Rican and very respectful, good people. For much of my adult life, I worked two jobs, at Hebrew Home for the Aged and Daughters

of Jacob. I worked for Hebrew Home for thirty-one years, retiring five years ago. The work was often hard, I had to lift people and many were confused with dementia. Working nights is a very hard adjustment.[46]

In 1988, in response to the changing demographics, CAB created a free immigration program, the first in the Bronx. An attorney and paralegals were hired to help immigrants with legal problems related to their immigration status. Most common were applications for citizenship, applications for or renewals of green cards, relative petitions, securing U visas for crime victims, and occasionally representation in deportation hearings. We had a handful of asylum cases. In 2012, we helped young people brought to this country as children apply for DACA, Deferred Action for Childhood Arrivals, a federal policy that lifted the fear of deportation and allowed them to work and often attend college. I came to appreciate that an important service was for our attorney to review undocumented immigrants' situations and, if they were here illegally with no alternatives, tell them straightforwardly that they had no legal remedy. This was to prevent them from filing an erroneous application. All too often, a desperate undocumented immigrant will pay an unscrupulous attorney or "notario" thousands of dollars to file an application that will not be approved and could lead to deportation.

We also offered free English classes and citizenship classes. These classes were always in high demand, and the adults were very eager to learn. The funding for these programs was often very hard to maintain, but we always kept the program open—sometimes, it seemed, through plain stubbornness. CAB organized a Bronx Immigration Task Force to share information and resources for immigrant groups moving to the Bronx. In the 1980s and early '90s, funders had not yet recognized that the Bronx was again becoming a borough of immigrants, probably because the borough did not have neighborhoods identified with immigrants from one country, such as Dominicans in northern Manhattan or Koreans in Flushing, Queens. In the Bronx, people of diverse backgrounds live together in the same buildings and neighborhoods.

Research indicates that cities with large percentages of immigrants have comparatively lower crime and higher wages. These include San Jose, San Francisco, Miami, New York, and Washington, D.C. Cities with low percentages of immigrants, such as St. Louis, Cincinnati, and Buffalo, are doing less well. This correlation does not prove that immigrants necessarily cause the crime rates to be lower or the wages to be higher, but it does certainly indicate that immigrants are an integral part of thriving cities.[47]

BRONX ARTS EXPAND, CONTINUING TO CONTRIBUTE TO THE WORLD'S CULTURE

Already home to legendary salsa and Afro-Cuban musical artists such as Machito, Charlie and Eddie Palmieri, La Lupe, and Ray Barretto, the Bronx played a significant role in the development of Latin jazz, a fusion of Afro-Cuban and Afro-Puerto Rican music. Brothers Jerry and Andy González formed the trendsetting Fort Apache Band in 1980, which brought attention to the borough. The band's first two albums were recorded live from European festivals.

The late Dave Valentin, a lifelong resident of the Bronx born in 1952, established himself as one of the premier Latin jazz flutists. His talent was obvious when, as a young child, he learned to play the congas and timbales. At the age of ten he was playing with a band of adults, earning ten dollars for each show. He switched to the flute to impress a girl. He studied music in high school and afterward, and as a young adult he taught music in the South Bronx, at a middle school for three years and at Casita Maria. He performed professionally throughout the world, released many albums, and won a Grammy.[48]

Another star from the Bronx was Luther Vandross, the singer and songwriter. His family moved to the Bronx in 1960, when Luther was nine, a year after his father died. He was one of the last students to benefit from music teachers at Taft High School. After graduating from Taft and attending college for a year, he became a background vocalist for stars such as Diana Ross, Judy Collins, and Barbra Streisand. With his satin-smooth voice, he went on to win eight Grammys, and eight of his albums ranked number one on the R&B charts. In 2004, his song "Dance with My Father," describing the impact his father's death had on him and his mother, won a Grammy for Song of the Year.

Well known in the Bronx is jazz pianist and composer Valerie Capers. She lost her sight as a young girl but went on to become the first blind graduate of the Juilliard School of Music, earning both a bachelor's and a master's degree. She has performed with many of the jazz greats. She taught at the Manhattan School of Music and at Bronx Community College, where she became chair of the Music and Art Department.[49] She continued to perform after retirement.

The rapper KRS-One, born Kris Parker, has roots in the Bronx, including forming a partnership with social worker Scott Sterling (aka Scott La Rock) while Parker was homeless and staying in the Franklin Street shelter. They formed Boogie Down Productions in 1987, shortly before Sterling was killed while breaking up a street fight. In response, KRS-One started the Stop the Violence movement. KRS-One has continued to perform for many decades.

Sotero Ortiz, known as BG183, is a member of Tats Cru, an influential, successful graffiti crew working out of space rented from the Point CDC in Hunts Point. Major news media have published features on Tats Cru, and both local businesses and large corporations in many countries, including England and China, have hired them. BG183 describes how their art meshed with hip-hop music through parties:

> High school was when I started doing graffiti. I met Bio, he lived in Bronx River Houses. The concerts, the DJs, hip hop, Bronx River Center, going to the parties, meeting Grandmaster Flash, Afrika Bambaataa. They performed for free at Bronx River Center, had at least fifteen groups, for free. They wanted to perform, they got bigger and bigger, performing for free. Always artwork, people dancing around our artwork. I painted the inside of Bronx River Center in the early '80s. If you ever look at old footage of Bronx River Center, you will see my art.[50]

The establishment often viewed hip-hop culture, including graffiti art, as a bad influence on young people and a link to gangs. A *New York Times* article in 1995 described the banning of the Zulu Nation from the Bronx River Houses and the removal of BG183's graffiti art. Most of the young residents of the project were adamant that the Zulu Nation founded by Afrika Bambaataa was a positive influence on young people.[51] BG183 describes what happened:

BG183 in front of his mural, *I Live in Hunts Point,* in December 2017. Three talented artists, BG183, Nicer, and Bio, met in high school and formed the well-known graffiti art group Tats Cru. They moved from tagging trains to painting murals, movie backdrops, banners, and canvases. Their art can be seen in music videos and commercials and has been exhibited in major museums. Photo by author.

> The housing project took them out, we had positive murals on the outside, they took the murals out, thought they were gang related. The housing cops went in, took kids from school, "This is bad graffiti, you have to help paint this over." But they weren't painting, just blanking it out. We said they should paint something else, they said it should be blank. We thought it should have color. Everything was painted over. The stuff I painted inside was like music, the Bronx River, people dancing, the Zulu Nation.

The three main members of Tats Cru—Bio (Wilfredo Feliciano), Nicer (Hector Nazario), and BG183, all very talented artists—met in high school and started tagging trains. They had no money and often had to jump turnstiles to get on the train and find a place where they could procure spray paint. They spent hours in the underground tunnels, painting and avoiding police. They didn't call their work graffiti, but writing. They wanted to bring color to what was otherwise a drab environment. BG183 recalls:

In the beginning, we wanted to be the best bombers, writing on the trains, then doing colors on the trains. From '86 on, we could not do trains. We had to move to painting in the streets. We became the Mural Kings. While growing up, you tried to avoid the police. For us, painting in the street in the late '80s and early '90s, some cops would stop you, be nasty, tell us to get out, but wouldn't arrest us.

In the '90s, a lot of street art was getting crossed out, even commercial advertising was getting crossed out. We started doing street art advertising and it survived, people were not crossing it out. We asked permission from landlords. Cops would see us painting, cops would say you have to stop painting, and we would say we have permission. They would say don't do it around me, not on my beat. That was the early '90s. In the 2000s, police would say, "What's up, Tats Cru, nice work." Now the police and fire department know about us, more love. They know it is not a crime.

Tats Cru became known for their memorial walls, large murals commissioned often in memory of young people who died from the plagues of drugs, AIDS, and gang violence. Nicer explains that the walls were a way to keep the person in the community. Tats Cru often added antiviolence messages to the walls. Sometimes when people saw members of Tats Cru in a different neighborhood, they would ask, "What happened, did someone die?" Other walls were commissioned in memory of community leaders or tragic events. BG183 continues:

Steve Sapp and Mildred Ruiz, Paul Lipson and Maria Torres of the Point asked us for two murals, towards the entrance of the theater, comedy and tragedy, a painting. They kept telling us, "We love you guys, we want you to use the facility. Yo, we are going to turn this into ballet dancing, a theater, after-school programs." We laughed, and they made it happen. "You guys should rent out a space." We were not making money, we were struggling, we were knocking on doors. Little by little we started getting contracts. In '93 and '94, we got contracts with Coca-Cola, we were working in L.A., Miami, Chicago, with Coca-Cola. We could rent out the space in '96.

Now we don't do commercial advertising, that died out. We do work with health plans, we do banners, movie backdrops, commercials, events. People want live events. In T-Mobile ads, we are painting in the background.

Everything has changed. We are going into the gallery, putting artwork on canvases. Now each of us are selling ourselves. They know Tats Cru, but now get to know the individual artists, that is how we are making it.[52]

Maria Torres talks about the significance of Tats Cru, proud of their association with the Point:

Tats Cru, one the most successful graffiti crews, is housed with the Point. They created a very successful business and brought their art to the masses. That was one of the ideas behind the Point, for people to create art and to own it, not have it controlled by Park Avenue. They took something, an art form, born from the streets and took it to the next level.[53]

Bill Aguado is a forceful advocate for the arts. Bill talks about the importance of two art galleries, both opened in the early 1980s: Fashion Moda and the Longwood Gallery. The area had been largely abandoned, and PS 39 had closed for lack of students. The Longwood Arts Project, established in 1981 by the Bronx Council on the Arts, obtained the use of ten rooms in the vacant school building. The gallery component was added in 1986. In 2002, when the neighborhood population rebounded sufficiently that the building was needed for school space again, the Longwood Gallery moved to Hostos Community College. Fashion Moda closed in 1993. Bill speaks of the galleries' significance:

Fashion Moda, a gallery on Third Avenue, had a dramatic impact on the arts. A whole generation of artists emerged from Fashion Moda, including Charlie and John Ahearn and graffiti artists Crash and Daze.

Two artists that had strong affiliation with the Longwood Arts initiative won MacArthur awards in 1998: Fred Wilson, who cofounded Longwood Gallery with me, and Pepon Osorio, now a professor at Temple. Longwood Gallery made a major statement as a voice for artists of color. Funders said what I was doing was [duplicating] the Bronx Museum. I said we have over one million people in the Bronx, why can't we have galleries?[54]

Hostos Center for the Arts and Culture opened in 1982, featuring performance arts, dance, theater, and music. Many music greats have performed there over the years, including Dizzy Gillespie, Rubén Blades, and Tito Puente. The center now has two wonderful theaters: an 884-seat main theater and a 367-seat repertory theater. Low ticket prices make attendance accessible to community residents as well as students.

Ricky Flores, the photojournalist, explains the flourishing of Bronx arts this way:

> We were hit with drugs and AIDS. There was a lack of services, no contin-
> uum of care. Lack of social services, lack of quality education, lack of medi-
> cal care. People pushed back as best they could, with advocacy and with
> cultural revolution. That culture has had an impact today and the impact is
> worldwide.[55]

ALMOST LOST

Despite much growth and a strong reputation, CAB almost lost its core funding, the funding for our walk-in offices, in 1988–9. In a labor agreement, the City had agreed to pick up the cost of Medicare Part B for retired City workers. Our funding was going to be sacrificed as a small contribution to this big, new City expense. Community members, fearing the loss of the help they needed, rallied to support CAB. Elected officials and the Human Resources Administration (HRA) were flooded with thousands of letters, and names on petitions, demanding that our funding remain intact.

The HRA commissioner, Bill Grinker, made a surprise visit to CAB to check us out at lunchtime one day when I had to be at HRA for a meeting. Later I was surprised to learn that Dorothy Peters, our director of senior citizen programs, had cornered him, wagged her finger at him, and told him, "Don't you dare cut the funding." When I spoke to Bill, he told me that the funding threat was not coming from him, but from Deputy Mayor Stanley Brezenoff—who, in turn, told me it was Bill Grinker! Somehow our funding survived. (In later years, when Bill was the head of Seedco, a national intermediary, we worked closely with him on our workforce development programs.)

For years our funding was threatened for one reason or another, but never for poor performance. I spent many days in June for several years on the steps and in the hallways of City Hall, lobbying for continued funding of our programs. One year in the early '90s, while lobbying on a Saturday, I had my daughter Johnicka with me. Mayor David Dinkins stopped to chat with her. I was touched by how much he respected and liked children.

BUT WHAT ABOUT THE CHILDREN?

By the close of the 1980s, CAB had earned a strong reputation that brought resources for expanded services. Our model remained the same: easily accessible storefront offices, friendly staff, on-the-spot help. The budget had grown to $1 million. We had an office specializing in services for senior citizens, an office for homeless people, an immigration office, two offices serving other geographic areas, and were opening a few new offices located with housing sponsors. But we were still very far from being able to meet residents' requests for assistance. High-quality advocacy help was now available to some segments of the community, but we weren't doing much for the children, and not enough for the homeless.

6 Not Yet Paradise, but We've Come a Long Way

1990s

I had lived in Brooklyn all my life. We relocated to Avenue
St. John, near 149th Street. It was an adjustment.
Uprooting and moving to a new borough was kind of scary.
I didn't know anyone and, at the time, it was a predominantly Latino neighborhood. The tenants who were already
here had mixed feelings about us because they had heard
that we were from the shelter. It was difficult.

Carolyn Pelzer

RESTORING A SENSE OF COMMUNITY

Restoring communities required far more than bricks and mortar. As dev-
astated areas of the South Bronx were rebuilt in the late 1980s and early
'90s, people moved in to take advantage of available housing, but both
formal and informal support systems for the new tenants were often non-
existent. Extended families were not likely to be able to move to new
buildings en masse. Many religious institutions were still in transition.
Social services were lacking in many areas. In 1990, the NYC Department
of Housing Preservation and Development (HPD) asked CAB to open an
office to help the new tenants of ten city-owned, recently rehabbed buildings on Avenue St. John and Southern Boulevard near 149th Street.
Because of the rapid increase in the number of homeless families, the City
was renting all the apartments in these ten buildings to families who were
homeless. The City knew it was not ideal to fill the buildings with all very

low-income tenants but was under intense pressure to close the welfare hotels. Nicole Levin was then working at HDP and funded CAB's work with this project:

> Families were rehoused without any consideration to where they had support services or other family members. Some were young mothers who had never lived independently. I aggressively sought out partnerships with community-based organizations to fill in the service gaps.
>
> CAB was one of the first of these HPD partnerships and they were charged with the task of working with one of the homeless housing projects. No one wanted to see people cycling from shelter to permanent housing back to shelter. No one wanted a tenant's electric shut off, candles burning into fires. CAB was the safety net of that time.[1]

John Weed, an assistant executive director at CAB, was in charge of developing the office:

> It was a very tough neighborhood with a lot of violence. No stores even. Many of the families had a lot of problems. The tenants were from all over and didn't know the area. Most did not have family members nearby. There was no format for our work. We had to figure things out as we went along, as needs and issues presented themselves.[2]

Carolyn Pelzer (the fire victim quoted in chapter 3) and her seven children were one of the families that moved in. She worked full-time for a Head Start program while she was living in the shelter and commuted back to Brooklyn for a year after moving to the apartment in the Bronx. She thinks back on those early days:

> CAB had opened an office in one of the buildings. That is where I met John Weed and started to volunteer. We started a tenants' association. I starting liking everything that was going on at CAB. It made you feel less alone. It was a great resource for me and my family. I started with a stipend for work in the community. The money wasn't a lot but it helped.[3]

John says:

> Our work with families was largely community building. We became very close to people who lived there. They trusted us. They were isolated, there were no services in the area except for CAB. We set up community activities, play streets, block parties. Many of the buildings had planters. I got the kids involved in planting trees. We did graffiti removal. Then I got them stipends.[4]

Carolyn Pelzer, a widow and a fire survivor, settled into a City-owned building in the Longwood section of the South Bronx with her children in 1989, when the area was just being rebuilt. While working full time at CAB helping others and raising her children, she earned her college degree and became an educational activist. Photo by author.

Carolyn remembers how successful this was:

> The trees in the planters, the ones at the dead end of the block, are still there. Organizing the play street was a lot of fun. The street was closed and we didn't have to worry about traffic. People looked forward to the play street and block party every year. We had groups that put on dance acts. When we went to local grocery stores, they donated food for the special events. School lunch was important with the play street. The play street was amazing. The kids came from all over.[5]

As John points out, this was the first time CAB did programs for children:

> I got HPD to give us access to the community room for an after-school program. We used volunteers, parents, and staff because we didn't have much funding. Then we started the family child-care program. Five or six parents from these ten Special Initiatives Program buildings became child-care providers, which gave them a steady income while offering working parents reliable, educationally sound child care.[6]

Carolyn was able to earn her college degree while working for CAB and received several promotions. She found the work rewarding:

I came on full time as an information and referral specialist. I really liked the work. A lot of clients received entitlements and were having issues. Their public assistance case was closed or they didn't get their food stamps. You could really make a difference. I lived in the neighborhood and people sent others to me. I had a lot of pride and my kids had a lot of pride in my work.[7]

Her story illustrates one of the many examples of community building that took place in the South Bronx and the benefits that residents derive from community-building activities. The Avenue St. John office was an effective partnership between the City, a nonprofit, and the community.

HOUSING CONSTRUCTION REALLY TAKES OFF

Picking up the story of his Gateway Initiative from chapter 5, Freddy Ferrer discusses how the Bronx went on to secure seventy-five thousand units of either rehabbed or newly built housing from Mayor Koch's city-wide commitment of $5.1 billion for 208,000 units citywide:[8]

The Bronx took the lion's share of the housing money. The money went to the squeaky wheel. We came out with a plan every other month and presented it to them for funding.[9]

Life in the South Bronx improved significantly during the course of the 1990s. The City's economy improved, and with it the job market. Now that funding was available, housing production moved into full swing. Vacant lots were snapped up by both nonprofit and for-profit housing developers, producing eleven thousand units of new housing.[10] Infill housing, private two- and three-family homes, were built to fill in between apartment buildings where lots had sat vacant for twenty years. Sometimes whole blocks sprouted private houses. Unlike Charlotte Street, they were attached houses—row houses with very small front and back yards. The owner could use the rental income from the other units to pay the mortgage, thus making the houses affordable to working families without large incomes.

Guillerma Velázquez, who had moved into one of the New Settlement Apartments units, was ready for home ownership. Like many immigrants, she kept her family close:

Guillerma Velázquez (second from left) and family members in front of the three-family townhouse on Mt. Eden Parkway that she purchased in April 2004. Guillerma emigrated from the Dominican Republic in 1979, learned English, then earned a college degree. Photo credit: NYC Housing Partnership Development Corporation.

> I own a three-family house. I live with my daughter in the first floor and half of the second floor, one of my sons is living in a studio apartment on the other half of the second floor, and I rent a two-bedroom apartment to a mother and her child on the third floor.

Guillerma had significant help from Bronx-based and citywide organizations, including nonprofits and for-profits. It all came together nicely for her and for many others seeking to invest in the Bronx by buying a home:

> In 1998, I heard about the program at Mount Hope through CAB. The Mount Hope Housing people helped me in finding the house, the purchasing paperwork, and the mortgage application. They also provided training about responsibilities in owning and maintaining a house. NYC Partnership

provided tax and money subsidy incentives. Citibank offered discounted closing costs. Without the help from these organizations, I would not have accomplished my dream of home ownership.

She is active in her community:

> I serve as treasurer of my block's neighbors association. We take actions when necessary towards the betterment of the community by bringing any issues or concerns to the attention of our local community board, the park administration, or the local police.[11]

Although the South Bronx had private houses as part of its housing stock, historically the vast majority of the units were in large apartment buildings. The construction of so many private homes was controversial. Some thought private home ownership would help stabilize neighborhoods, as homeowners have a financial stake in the health of their area. Others thought that the higher numbers of apartment units created by large buildings would be needed in future years to house the growing population. The mix of rental and private housing has worked.

STOP—WE DON'T WANT THIS PLAN

Rebuilding in the Bronx took off—so much so, that one community slated for massive rebuilding told the City to stop, that they had to be the ones who decide the future of their neighborhood. Melrose Commons, a large-scale redevelopment of twenty-six hundred units, was planned for a thirty-block area. Fearing that the project would displace thousands of residents and businesses, concerned residents formed an organization they called Nos Quedamos ("We Stay"), led by Yolanda Garcia. They would have a strong voice in deciding what would happen in their community.

Freddy Ferrer remembers the process, now considered by many as an example of successful community involvement in planning. It started off rough, with the community rebelling against the plan:

> The urban renewal plan for Melrose Commons was begun under Mayor Koch. I didn't care much for the plan. When I became borough president, I asked that the plan be tweaked. When the tweaked plan was released,

I called public hearings for Melrose. The neighborhood went ballistic. I held a meeting with area representatives. Yolanda Garcia, who owned a floor-covering store in Melrose, was among them. After a series of meetings with Nos Quedamos, we agreed to fund a Melrose community planning group and work together toward a new urban renewal plan. We made an agreement: they would be our equal in decision making and we would support each other as others criticized the plans. It worked and held up.[12]

A summary report, issued in 1993, of a Bronx Center concept that Melrose Commons was to be a part of, stated that "many Bronx Center residents fear that housing construction will force them from their homes and they will be unable to afford other places to live. We fully recognize the reality of these fears. Current residents must have the right to continue to live in their own community."[13] Included in the report is a photo of residents holding a sign that reads "We Are Staying."

The residents played a major role in designing Melrose Commons. They had input into overall design, project density, building height, and income levels of new tenants. Their existing homes and businesses were largely saved, with 90 percent of the existing residents able to stay in the area. The larger Bronx Center plan was not implemented at that time because of a change of mayors. Mayor Rudy Giuliani was not interested in funding it.[14] Melrose Commons is home to several community gardens and is a U.S. Green Building Council LEED-certified neighborhood.

MOTHERS STILL ADVOCATE FOR BETTER SCHOOLS

Poorly performing schools still plagued the South Bronx. Parents, particularly mothers, continued to organize to advocate for better school leadership. Carolyn Pelzer, despite being a widow raising seven children and working full time, felt so strongly about education that she became involved with an organizing group called Mothers on the Move (MOM). The issues were not identical but also were not dissimilar to the ones that Evelina Antonetty and Aurelia Greene had worked on decades earlier. Carolyn describes her initial work with MOM:

> There were concerns about the children not getting a quality education. MOM was fighting for change. It started with parents who attended a school

on Longwood Avenue and realized that the same problems they had faced when they were students at the school, their children were facing. Superintendent Max Messer of District 8 was there over twenty-five years, a long time, and nothing changed. With MOM, we went to school board meetings, started a campaign to get him out, and to bring someone in who was more in tune with what was needed.

Determined to be taken seriously and to demand a voice, MOM adopted many of the same practices once used by United Bronx Parents and the Northwest Bronx Community and Clergy Coalition. Carolyn recalls:

> Ramon Cortines, a Board of Education chancellor, canceled a meeting with MOM. I don't think he dreamed we would show up at his door. We met with Rudy Crew when he first became chancellor. Sometimes you have to act out to get attention.[15]

MOM was a key factor in getting Superintendent Messer removed and replaced with Betty Rosa, who is now the chancellor of the New York State Board of Regents. Through her leadership on the board of MOM, Carolyn had the opportunity to visit other states to see how they were tackling issues of school quality. She learned that they were facing many of the same issues that the Bronx was dealing with. She also realized that children need to have options, that they don't all learn the same way, that the schools were too rigid. MOM began to fight for the breakup of large failing schools.

A long article in the *New York Times* in 1995 on alternative schools described the miserable experiences of Carolyn's children in large public schools. Three of her children were attacked or injured in school. The article describes Carolyn advocating for better educational options for students. A well-regarded small public high school, named for the great activist Fannie Lou Hamer, was established as a result of MOM's effective advocacy.[16] Carolyn describes what a difference this made:

> Two of my sons went to Fannie Lou Hamer. The kids keep in touch with some of the teachers. Peter, the principal, was like a father to the students. He knew them all. There was a conflict with kids from another school and he was out there walking them to the train stations.[17]

After these victories on educational issues, MOM became involved in housing and with environmental issues in Hunts Point.

FIGHTING THROUGH COALITIONS

CAB formed and led groups with other social service and legal providers to advocate for progressive policies. Staff was helping many people, one by one, with individual case advocacy, but to have more impact, we knew that class advocacy was important. One such group was the Bronx Welfare Advocacy Network, which argued against policies and practices that made it difficult for people to get benefits they were legally entitled to. For example, the City's Human Resources Administration would randomly close a percentage of welfare cases each month. All of a sudden, people were left without income and had to go through the lengthy and often difficult process of reapplying. Not all the cases were reopened, which saved the system money. The argument was that the cases that were not reopened were either no longer eligible for assistance or no longer needed it. We countered that the people who were the frailest and needed assistance the most had the most difficulty with the application process. This "churning" practice was discontinued.

Another group formed by CAB was the South Bronx Coalition for Relocated Families, concerned with making the transition from homelessness to stable housing smoother for families. We provided training for housing and social service providers, published directories, and held meetings so that groups could get to know each other's resources.

CAB didn't really have the resources to staff coalitions. But I believed in collaborations and advocacy, and we did the best we could to improve delivery of services. Leta Weintraub, who staffed the coalitions, remembers her start with CAB and her unusual introduction to the Coalition for Relocated Families:

> I was asked to attend the first meeting of the coalition as an observer and then I was to meet with you to formalize my hiring with CAB. The room was crowded with representatives of many agencies; however, there was no one from CAB leadership. You had called to say you had a migraine and would get in as soon as you could and James [another staff person] was mired in a traffic problem. You asked if I would start the meeting. There was a well-prepared agenda and I ran the meeting until James arrived.[18]

The third group was the Bronx Unity Coalition. Soon after the inaugurations of Rudy Giuliani as mayor in 1994 and George Pataki as governor in 1995, large budget cuts were proposed for nonprofits, for the public hospital system, and for the benefits that people on public assistance received. Although we certainly cared about cuts that would affect our services in the Bronx, one of the worst proposed cuts was to limit public assistance for people without children to ninety days a year. Additionally, families on welfare would see their grants cut by 15 percent. With the support of other Bronx nonprofits and Borough President Ferrer, we formed the Bronx Unity Coalition to fight cuts that would affect the people of the South Bronx and the borough's organizations. We met with elected officials, gathered names on petitions, held rallies, got articles published in newspapers, and lobbied City Hall and the halls of state power in Albany. The effort went on for several years of budget fights, and we undoubtedly had some impact in helping to moderate the worst of the proposed cuts.

MORE HOUSING, MORE PEOPLE, MORE DIVERSITY, MORE VITALITY

Although the first building in Melrose Commons wasn't finished until 2000, so many other housing developments in the Bronx did open that the population increased by 128,000 people from 1990 to 2000.[19] Most of the new residents were immigrants from the Caribbean, Central and South America, West Africa, and South Asia. A 2013 report by New York State Comptroller Thomas DiNapoli states the importance of immigrants to the state's economy; they represent 44 percent of the workforce, although most are in lower-paying positions.[20] In a 2015 report, DiNapoli values the economic contributions of immigrants at $257 billion annually.[21] Close to half the small businesses in NYC are owned by immigrants. These include most of the taxi services, dry cleaning, laundry, grocery stores, beauty salons, and restaurants.[22]

In the year 2000, half of the Bronx's population was Latino. Puerto Ricans, although still the largest Spanish-speaking group in the Bronx, no longer made up the majority of Bronx Latinos. Puerto Ricans numbered 319,000, as the numbers of Dominicans (133,000), Mexicans (34,000), and Central and South Americans grew rapidly.[23] The African American population remained at roughly one-third of the population, while the white population declined further. Also by the year 2000, over 36,000 Sub-Saharan Africans lived in the Bronx.[24] And Bangladeshi families were settling near BronxWorks Community Center.

The South Bronx has a mix of documented and undocumented immigrants; the latter risk everything, including their lives, to seek opportunities for themselves and their children. I interviewed several undocumented immigrants and some people whose immigration status I am unsure of. I have signed releases from them. Because of the federal anti-immigrant policies now in effect, I have omitted their last names here, and changed their first names and a few minor, possibly identifying details.

Margarita is an undocumented immigrant who risked her life to come when she was still a teenager. She shares her story about crossing the desert from Mexico near Nogales twelve years ago:

> It took us two days and two nights to get to Arizona. We had to carry our water and food with us. We ran out of water and had to drink dirty water. We fell, we were so tired. We had good luck because immigration never saw us. Now it is much harder to cross.

Although initially she wanted to go back because she missed her family, she saw that life here has opportunities:

> My husband has his own business. He makes enough to live. We have a small apartment, we sleep in the living room and the girls have the bedroom. We still have relatives in Mexico. When we talk, we see that we are doing better here.[25]

Juana is also an undocumented immigrant living in the Bronx. Her route to the United States included crossing the Rio Grande River:

> We came across the border. It was hard. We had to cross the river in Texas. The river was too deep. I was worried we would drown. We had to make a decision, to go back or keep going. If we want a better life, we had to come over here.

Juana is happy they kept going. Her oldest son is in college, studying computer software. He plans to get a master's degree and hopes to work for the FBI. All of her four children are doing well in school:

My hopes are for my children's futures, that they all finish school and go to college. The children have a lot of opportunities. They are citizens. Here, if you work, they pay you.[26]

Kabba followed his wife to the Bronx from Sierra Leone. He overstayed his visa and thus was undocumented for many years. He lives in a well-kept building that has tenants from Senegal, Guinea, and Ghana. There are also several Latin families. Although he left before the vicious civil war in Sierra Leone, politics was becoming unstable. He describes the heartbreak of living separated from members of his family, including some of his children:

> During the civil war, my oldest son got malaria from a mosquito bite and died because there was no medical care. My son passed away, my father passed away, my mother passed away and I couldn't go home for any of the funerals because I didn't have papers. Saddest time of my life.

Kabba describes working without legal status and his feelings about being in America:

> It took me a long time to get my papers. The hardest part was having to wait for so long but you have to go through that. I worked as a printer for over twenty-three years. When I finally got my green card in 2014, it was time for me to retire because I had a heart attack. A stent was inserted. When I was working, no pension, no nothing. I did pay into Social Security and am now eligible.
>
> America is the country that looks out for everyone who is suffering. As long as you are not involved with things, don't join with bad people, you will be safe. The Bronx has always been welcoming of immigrants. Thank God, I am in America.[27]

Isabel Butos worked as a live-in nanny. The family she worked for sponsored her and she was able to receive a green card, after returning to Ecuador and reentering the United States from there. Now a senior citizen, she reflects on her life:

> Everyone tells me the Bronx is bad, but there is crime everywhere. I like living in the Bronx. I am very appreciative of being here because I was able to take care of my family. I come to the senior center and then go home. I will stay here until I die, until God takes my life.

I don't have an education but I know how to express myself, how to talk, how to treat people. I would never complain about my life. I worked hard. I am very happy. I never had any riches. I raised my kids. My children would not have had the same opportunities in Ecuador. I am forever grateful to this country.[28]

Women who came to the Bronx more recently described to me their hopes for the future:[29]

Aicha, age twenty-four, from Burkina Faso, wants to be an accountant; her father wants her to be a nurse. She is not sure which she will do. She has friends from many countries, including Nigeria, Ghana, Senegal, Guinea, and the Dominican Republic, and says, "We are like one big family."

Isabella, age twenty-seven, from the Dominican Republic, works part-time as a home attendant. She wants to attend Hostos Community College and become a medical assistant.

Nadege, age twenty, from Ivory Coast, had only religious education in her country. She hopes to become a citizen.

Yusra, age forty-five, from Yemen, wants to learn English so that she can pass the citizenship interview. She cries a little when she describes how hard it is for her to learn English. Her six-year-old daughter tells her it is easy.

CRIME PLUMMETS

The press often describes poor relations between the police and low-income communities, based on resentments from aggressive police tactics such as stop-and-frisk, high arrest rates, police shootings, and cultural differences, among other factors. But some residents actively try to promote positive connections with the police. Louella Hatch worked closely with community affairs officers and the 46th Precinct Community Council for over forty-five years. She helped CAB sponsor Night Out Against Crime events and was involved with CAB-organized shopping trips for senior citizens, with police escorts, during the rough years. She often lectured neighborhood youths that they had to respect the police and vice versa. For many years, she ran a play street in the summer and was active with Community Board 5. When she died, hundreds of people attended a

A street was co-named for the late Louella Hatch in June 2018 to honor her forty-five years as a community activist. She worked to improve police-community relations and also ran activities for children. Family members, Bronx District Attorney Darcel Clark, Bronx elected officials, NYPD Chief of Department Terence Monahan, and many community members and police officers attended. Photo by author.

candlelight vigil for her. A street was co-named after her in June 2018. NYPD Chief of Department Terence Monahan spoke at the street naming, along with elected officials, family members, pastors, and other police officials.

David Dinkins, the city's first African American mayor, took office in 1990 and increased the size of the police force under his "Safe Streets, Safe City" initiative.[30] Whether because of increased arrests, the improving economy, or the lessening impact of crack cocaine as people came to fully realize its dangers, the crime rate started to fall. Following Dinkins as mayor was Rudy Giuliani, who applied the "broken windows" approach to policing: minor quality-of-life violations such as panhandling, drinking beer in public, subway turnstile jumping, and public urination would be dealt with by the police and could lead to arrests. This policing approach, now often discredited, may have led to an improved quality of life in some areas but also to needless criminal records for thousands of young people and adults.

According to the Bronx District Attorney's Office, from 1990 to 2014, violent crime fell by 73 percent. Homicides fell to rates comparable to the 1960s, from 653 to 95—an 83 percent decline. The Bronx set up special domestic violence, drug treatment, and mental health courts in an attempt to get people appropriate help. During this period, crime rates fell throughout New York City; the Bronx's rates, although low, were still slightly higher than those of the other boroughs. Crime also fell in other major cities during the 1990s but stayed lower in New York than in many other cities. The DA's office also states that illegal guns and gangs are currently still a problem.[31]

A report by John Jay College of Criminal Justice suggests two reasons for the decline in crime during the '90s. One was that young people saw the effects of crack, stayed away from it, and used marijuana instead. The other reason was that drug dealing moved off the street and into underground places. Dealers used delivery services and beeper services, not street-corner interactions.[32]

According to a recent study, another cause of the decrease in crime is the rise of nonprofits in low-income communities offering mentoring, employment, community improvement, and related programs.[33] These efforts, often arising within communities and similar to the ones described in this book, build social cohesion and solve common problems. This is almost certainly a factor in the decrease in crime in the South Bronx.

One of the consequences of the high incarceration rates in the Bronx in the '70s, '80s, and '90s is the high percentage of men who had prison records, making it extra hard for them to find employment upon release. Eileen Torres oversaw CAB's human resources department until she became executive director. She took a progressive approach to hiring:

> We have always hired people with criminal justice records, even when we started doing criminal background checks. I weighed the type of offense, how long ago it was, its relevance to the job they applied for. We hired people with murder convictions. For example, a murder committed when he was young, and he came to us for a job when in his forties might be OK.

Sometimes things are not as clear as murder—drug convictions, assault, burglary. Most of the employees with these backgrounds work out well. They may feel they have something to prove and work harder. A misdemeanor three years ago would not likely affect their employability with us now.[34]

New York City has since passed the Fair Chance Act, forbidding employers to ask about criminal backgrounds until they have made a job offer.

One horrific crime, however, is burned into the memory of many who lived in the Bronx at the time. A tragic fire at an illegal social club, called the Happy Land, caused the death of eighty-seven people,[35] mostly Garifuna.[36] It was one of the worst fires in the city's history. I remember how sad and helpless I felt, wanting to help but not knowing how to.

After the fire, Astin Jacobo, who had created ball fields in the Crotona area, had an idea of what he could do to show support for the grieving community. He and his neighbors laid out a soccer field for the Honduran community; Honduras is the home country of many of the Garifuna people who lost family and friends in the tragedy.[37] Bobby Sanabria describes the tragedy's unexpected impact on the Bronx music scene:

> All this great music was happening in illegal clubs. From watching my parents getting dressed up to go dancing as a kid, now I was playing at these places. It all started to end with the Happy Land fire in 1990. It was a second-story club in the Bronx that many people from the Garifuna community would go to for dancing. A Marielito [i.e., a Cuban who left the island through the Mariel boat lift] had a fight with his girlfriend. He filled a canister with gasoline and spread it all over the only exit in the club and lit it. No one could get out. They had to line up the bodies on the sidewalk. The next day the mayor started closing every club that wasn't up to code in the city. The problem was those clubs provided work for hundreds of musicians, particularly in the 'hood. It killed the salsa scene.[38]

HUMAN SERVICES PROGRESS LAGS AS HOUSING REBOUNDS

A colleague, David Rubel, wrote a study he called "Unequal Slices: A Study of the Distributions of Government and Private Funding Sources to New York City Neighborhood Service Providers and Community Districts."

Predictably, it showed the areas of the Bronx where we worked to be very underfunded, with the exception of services for the aging. The South Bronx was being drastically shortchanged in funding for youth services and employment services, and in funds from the United Way and even state legislators' "member items."[39] Released in 1997, the study was based on data from the early 1990s. The area of the city that had the most need was not getting the resources that better-off areas were.

Part of the reason for the underfunding was the lack of strong agencies in the South Bronx in a position to bid on grants.[40] In fact, most of the agencies that cosponsored with us the 1986 study "Tenants on Their Way Out but No Place to Go" were small and did not survive. Most of the housing groups were not social service providers at that time. I knew that part of what CAB could do, as we built a strong reputation, was attract government funding to the area, thus bringing needed services and jobs. The challenge with foundations was much harder; a good track record and a well-written proposal were not enough. Usually connections were needed, and these were not easy to make.

Maria Torres, CEO of the Point, describes the severe lack of resources for children in the early 1990s in Hunts Point, when she started developing youth programs:

> There was a laundromat close by that had video games. If you ever needed to find a kid, you knew to look in the laundromat. That was really the main recreation available to them. We are on a peninsula surrounded by water, but there was no waterfront access, no parks. Kids would talk about jumping into the Bronx River in the summer, which, of course, was not safe. We wanted the children to have much more than this.[41]

BOYS IN THE GIRLS CLUB?

The situation for youth was not much better in the West Bronx than in Hunts Point. The main youth center, run by the Girls Club of New York, was failing for lack of funds. In the early 1980s, the Girls Club had purchased a large YMHA building no longer used by the rapidly declining Jewish population. Ten years later, the Girls Club was in debt and the building was in serious disrepair.

Originally built as a children's shelter, 1130 Grand Concourse became a YMHA, then the Girls Club of New York, and finally BronxWorks' main community center. It is shown here when Citizens Advice Bureau was changing its name to BronxWorks in 2009. In 2013, it was named the Carolyn McLaughlin Community Center. The building next door is the housing court. Photo credit: Jim Henderson.

The four-story building on the Grand Concourse was constructed in 1926 by the Society for the Prevention of Cruelty to Children as a children's shelter, but most people remember it as the Jewish Y. The Y added a swimming pool, gym, and office space in the 1955, bringing the size to over forty thousand square feet. One memorable feature was a bullet hole in the window of what had been the executive director's office. The front stairs were crumbing and partially closed off. The Girls Club had lost much of their funding and the building was only lightly used.

The Girls Club's board of directors had decided to either merge with another organization or just close up shop. CAB had been rapidly expanding and we were in desperate need of space for our AIDS and eviction prevention programs. I knew the building because my son Kamau, when he was six years old, had attended an after-school program there when it was a Y, and I had attended various meetings in the building over the years. CAB's board of directors and I jumped at the opportunity to merge, although taking on the Girls Club's debt scared me. The Girls Club was represented in the merger negotiations by the law firm of Davis Polk and by Girls Club board member Bruce Phillips, an architect. Sean Delany and Marshall Green represented CAB. After the agreements were signed, a partner at Davis Polk, John Fouhey, joined CAB's board. Davis Polk provided important legal support and guidance to CAB for many years.

The merger was the impetus for board expansion. All Girls Club board members were invited to join CAB's board, but only a few did. But those who joined were excellent members, including Bruce Phillips, who provided essential guidance to staff in managing the large building, and Judith Leonard, an attorney who helped with everything. We formed working committees of the board and alternated meetings between the Bronx and Manhattan. The board began to engage more actively in fundraising, besides continuing to provide excellent governance.

As ownership of the building and the programs was transferred to CAB, we realized that the few programs that still existed were mediocre. We needed to develop high-quality youth programs, but we were still relatively inexperienced with running children's programs and, of course, we lacked funding. Robin Hood Foundation, known to be a generous but very demanding funder, was accepting proposals for a model teen-pregnancy prevention program based on the work of Dr. Michael Carrera of the Children's Aid Society.[42] Ken Small, our development director, tells me I made him rewrite the proposal thirteen times (I think it was only seven times), I wanted so badly to be one of the six organizations in NYC to pilot the program, which had a rigorous research component. We received the funding, developed a youth program we called Higher Visions, and had intensive guidance from Carrera's skilled staff. For over ten years, we had the level of funding support needed to provide the teens with the help they needed to get through high school and into college.

The researchers allowed us to take two extra participants who were not part of the study. One was Johnicka, who had recently started living with my husband and me when her mother could not care for her. I had known the family for years, during which time they had been in and out of homeless shelters. Johnicka had visited us on weekends. I loved her and admired her strength and determination. Kamau was in medical school by then and our younger son, Jimmy, was in college. Jim agreed that I should become her legal guardian. Johnicka remembers her years in Higher Visions:

> The staff of Higher Visions were very involved, did not let go of us, and really tried to work with us. They were not afraid of us. To most people we were seen as rough kids, but to them we were just kids. The academic support they provided was intense. We had to do our homework every day and they had tutors to help us. I didn't like math at all; I felt like I couldn't do it. Ramon would come to meet me on Saturdays to help me prepare for SAT. That was so nice.
>
> The work-experience internship was great. I worked for the Bronx DA's office doing clerical work and for a while helped with a big drug case, but they took me out of it for my safety.
>
> The sex education was one of the most helpful things. I don't think any-one from the program got pregnant or became a father. Boys felt that getting a girl pregnant was the only way to get someone to care for them but in the program, we were friends with the boys without being sexual. There were some couples in the program but they were watched very closely and they were taught about being responsible. We learned about STDs and AIDS.[43]

Higher Visions helped the other fifty-one participants as much as Johnicka. Almost all went to college and most graduated. In college, Johnicka was elected to be president of the student government. She was chosen to give the speech at graduation. She joined Teach for America and became a special ed teacher. She is now a supervisor of special ed teachers. Married with a young son, she is an amazing mother, constantly delighting in her son's accomplishments. Her success and that of the fifty-one other participants demonstrates the impact that an intensive youth development program can have. It also is an example of the resiliency of young people when given the opportunity to achieve.

Vivian Vázquez, who was CAB's assistant executive director for children and youth programs for many years, discusses the challenging work needed to create quality after-school programs for primary school children:

> There was a strong movement to strengthen literacy skills in after-school programs. Foundations such as Robert Bowne and Altman were funding

programs that would incorporate Whole Language, which meant that after-school program staff had to understand a conceptual framework for reading and develop a commitment to make reading a priority in our programs despite having limited backgrounds in this field. Receiving technical assistance from consultants and literacy organizations helped to guide our work as we developed goals around structure and content.[44]

In addition to the after-school programs being educationally sound, we wanted them to be fun and enriching—a place where children would be welcomed and would continue to learn in a relaxed, friendly environment. CAB board member Lena Townsend, an expert in literacy programs, provided wonderful guidance in shaping the after-school programs. Of course, like Evelina Antonetty, we knew the importance of food and provided the children with a nutritious, hot meal.

It took lots of work, but the Girls Club became a very busy community center used by hundreds of people daily, always both boys and girls. After several years, we discontinued using the name "Girls Club" out of consideration for the many boys who attended, calling it simply CAB's main community center. Both girls and boys face significant challenges growing up in poor communities. Comprehensive youth development programs do not "level the playing field" but are steps toward that goal.

Emily Menlo Marks, then the executive director of United Neighborhood Houses (UNH), the association of settlement houses in NYC, encouraged CAB to join UNH and helped CAB develop children's programs. Emily later became a valued CAB board member. Settlement houses are agencies based in neighborhoods that seek to develop a comprehensive range of programs to meet residents' needs. These include child-care and after-school programs, senior centers, and social services. Some agencies, like Henry Street Settlement in the Lower East Side, are over 120 years old, while others are more recent. CAB joined UNH in 1992. Being a member of UNH gave senior staff a circle of colleagues who worked on many of the same issues as we did. UNH's strong advocacy capacity allowed us to support citywide efforts and relieved us of having to directly lead advocacy efforts for which we were not adequately staffed. Emily joined CAB's board of directors after she retired.

In 1992, with UNH's help and in partnership with the National Council of Jewish Women (NCJW) New York section, CAB started a HIPPY program—Home Instruction for Parents of Preschool Youngsters. Depending on resources, from fifty to a hundred low-income parents each year received training on how to become their child's first teacher. Provided with lesson plans, books, and materials, in English or in Spanish, the parents work with their three-, four-, and five-year-old children about twenty minutes each day doing preschool activities. Individual meetings with parents are supplemented with group meetings and workshops. Studies have shown that HIPPY children do better when they enter school and that their parents are more engaged in their children's education. Over two thousand families have benefited from HIPPY over the years, and NCJW continues to support the program, the only HIPPY program in New York State.

Shortly after we acquired ownership of the Girls Club, the City started constructing a large housing court building next door. Both properties sit on bedrock. The blasting of the bedrock shook our building, causing further damage to the old swimming pool, which started leaking into the basement of the courthouse under construction. Bad feelings intensified when a portion of a wall being built fell on and damaged our roof. We then refused to allow the City access to our roof to put up scaffolding; they sued to force us to do so. Our volunteer lawyers and architect Bruce Phillips went to great lengths to draft a detailed response to the suit. At the hearing our board chair, Marshall Green of Legal Aid, represented CAB. The judge knew him from his work on behalf of tenants facing eviction and, only glancing at the legal papers, ordered the City to give us a new roof. There can be advantages to being community based.

The pool leaked for years and we patched it up as best we could. I was determined to keep the pool functioning, as there were only two other indoor pools in the South Bronx and very few children or adults knew how to swim. We offered swimming lessons and access to the pool for children in our programs. It took many years, but we were finally able to develop a swim team, the Blue Waves. The team is part of Metro League. Besides competing in New York and New Jersey, team members have traveled to Puerto Rico, North Carolina, Washington, D.C., and Buffalo for competitions.

Jeanne Tibbets, a long-term director of children's programs, supervised the development of the swim team:

The 2015–16 season had fifty swimmers on the Blue Waves, all of whom were registered with USA Swimming memberships. Eighty-eight percent of the swimmers on the team received some kind of public assistance. The team started in 2012 with about twenty swimmers, most of whom had just finished the intro swim class. In September 2015, the Blue Waves were accepted as a member of the USA Swimming organization, making our swim team one of only three nationally recognized swim teams in the Bronx. The team's parents were incredibly active and involved and supportive of their children and the team as a whole.[45]

In 2016, Anthony Ervin—Olympic four-time gold medalist and the world's fastest swimmer—gave a swim clinic for the team. This was a wonderful affirmation of the children's progress and aspirations.

MAYOR DINKINS BUILDS PARTNERSHIPS WITH NONPROFITS

Mayor Dinkins was a friend to nonprofits in several ways during his term from 1990 to 1994. I was frequently invited to Gracie Mansion for input into policy decisions, including the issue of increasing incidence of family homelessness. Very significantly for local communities, he accelerated the contracting out of New York City's human services to nonprofits—rather than being staffed by City workers, services would be delivered by nonprofits. Contracting out saved the City significant amounts of money, shrunk the size of its workforce, and increased accountability. If the nonprofit did not meet the requirements of the contract, the City could yank the contract and give it to a different provider. The contracting relationship with government worked best when it was a partnership, with the government providing funds and monitoring results to hold the nonprofit accountable but allowing the nonprofit flexibility in program design.

City-run senior citizen centers, shelters for families who are homeless, and outreach to individuals living on the street were some of the first programs the City put out for bid. Government contracts provided financial resources for the development of community-based services, now the backbone of human services in New York City. Foundation support and private donations could enhance services and fill gaps but would never be nearly enough to develop a comprehensive network of services in a poor area like the South Bronx.

"MY SECOND HOME": SENIOR CITIZEN CENTERS

As the City contracted out the city-run senior services, CAB was in a good position to bid on the contracts to operate senior citizen centers. We had many years' experience working with senior citizens. In addition, many of the seniors knew us, liked us, and wanted us to run the centers. We didn't have experience preparing meals, an important aspect of the centers, but the staff we hired knew this aspect of the work.

When we were awarded the contract for our first and largest senior citizen center, Morris Senior Center, we hired three staff (out of a total of four staff members) who were welfare recipients placed at the center through a program requiring that they work to pay off the value of their welfare grants. They were delighted to get off welfare and become employees of BronxWorks with paychecks and benefits. They all did an excellent job and stayed in their positions until they retired.

BronxWorks sponsored four senior centers and three other, smaller programs for seniors under the capable leadership of the department director, Maria Rivera. The centers play an important role in the lives of the seniors, providing nutritious meals, educational and health-related activities, recreation, trips, and friendship. Many seniors refer to the center as their second home. Numerous studies have shown that seniors who stay active and engaged with others remain healthy and independent longer.

Solomon Smart is the director of BronxWorks East Concourse Senior Center, a position he has held for over ten years. Solomon's first job upon graduating from Cornell University was with CAB's community-building project; then he transferred to the eviction prevention program before being promoted to his current position. The day I met with him, besides overseeing lunch for 110 seniors and getting some reports done, he was filling in for the DJ, whose wife had just had a baby (the seniors at his center love to dance). Solomon describes his job:

We get to help people age sixty and older remain active and vibrant. The parties, the trips, we celebrate everything, all kinds of activities. It's as if people live their work lives and after they retire, they get to do things they always wanted to—sing, act, dance, be a photographer, learn to use computers. We are in a poor community, so we are able to offer these activities free to people who might not be able to afford them anywhere else. Working with older people is a great joy for me.[46]

Lauret Lewis is a member of East Concourse Center. She came to New York from Costa Rica in 1969 to work as a live-in housekeeper for a family in Long Island who sponsored her. She later worked as a home attendant and as a nurse's assistant:

We moved to the Bronx about fifteen years ago. I love it. As a senior, they take us to the Botanical Gardens, the Bronx Zoo. I come to the senior center every day. I help. I volunteer at the center.[47]

Divina Rivera came to the Bronx from Puerto Rico in 1953. She has children and grandchildren, but—like those of many Bronx seniors—they moved away and she lives alone:

It is important to get dressed every day, to look nice, and go out, like when I was working. At home, what do you do? Stay in your pajamas all day and eat. That's no life. I take three buses daily to Morris. I think it is the best center and I have been attending for years. I love my center.[48]

Ata Aduna from Ghana shares his feelings about the center he attends:

I come to the center every day, even in the snow. There are several of us from Ghana. After lunch, we sit around and talk about the old days. The center is very important to me.[49]

More recently, health and wellness has been added as a third major focus for the senior centers, in addition to the recreation and meals. Two of the BronxWorks centers have well-equipped gyms, one with a physical trainer. Members can bring in all their medications a few times a year for medical personnel to review to make sure the person is not over-prescribed or taking medicines that interact negatively with each other. Two of the centers also have food pantries that assist both seniors and younger people once or twice a month. One center has several pool tables, providing an activity that the men enjoy.

HELPING PEOPLE WHO ARE HOMELESS

Since society tends to look down on people who are poor, people who are homeless are stigmatized even more harshly. Some municipalities view people who are homeless as a law enforcement issue, not as people who need help. Fortunately, New York is more enlightened. Over the years, NYC developed a comprehensive network of services for people who are homeless, more than any other place in the country. New York has somewhat different systems depending on the person's circumstances. Homeless families, by and large, are homeless for economic reasons; rents are sky high and their incomes are very limited. Generally, they need temporary shelter and assistance in renting an apartment. Some may have other needs, such as help in finding employment, academic support for the children, and untreated health problems, including depression—but they don't differ substantially from other low-income families.

More variation exists among *individuals* who are homeless. Some may be young people who aged out of foster care or are estranged from their families. Some are employed but cannot afford rent. Others are unemployed. People in these situations can often stay in NYC's shelters until they can get on their feet and move forward with their plans. On the other end of the spectrum are people with severe addiction and/or mental health problems. These are often the people who end up living on the street. They need far more in the way of services. BronxWorks is successful in working with both individuals and families who are homeless.

Due to pressure from the *McCain* lawsuit (see chapter 5), public opinion, and the State, the City closed the congregate Tier 1 shelter at Roberto Clemente State Park gym and worked to close the welfare hotels. As the numbers of homeless families continued to grow, the City funded nonprofits to operate Tier II shelters. In Tier II shelters, families have their own private living space, with cooking facilities and a private bathroom, as well as social services to help stabilize the family and assist them to move to permanent housing as quickly as possible. As was the case with senior citizen centers, CAB was also in a good position to run these facilities, having worked with many homeless people through our walk-in offices and having learned what kinds of assistance they need.

The first shelter CAB applied to run was the newly renovated Nelson Avenue Family Residence, a large, previously abandoned apartment building in the West Bronx that the City decided to convert to a shelter for seventy-eight families, due to the pressing need for shelter space. It was a big step for CAB. Writing the multi-million-dollar, hundred-page proposal required help from board members, many staff members, and people outside the agency. How to structure the twenty-four-hour security? What was needed in terms of maintenance staff to clean common areas, but also to quickly turn over living units as they were vacated? What pay scale and credentials for the child-care staff? The local community board supported our proposal because they had a history with us.

A few years later, CAB was granted a contract to run a second shelter, the Jackson Avenue Family Residence in Mott Haven, for ninety-five families (although we came frighteningly close to not getting the proposal in on time). Each of the shelters has a child-care center, an after-school program, case managers, social workers, housing specialists, a health-care provider, and twenty-four-hour security. An ancillary benefit for the community is that the security, maintenance, and teacher's aide positions offer good entry-level employment opportunities with benefits. Depending on what rent subsidy the City was offering, our organization's close connections with local landlords often facilitated finding apartments for the families. Since BronxWorks is a South Bronx agency, communities can easily hold it accountable if any neighborhood problems arise from the facilities.

NINETY PERCENT DECLINE IN STREET HOMELESSNESS!

In 1995, CAB started building a comprehensive continuum of services for unsheltered individuals. This effort was led by Scott Auwarter, an assistant executive director with a special passion for working with homeless people. Through a contract with the City, staff from CAB's Homeless Outreach Team (HOT) worked from vans operating twenty-four hours a day and got to know the people as individuals as they offered them help. They mapped where individuals usually stayed so they could keep track of them, whether it was in a park, under a bridge, in an abandoned car, or in a tunnel.

Staff became expert in helping people obtain identification and government benefits, and gave them an address to receive mail (the agency's). We added a part-time psychiatrist and medical doctor to the team so that clients' health issues could be treated immediately. Some of the older white alcoholics were the hardest to help, as they suffered from alcohol-related dementia. I remember a day riding in the van with two HOT staff members, checking the sidewalks on the underpasses beneath the Grand Concourse. The staff found an older man, probably only in his late fifties, but people age earlier when they live on the streets for many years. He was unbelievably dirty, smelly, and pretty confused. After speaking to him with the utmost respect and compassion for about thirty minutes, the staff persuaded him to come with them to the office to get cleaned up and have a meal. That was the beginning of his journey out of homelessness.

The underpasses were later closed off by the City to prevent people from living in them. When the sanitation department was going to remove encampments in parks, our staff was notified ahead of time so we could give the people warning and urge them to let us help them.

By 1997, we had garnered the resources to open the borough's only drop-in center. Scott named it the "Living Room" and Noel Conception, with a master's degree in social work, was promoted to direct it. The center would offer showers, three meals a day, laundry, professional social workers, a harm reduction program, and linkages to housing. We knew if we could open it, people could really start moving ahead with their lives. We also knew it should be in Hunts Point, as that was the area of the Bronx with the largest number of people living on the street, attracted by the possibility of work as day laborers.

Finding the best location for these types of facilities can be difficult. Luckily, we met a wonderful man, Max Blauner, who owned two buildings in Hunts Point. One was the huge, famous American Bank Note Company printing plant (now called the BankNote Building), the other a smaller one nearby. Max was eager to rent to us because he wanted to do something meaningful for homeless people. Max had personal experience being homeless in Europe during and after the Holocaust. He had fled from his native Poland to Russia, was forced to work in a Siberian labor camp, then fought with the Red Army against the Nazis. Upon coming to the United States, he lived with his wife and children on the Grand Concourse for several years. Max was passionately in favor of the drop-in center. (A few years later we honored Max as a Living Legend.) But, understandably, there is always community resistance to these types of facilities. The borough president's office offered to broker a meeting between us and the neighborhood residents in a local church.

I remember the sinking feeling I had viewing the very long line of people in the church waiting to get their turn at the microphone to denounce the project. Most did, but to my surprise some spoke in favor of it, including some religious leaders and a local homeowner. We worked with the community and agreed to move the site from Max's smaller building to the front of the BankNote Building, a long block farther away from the neighborhood's private homes and apartment buildings. Zoning issues made the BankNote Building less desirable for us, but it was better for the neighborhood. Over the years, we kept the community's support as the number of people living on the streets dropped dramatically.

Manny is one of the thousands of people who benefited from this work. He lived on the streets of the South Bronx for six years after he was released from prison. He had grown up in the area and attended a high school for special ed students but had not graduated. At one point in our meeting, he started to cry when talking about how hard it was to live on the street:

> It was horrible living on the street. Gangs. Growing up there were gangs. Growing up was hard. Only the strong survive. I became homeless because I got incarcerated, got separated from my family. I went to Dannemora, New York. When I came out, I could have lived with my mom and dad but I just didn't feel like I should go home. Oh my god, the winter, it was awful. Eating out of the garbage cans.

Manny describes his engagement with a member of HOT:

> HOT, they got to know me on the streets, Southern Boulevard and Tremont, near where I grew up. They were passing my area for a while, asking me to go with them and I didn't want to go with them. Finally, I realized they

really wanted to help me. The outreach person who picked me up, his name was Eugene. Eugene was nice, he always treated me good. He helped me in any way he can. Just a nice person. Very generous.[50]

HOT took Manny to the Living Room, where he lived for years, although he still spent some time on the street. He made friends, liked the staff (particularly Noel Conception), felt comfortable at the Living Room, and was resistant to leaving until he had a good option.

Another very significant contract awarded during the '90s was for eviction prevention. CAB's skilled staff, led competently by Julie Belizaire Spitzer, worked with landlords, housing court, and the welfare department to prevent evictions of thousands of low-income families each year, saving the City millions of dollars in shelter costs and, even more importantly, preventing the disruption to families and the pain to the children that homelessness causes. Over the years, Julie, a professional social worker, gained the confidence of the housing court judges, legal service attorneys, and even landlords' attorneys. When funding for this work was threatened, all these parties rallied to save the program. The court valued the program so highly that it provided an office for our staff, despite there being a severe shortage of space.

SCALE AND QUALITY MATTER

To its credit, despite CAB's strong advocacy stance, the City did not retaliate against us and we continued to grow. This growth was important because scale matters in a huge area like the South Bronx. It is not enough to assist ten, twenty, or a hundred people when thousands need help. By 2000, CAB had an annual budget of $15 million and 365 staff members working from over fifteen locations. Some of CAB's achievements:

130,000 meals served from senior citizen centers annually

4,500 people helped from walk-in assistance offices each year

500 children and teens in after-school programs daily

175 families housed in Tier II shelters daily

200 people placed in jobs

900 people helped by HOT and the Living Room, including being placed in temporary or permanent housing, drug treatment, or other services

700 people with HIV/AIDS helped with housing, case management, and/or meals

5,000 evictions prevented annually

ENVIRONMENTAL JUSTICE MOVEMENT

A strong environmental justice movement developed in Hunts Point. In many ways, Hunts Point was the most disadvantaged section of the South Bronx, having the same housing and poverty problems as other areas plus a very heavy dose of pollution. Its population had fallen from 99,500 people in 1970 to 35,400 in 1980.[51]

The Hunts Point Produce Market was opened in 1967; the Hunts Point Cooperative Market, which distributes meat, in 1974; and the New Fulton Fish Market in 2005. These three markets, set on sixty acres, comprise the largest food distribution center in the world. Sixty percent of the metropolitan area's produce passes through the markets, as does half of the meat and fish. The markets employ fifteen thousand people.

However, twenty thousand truck trips are made through local streets in Hunts Point daily. Many of these are large tractor-trailer trucks hauling produce and other food to the markets, which is then distributed by smaller trucks throughout the region. Additionally, six thousand tons of trash are hauled into and out of the South Bronx daily from nine waste transfer stations in Hunts Point and Mott Haven. This represents a third of the entire city's trash. Also transferred is noxious construction debris. Add four power plants and a huge wastewater treatment plant, and it is clear why the 52,200 people who live in Hunts Point suffer extremely high rates of asthma.[52]

Dr. Hal Strelnick, chief of community medicine at Montefiore Medical Center, has studied the relationship between air pollution and asthma:

> Half of the particulate matter in the air in the Bronx comes from power plants in the Midwest and half locally, from trucks and buildings. Nationally, there has been a lot of improvement in the overall quality of air in the past forty years with the Clean Air Act. The paradox is that asthma has gotten

worse in the Bronx, with the concentration of the deteriorated private hous-
ing and the risk from truck traffic in Hunts Point, and along the Deegan and
Cross Bronx Expressways. A lot of the city's construction waste goes to the
South Bronx. A lot of the Hunts Point traffic happens at night. The City and
State have no control over the interstate highways or the pollution. No ques-
tion that asthma is epidemic in the Bronx.[53]

Despite the recognition of the problems of this community, the City
kept eyeing Hunts Point as the site for more undesirable plants, such as
waste transfer and incineration facilities. After all, the area had miles of
waterfront and train tracks, and the population was poor—and thus less
likely to object than those in wealthier areas. Led by Paul Lipson and
Maria Torres from the Point, Alexie Torres-Fleming and David Shuffler of
Youth Ministries for Peace and Justice, Majora Carter from Sustainable
South Bronx, and others, community members fought and won important
environmental justice victories.

Paul Lipson, who fought these battles when he was Congressman José
Serrano's chief of staff, as well as when he was at the Point, discusses three
significant campaigns and the relationship between the evolving environmental movement and crime:

> By the '90s, crime was coming down under Mayor Dinkins's Safe Streets
> initiative. When mothers could safely take their kids to school and back,
> they could start noticing other things that greatly affected life on the penin-
> sula, like how bad it smelled when the New York Organic Fertilizer Company
> (NYOFCo) plant was operating.
>
> The first significant environmental justice effort in the South Bronx was
> the fight against the BFI medical waste incinerator in Port Morris. People
> started asking, "Why do we have to breathe this stuff?" It was closed in 1997.
> BFI agreed to pay $50,000 in fines and $200,000 to community groups in
> penalties for its violations, including excessive carbon monoxide.
>
> The second major battle was with NYOFCo. It opened in 1993 and peo-
> ple began to complain about strange odors, headaches, and even shortness
> of breath. Louise Mathies, Marie Davis, and Eva Sanjurjo started the Hunts
> Point Awareness Committee to educate community members about the
> source of the smell and the suspected links between Hunts Point's bad air
> and the alarming increase in childhood asthma rates. They galvanized the
> whole neighborhood. The Natural Resources Defense Council sued in 2008,
> along with Mothers on the Move and ten residents as plaintiffs. Wanda
> Salaman from MOM was really a leader in pursuing a legal strategy and

organizing the community during this phase of the campaign. It closed in 2010. The settlement included $0.5 million for the new Barretto Point Park and $0.6 million towards eliminating odors from the Hunts Point Sewage Treatment Plant.

The third major fight was the American Marine Rail battle, 1998–2000. The proposal was to build a barge-to-rail transfer station that could handle up to five thousand tons a day of waste. Over eight hundred people came to public hearings, stating that the Hunts Point waterfront "was for the people of Hunts Point," not for the other boroughs' garbage. Why did Manhattan get a continuous greenway around its waterfront but the Bronx got transfer stations to handle Manhattan's waste? The company withdrew the project in 2000.[54]

THE BRONX: ALL-AMERICA CITY

After thirty years of struggle to survive and rebuild, the Bronx won the prestigious All-America City Award in 1997. The award, given by the National Civic League, is based on evidence of grassroots community problem solving that produces tangible results. It is given to ten communities annually. The year the Bronx won, fourteen hundred cities from across the country competed, thirty finalists were interviewed, and ten cities were chosen as winners of the $10,000 recognition award. The borough president's office prepared the application. One of the groups that was highlighted was the Women's Housing and Economic Development Corporation (WHEDCo), founded by Nancy Biberman, who developed a vacant hospital building into affordable housing with community space. Nancy thinks back on the housing project:

> No one could figure out what to do with this huge hospital building after it was closed in 1976. We met with a group of neighborhood women every month for two years to understand how they were making ends meet, and their ideas about important community needs that we might be able to address in the hospital building. Many women were selling meals prepared in their homes, so including a licensed commercial kitchen would help them professionalize their home businesses. They also wanted a school. Our proposal included apartments, but also forty thousand square feet of community space for a Head Start center, a health-care clinic, the commercial kitchen, and classrooms. A school was planned for the adjacent three lots. We opened in 1996 with 132 units of affordable housing.[55]

The other groups included in the application were the Mid-Bronx Senior Citizens Council for rebuilding residential housing and for restoring the block-long Andrew Freedman Home; and the Undercliff-Sedgwick Neighborhood Safety Service Council, which had cleaned up a section of the West Bronx. By this time, thirty thousand housing units had been built or renovated and crime had declined by 25 percent.[56]

Freddy Ferrer says:

> The All-America City Award was a big deal, it was an affirmation for us. People noticed what we were doing. We were not paradise yet, but people acknowledged we had come a long distance.[57]

7 Many Faces of Success

2000–2018

It was great sleeping in my own bed. I am happy.
Manny

The Bronx is a city of artists. I love the Bronx.
Muhamadou Salieu Suso

Not in my wildest dreams did I think I would come back
and live in the Bronx.
Bobby Sanabria

We were the key in bringing back our parks.
Maria Torres

We are now middle-aged adults and take ownership of the
work we did for the river.
David Shuffler

I can excel beyond the expectations of my circumstances.
Jeniffer Montaño

I am a single mother of two kids, I am in college, I am
working, I am doing it.
Donnisha Wright

I have accomplished all of my dreams. I am very grateful to
live in the Bronx. I love it.
Guillerma Velázquez

By 2015, building on the work of the previous four decades, real progress had been achieved toward bringing the South Bronx back. Crime rates stayed low. With most vacant lots already developed, housing construction slowed. Immigrants were absorbed into neighborhoods without overt tension. The number of businesses in the South Bronx increased significantly.[1] Comprehensive support was increasingly available to people who were living on the street, but housing affordability was a large and growing concern. Educational and recreational opportunities for children were improving although still not meeting needs. Senior citizen centers were easily accessible to most seniors. The South Bronx was a better place to live than it had been for decades.

THERE SHOULDN'T BE CARS IN OUR RIVER (OR 250 TONS OF GARBAGE)

> I was fifteen, going down to the Bronx River waterfront, sitting on a partially submerged car, planning how to clean up the river. There shouldn't be cars in our river or tons of debris. We had canoes before other groups had canoes. We mapped out all the cars that were submerged before the National Guard came to get the cars out. We mapped trees that needed to be preserved. When the National Guard came, we were there. We took pictures of the cranes pulling the cars out of the river. Yes, we reclaimed the space, cleaning up the river and bringing back wildlife.
>
> David Shuffler, Youth Ministries for Peace and Justice[2]

As the Bronx stabilized, residents continued their efforts to strengthen their communities, knowing they deserved the opportunities and livable environment that most other Americans enjoyed. Visionaries living in congested, polluted areas saw the potential for more parks and for bringing back a healthier natural environment. They knew it wouldn't be easy and could take years.

For over two hundred years, the Bronx River, flowing south from Westchester County and through the Bronx for eight miles, was often compared to an open sewer, heavy with industrial waste and overflow sewage. For the past fifty years, the southern three miles were the worst, close to where the river flows into the East River. Tens of thousands of tires, refrigerators, shopping carts, air conditioners, and hundreds of cars were illegally dumped in it. The Westchester County section had been improved in 1925 with the creation of a linear park alongside the Bronx River Parkway, although pollution continues to enter the river from the surrounding towns. In the North Bronx, the river also had parkland beside it and beautiful surroundings where it flows through the New York Botanical Garden and the Bronx Zoo. But south of the zoo, in the area where David Shuffler lived, the river was a disaster.[3] Industry lined the river and junk filled it. Because of the extent of the pollution and lack of access to the river, many people who lived near it didn't even know it was there. Occasionally teenage boys, looking for something to do, would venture in. Rubén Díaz Jr., borough president of the Bronx, remembers the lure of the river when he was a teen:

> As an adolescent, I lived blocks away from the river. Leaving our home territory, we had to be careful going around the Bronx River Houses. Once we got to the river, we had to see who was there. If it seemed OK, we would swing on a Tarzan rope over the river and jump in. It wasn't as clean as it is today.[4]

Community residents and organizations, particularly Youth Ministries for Peace and Justice (YMPJ) and the Point, started advocating for the river and for new parks. They wanted the river cleaned up and they wanted access to the river in the form of parks, paths, and canoe launching sites. Working with the parks department, they came up with a plan to clean up the river, build several new parks, construct walking and biking trails, and restore native plans along the riverbank. Henry Stern, the parks commissioner, estimated it would take ten to fifteen years and cost $60 million.[5]

In 2001, as funding started to become available for the river, local leaders—including Alexie Torres Fleming of YMPJ, Majora Carter of the Point, Dart Westphal of Mosholu Preservation Corporation, and Jennie Hoffman of the Bronx River Working Group—formed the Bronx River Alliance. They realized that there was a need for one organization to focus exclusively on the river and that a public-private partnership with the City was the best option. The alliance would raise funds, coordinate efforts, and often receive and handle the grants. Linda Cox, who served as the first executive director of the Bronx River Alliance from 2002 to 2017, sums it up this way:

> To me the work is emblematic of the sophistication of the founding organizations. They realized if we can make the river a positive attribute, it could

be used as a cudgel against the environmental destruction. They were right and it worked. It said something about the environmental justice community in the Bronx that they could be that smart and that ambitious.[6]

What stunning progress has been made! All the garbage dumped in the river, all 250 tons of it, has long since been removed. Booms now catch much of the trash that floats in from storm drains and down the river from Westchester. Water quality is much improved and is regularly monitored through citizen science projects. The alewife, a native fish that had not lived in the river for two hundred years, has been reintroduced. A fish ladder now helps the native fish navigate the first dam in the river so they can spawn in the quiet river waters in the Bronx Zoo. Eels are using a new eel passage in the dam. Over a thousand volunteers plant trees and native plants, collect trash, and participate in citizen science projects. About fifteen hundred people canoe the river annually, and many others use it for recreational boating. A group called Rocking the Boat teaches teens to construct wooden boats and launches them in the river. Several of the parks offer fishing spots. A hiking and biking path along the entire length of the river, including the Westchester portion, is 90 percent complete.

Very significantly, three new parks—Hunts Point Riverside Park, Starlight Park, and Concrete Plant Park—offer river waterfront access and beautiful parkland. Soundview Park's 205 acres have been improved with the addition of trails along the river, the creation of three acres of marshland, landscaping, and the establishment of oyster beds.

David Shuffler is now the executive director of YMPJ, which offers youth development and social-justice-oriented programs. Between a stretch of the Sheridan Expressway and the Bronx River is Concrete Plant Park, with its restored industrial structures, a reminder of the park's history. David discusses YMPJ's long, persistent drive to make the Concrete Plant Park a reality:

> "Replant the Cement Plant" was a fifteen-year campaign to turn the 7.8-acre brownfield (from an old cement plant on the Bronx River) into a park. It was about making a bold statement and transforming the space. It was about allowing people to start seeing the space in a different way, using art to help people see it differently. We are now middle-aged adults and take ownership of the work we did for the river.[7]

Canoers paddling down the Bronx River during the Bronx River Alliance's annual flotilla in 2015. Community groups, particularly Youth Ministries for Peace and Justice and the Point, advocated for years for parks that would provide access to the river. In the background, structures from an old concrete plant, now part of Concrete Plant Park, are visible. Photo credit: Nilka Martell.

At $144 million and counting, the cost was considerably more than Parks Commissioner Stern anticipated, but the Bronx River has become one of the gems of the borough. The ongoing support of Congressman José Serrano and other Bronx elected officials has been crucial to reclamation of the river. The first beaver to inhabit the river in hundreds of years was named José after the congressman as a way of acknowledging his support. The Bronx River Foodway was incorporated into Concrete Plant Park in 2017–18, demonstrating that a sustainable food landscape could be incorporated into a public park. Fruit and nut trees, berry bushes, and herbs and spices grow along the trail. Demonstration beds of familiar vegetables and a rain garden add to the educational aspect of the park. The Bronx River is seen as a national and international model of reclaiming an urban river. (As a disclaimer, I became a board member of the Bronx River

Alliance in 2014, after the heavy lifting was done, and deserve none of the credit for these accomplishments.)

However, a huge obstacle to having a clean river remains: New York City's combined sewer overflow system. When the sewer system was built, both sewage and rain runoff were to go through the wastewater treatment plants. However, when there is a moderate or heavy rain, the system can't handle the volume, and the overflow, including sewage, goes directly into NYC's waterways. There is no easy fix. Boston, a much smaller city than New York, had a similar problem, which is now significantly improved at a cost of $900 million and thirty-one years of litigation (plus a $3.7 billion water treatment plant).[8] Advocates for the Bronx River, including David Shuffler, want the river clean enough that it is safe to swim in, a standard that would allow people to safely wade in the water.[9] They are likely to keep fighting until that is achieved, despite the scope of the problem.

Activists began thinking even more broadly about the importance of parks and greenways along the miles of waterfront around Hunts Point and Port Morris, about the value of green streets with medians planted with trees and flowers, about access to existing parks. Paul Lipson, cofounder of the Point CDC, explains:

> Much of the Manhattan waterfront had already been converted into greenways and parklands. At the Point, we came up with the South Bronx Greenway idea. You can't have a waste transfer station within five hundred feet of a park, so we thought it would be great to have greenways in a ring around the Bronx as well. On the East River, where Barretto Point Park is now, Mayor Koch had wanted to place a waste incinerator. The City is building a transfer station in Manhattan at East 91st Street, not far from Gracie Mansion, that will soon export Manhattan's garbage by water. That was a victory for the Bronx.[10]

The Point and YMPJ are members of the Southern Bronx River Watershed Alliance, which has been working for over ten years to advocate and plan for the transformation of the Sheridan Expressway into a boulevard in order to ease air pollution from the heavy truck traffic. The other members of the watershed alliance are MOM, Nos Quedamos, Pratt Center for Community Development, and Tri-State Transportation Campaign. A significant federal grant allowed for a community planning process with City support that led to a plan for the transformation of the expressway into a boulevard with fewer lanes and traffic lights. A part of the plan calls for direct access ramps into Hunts Point. This would lessen the impact of truck traffic on neighborhood residents. New York State has decided to transform the expressway into a boulevard with traffic lights and pedestrian crosswalks, but it is not yet clear, at this writing, whether key aspects of the community's recommendations, particularly the location of the exit ramps, will be adopted by the state.

Randall's Island is a large island in the East River just a few hundred yards from the Bronx. It is a great resource, with sixty athletic fields, walking trails, and picnic areas as well as government facilities. But it was very difficult to get to from the Bronx. The Randall's Island Connector now provides walking and biking access to the island's recreational assets from the southern tip of the borough. The connector, which took years to approve and build, is another example of people from the Bronx, including Congressman Serrano and community groups, working to gain a share of the city's resources.

MANMADE AND NATURAL DISASTERS

Although the World Trade Center towers were in Lower Manhattan, the 9/11 attacks affected many people in the Bronx. Families lost family members—people who worked in the towers and firefighters who tried to rescue people trapped in the towers. For months, firefighters, construction workers, police, and others risked their health working on "the pile." Employees of businesses in Lower Manhattan lost their jobs. People were traumatized, afraid, insecure about their personal safety, and unsure of the future. Walking through Grand Central Station and seeing the National Guard with their automatic rifles was unsettling. Rigorous security was installed in most large Manhattan office buildings and virtually all governmental buildings. It was a tough time for New York City. At CAB, we thought about disaster preparedness but didn't really know what to do. But it felt much safer working and traveling in the Bronx than in Midtown or Lower Manhattan.

Another major disaster hit New York City eleven years later, in the fall of 2012. The superstorm Sandy, a mix of a hurricane and a powerful nor'easter, flooded much of Lower Manhattan, knocking out power for most of the city. Subways were taken out of service and many couldn't operate for days, weeks, even months. Offices of several NYC agencies, such as the Human Resources Administration, were displaced for a year. The Bronx, being on the mainland and hilly, was relatively unscathed, although the City did ask BronxWorks to help some people who lived in low-lying areas of the borough. Amazingly, the Hunts Point food markets, lying on a peninsula jutting into the water, were unaffected. If they had to close, the city would quickly be desperately short of food. Planning has been underway since Sandy to protect the food markets from major storms in the future.

POPULATION GROWTH CONTINUES

Although the economy suffered from the 9/11 attacks and later from the Great Recession of 2007–9, the Bronx continued to grow during those years as people, including many immigrants, moved to the Bronx, steadily increasing the population. The number of people living in the South Bronx is still not quite back to the 1970 level but is 28 percent higher than in 1980. And certainly, with all the new residential construction, the Bronx will soon surpass previous population records. Dominicans, Mexicans, Jamaicans, and other people from Central and South America and the Caribbean, along with large numbers of people from West Africa, are the main immigrant groups, along with smaller numbers of South Asians.[11]

As in previous generations, many longer-term residents moved to the suburbs as their incomes increased. Reflecting the population shifts, the ownership of small business, including bodegas, car services, beauty parlors, and barber shops, often changed hands. The service industry continued to grow, offering employment opportunities to people with limited education. Many of the jobs, like home health care, security, and restaurant kitchen staff are low paid but are available to immigrants. The immigrants tend to be poorer than longer-term residents and bring down the statistical average income in many community districts.

Life expectancy improved in the Bronx. From the period 1988–2010, life expectancy increased by an amazing seven years, while the national average increased by about four years. The Bronx's life expectancy is now close to the national average, unusual for a low-income area. Some attribute the improvement to the large number of immigrants in the Bronx who tend to be healthier than the native population. Others credit the extensive network of community health centers, with over a hundred sites. Several health centers operate school-based health clinics, offering health services directly to children and teens. The decline in deaths from HIV, the ban on smoking in public spaces, the increasing availability of social services, and the removal of trans fats in food are other major factors.[12] Dr. Hal Strelnick of Montefiore Hospital comments:

> It is hard to tease out what is attributable to what, but I attribute a portion of the increased life expectancy to the clinics. Improvements to the management of heart attacks and cardiovascular disease, access to emergency cauterizations, higher rate of surviving heart attacks. A big challenge is diabetes.[13]

Despite the increase in longevity and the now "average" ranking nationally, the Bronx is labeled as the least healthy county in New York State in a report by the Robert Wood Johnson Foundation and the University of Wisconsin's Population Health Institute. Factors included in the rankings are child poverty, quality of air, access to healthy food, obesity, smoking, high school graduation rates, and income inequality. People may be living longer but are not in good health. Seventy organizations are involved in an effort called #Not62—The Campaign for a Healty Bronx (for the sixty-two counties in New York State), which promotes healthy eating and exercise while also addressing socioeconomic factors.[14]

BLACKOUT, CHILDREN, GUNSHOTS

Thankfully, the blackout of August 14, 2003, did not have the looting and destruction of the 1977 blackout—but for staff at CAB, it was a surreal night and one we will always remember. About forty children from our day camp, coming back from a trip to Coney Island, were stuck in the subway when the power went out. The children and counselors were able to get out of the subway and to Bryant Park near Grand Central Station.

Although most cell phones were not working, we were able to learn of the children's whereabouts. Vehicles were forbidden to travel over the bridges into Manhattan. Vivian Vázquez (introduced in chapter 2) and Jeanne Tibbets, the summer camp director, made repeated trips to the local precinct, as did Eileen Torres (our general counsel) and I, pleading for police help to get the children back to the Bronx. Vivian recalls:

> I remember Jeanne being furious and insisting that they do something. She actually yelled at them. By the third time, I went to the precinct alone, in the dark. There were lots of people on the street, seeming to make the most of the dark. I must admit, I felt afraid.

More and more parents gathered on the sidewalk in front of the community center with the staff to wait for their children. Vivian continues:

> By 9 P.M. it was dark and parents were worried about their children and expressed impatience with our efforts to calm them. Some parents cursed at us.

I remember one father yelling in my face that it was my responsibility to get his child back to the Bronx. Since vehicles were not permitted to cross into Manhattan—and anyway, we only had one van—there was no way we could go get the children. Vivian:

> At one point a police van stopped by to ask about our situation. A parent asked the officer if he could drive to Manhattan to pick up the kids from Bryant Park. When the officer replied no, several parents yelled and cursed at them. Parents felt so frustrated at the police's inability to do anything, and I think they interpreted their response as lack of concern. The night was long, hot, and unsettling. By 10 P.M. some of the parents decided to walk to Manhattan to pick up their children. We pleaded with them not to go. They left anyway.

Finally, at 10:30, a bus arrived with the children. Most were immediately embraced by their waiting, worried parents. But the parents of several children were not there. Some had set off walking to Bryant Park, and perhaps the others were stranded themselves. We sat on the outside stairs of the building and offered the children sandwiches, apples, and reassurance. Scott Auwarter walked one child to her apartment several blocks away to see if a relative was there. Vivian tells what happened next:

Suddenly, a car came screeching towards the corner of our building and we hear gunshots. Everyone started to run inside the center, scattering food on the stairs. Staff and kids began to scream and cry. One of our camp counselors was in a state of shock because a bullet just passed her leg. She could not talk. Then another camp counselor suffered an asthma attack and did not have her inhaler. I remember trying to calm people down and especially sitting on the floor with the counselor having the asthma attack.

Scott, returning from taking the girl home, was caught in the middle of the crossfire. He ran and dove under a car. State troopers appeared and we asked them to call an ambulance for the counselor with the asthma attack. Eventually the counselor was able to control her breathing and an ambulance came for her.[15]

By around 1 A.M. all the children were with family, except for one little girl. I had a choice: take her home with me or find a neighbor she could stay with, neither of which was a great option. I drove her to her building and found a friend of her mother's. The girl assured me it was OK to leave her there. I did. When I got home, my husband was anxiously watching out the window for me. He told me gunshots had been fired at the Jackson Avenue facility, one of our family shelters, a few hours ago. I went to bed exhausted, knowing I would learn the details in the morning. I also knew that senior staff would figure out how to feed the residents of the Living Room drop-in center if power was still out in the morning. It was and they did.

HELPING YOUNG PEOPLE SUCCEED

Life for families living in poverty is hard. Stress on parents is unrelenting and affects children. Parents face impossible financial decisions: Should my inadequate income be used for rent or food or carfare? Should I keep my child with asthma home and miss work or send her to school? Fight with the landlord about leaks and inadequate heat, and risk his ire, or live with the bad conditions? Often people in poverty have physically exhausting work, and many suffer depression. Their children are often in overcrowded and under-resourced schools. As a matter of social justice, children deserve adequate, wholesome food, a stable home life in decent housing, preschool education, quality schools and after-school programs,

athletic and artistic opportunities, and being free from the effects of negative stereotypes. These were issues that Evelina Antonetty at United Bronx
Parents understood and fought for in the 1960s and '70s. At CAB, as soon
as we were able to garner resources from the City, the State, and foundations, we started offering more programs to support children's educational
achievement and social well-being.

Mayor Michael Bloomberg took office in 2002, three-and-a-half
months after the attack on the World Trade Center. He moved quickly to
put his stamp on many aspects of life in NYC. He championed the expansion of after-school programs for children. Along with the philanthropist
George Soros and School Chancellor Harold Levy, he visited CAB's
after-school program at PS 130 in 2002. The occasion was to announce
significant new funding for after-school programs in public schools.
The children in our program performed a hip-hop dance routine for the
guests.

My husband kidded me that I was hanging out, if only for an hour, with
three billionaires: Bloomberg, Soros, and Levy. We had started the program at PS 130 at the invitation of District 8 Superintendent Betty Rosa
(later chancellor of the New York State Education Department's Board of
Regents) and a wonderful principal, Danny Garcia. The funding was from
the After-School Corporation, supported by Soros's Open Society Institute.
The program represented a model partnership between a public school
and a youth organization. We provided music, theater arts, homework
help, and other activities for two hundred children. I remember parents
telling me that the number one thing they wanted was for their children
to be safe after school while they were at work, and the second was for the
homework to be done. We were able to provide a lot more than that.

After-school programs run by nonprofits remained a funding priority
during Mayor Bloomberg's administration. Principals and nonprofits had
to learn to work together to successfully run these programs, which was
often not easy. Schools wanted the after-school programs to help increase
the students' test scores. Nonprofits often wanted to bring in arts, music,
sports, and fun, which were often lacking during the school day. The after-
school programs used classrooms in the schools, and the teachers would
get understandably upset if things the next morning were not exactly as
they had left them at the end of the regular school day.

When the collaborations worked, as did the one at PS 130 with Principal Garcia, they were great. Children were cared for until 6 P.M., when most working parents got home. Children were exposed to creative enrichment programs. Schools performed better. Over the years, we worked closely with several schools providing after-school programs and social services.

Another very significant initiative during this period was the breakup of large high schools that were seen to have been failing the students. It was believed that smaller schools of no more than four hundred students would be better able to provide the individualized attention and support that students needed. The schools were also given more autonomy than they had under the school districts. Each small school had to partner with a nonprofit that could bring additional resources and a community perspective to the school. Often the new school would be located in a section of an existing large school building. The Bronx was chosen to pilot the first ten small schools, and CAB was chosen to be one of the ten nonprofit partners.

Along with a public school principal, we created our pilot school, the Community School for Social Justice, in 2002. Vivian Vázquez helped develop the theme and curriculum, hire the teachers, select the students, and prepare the space. With grants from major foundations (Carnegie, Bill and Melinda Gates, and Open Society Institute) interested in educational reform and with support from the NYC nonprofit New Visions for Public Schools, we were able to fund a few staff positions that would work primarily to support students and their parents. I lobbied Department of Education officials to move the school to a better space. However, after a few years, when the grant money ran out, the principal, who had never fully embraced the idea of a true partnership and wanted to keep control herself, declined to financially support our further involvement. She continued to run the school without a close community-based partner. Other partnerships between nonprofits and principals fared better, such as one with East Side House Settlement.

Rigorous research by the nonprofit, nonpartisan firm MDRC showed that students who attended these small schools did better than their peers in large schools. Ten percent more students graduated on time, and significantly more went to college. These results show that students need to feel that teachers and staff know them, care about them, believe in them, and will help them succeed.[16] More small schools were opened in the Bronx in subsequent years.

A few years later, we had our second opportunity to create a small high school, this time with a principal, Ann Fennelly, who really wanted our involvement. It was a transfer school open to students who were not accumulating enough credits to graduate—for example, a seventeen- or eighteen-year-old with so few credits she was technically still a ninth-grader. Students could transfer into our high school, earn credits more quickly, receive intensive support from our counselors, and have paid internships. The school was called the Jill Chaifetz Transfer School (JCTS) in honor of an educational advocate. It was a success, and every year students graduate who would otherwise have dropped out.

Jeniffer Montaño grew up in the Mott Haven section of the South Bronx. Although she had a close relationship with her supportive mother, she was affected by the negative stereotypes and low expectations that surrounded her. She hated the huge high school she attended. She needed a positive environment and people who believed in her:

> Teen pregnancy consumed my high school. Every morning I had to take off my shoes, belts, and empty out my pockets to pass through the metal detectors, so because of that, I felt like a criminal. I had just barely made it to my junior year when I decided that I was done—ready to drop out. So, each day I would kiss my mom goodbye, walk to the roof of my building, and wait for her to leave for work. Somehow staying home all day doing nothing seemed more meaningful than going to school.
>
> My mother refused to give up on me. She decided that my best option was a transfer school, and the search began. Then one day we came upon JCTS. We knew that this was the one. The staff, the environment, the energy felt different; it reeked of positivity. When I started at JCTS, I hadn't gone to school for several months. It was small, they checked up on me and showed me I had value. I was no longer invisible. JCTS took me from being a 55-average student to being an honor roll student.
>
> My whole outlook on education and my abilities changed. My outlook changed so much that I independently entered a writing contest sponsored by the NYC Department of Education.

Jeniffer's essay had to do with the labels we put on people. She asked people: What does it mean to be an addict, homeless, a teen mom, abused?

She wanted to look beyond the labels and the stigmatization and think about the causes. It was a winning essay:

> Out of over a thousand entries, I was one of twelve NYC students who won and would be going to South Africa to meet Nelson Mandela. On June 2, 2009, I did just that. I sat next to Nelson Mandela, shook his hand, and watched my name, Jeniffer, leave his lips.
>
> I was never the same after that. My aspirations, dreams, and goals for the future have drastically changed. I can excel beyond the expectations of my circumstances. I have to thank organizations like BronxWorks that establish schools like JCTS to give students like me, students who are ready to give up, a second chance.[17]

Another important priority at CAB was to help teens who had dropped out of high school. In some areas of the South Bronx, only slightly over 60 percent of students graduate in four years. Without a high school diploma—and, these days, without some college—a young person's prospects are very limited. The yearly earnings differential between a high school graduate and a dropout is $10,000 a year, and that between a college graduate and a high school dropout is $36,400 a year. Dropping out of high school confines young adults to a lifetime of poverty.[18]

Many young people who have dropped out can succeed if given another chance in a high school equivalency (GED) program. With intensive small-group or one-on-one remedial tutoring, coupled with social service support and possibly income from a part-time job, many young adults can overcome the barriers they faced in school and make significant academic progress. Those students with reading and math skills below the eighth-grade level need pre-GED remedial work for many months or even a year or two. The BronxWorks GED program helped over fifty students each year obtain their GED, get jobs, and/or start community college.

For several years, CAB administered GED exams at a space in one of our senior centers. One Friday afternoon, I was leaving a meeting at the center to walk back to my office. A young man who was leaning against the outside wall of the center inquired if he could ask me a question: If you multiply a positive number and a negative number, do you get a negative number? I was glad to have the opportunity to reassure him that he was right. I hope he passed the exam. It was one of the more unusual questions I have been asked on the streets of the Bronx.

Donnisha Wright, age twenty-four, lives in a public housing project with her mom and two young daughters. A special ed student, she dropped out of school in twelfth grade. She describes her frustration with the special ed label:

> When I was in special ed, it was always "You won't amount to anything, you are retarded, you are slow." So, I couldn't take it anymore and that is why I left. To hear that all the time, it sometimes wants to make you give up. You had so few people believing in you. And now that is a main reason why I keep going, to prove everyone wrong.

It took her several years and three programs to earn her high school equivalency degree. She was very determined, but the obstacles were significant:

> I went to night school at the Young Adults Borough Center and worked for the assistant principal in the office. Some of the kids who were abused would come to me and tell me what was happening to them. I wound up leaving when I had my oldest daughter.
>
> I was frustrated because I wasn't passing. Then I came to BronxWorks in 2013. I took the GED exam for the first time and passed two subjects. I left for a while to take care of my oldest daughter because I didn't have child care. I came back for a cycle or two. I had my second child in 2014. I finished my GED at Bronx Community College in 2015. I still come to BronxWorks to participate in activities and to study.

Donnisha is now a full-time student at Bronx Community College with a work study job. She has earned thirty credits and has another thirty to go. Then she plans to get her bachelor's degree from John Jay College of Criminal Justice.

> I am a single mother of two kids, I am in college, I am working, I am doing it. You are wrong about me. BronxWorks is my first resource, my second home, my counselors. I come here, I email them. If they have any functions, "Yes, I am coming." Sometimes I can help someone else—"This is what I went through. If I can get through it, you can."[19]

We were also able to gather funds to rehab the first floor of our community center in order to create a full-day early-childhood learning center for fifty-four children. We pieced together funding to operate the center, including a grant from the Robin Hood Foundation. The early-learning center opened in 2004, providing high-quality preschool education. Children from low-income families often lag significantly in language development compared to their middle-income peers. By the age of five, many are two years behind. Educators talk about the thirty-million-word gap, an estimate of how many fewer words poor children hear compared to other children. When they start school without an adequate vocabulary, many children never catch up—thus the urgency of providing preschool education.[20] Children in families that don't speak English and those with parents who have limited literacy—the majority in the BronxWorks early-childhood center—need even more help with language development. We were able to keep the program open from 8 A.M. to 6 P.M., which enabled parents to work, knowing their children were in a good place.

During this time, New York State provided funds to school districts for prekindergarten for four-year-olds for two-and-a-half hours a day. The programs could be in schools or at nonprofit sites. Mayor Bloomberg expanded free prekindergarten slots (pre-K) to the full school day in low-income areas and increased those slots by twenty thousand in 2012. The BronxWorks program qualified for that additional funding, which was a boon to our program. Shortly after Mayor Bill de Blasio took office in 2014, with additional funding from the State, he created full-day "Pre-K for All" for four-year-olds, making seventy thousand seats available throughout NYC regardless of a family's income.[21] In 2018, Mayor de Blasio started offering free pre-K seats for three-year-olds in selected school districts.

It took years, but BronxWorks was able to have programs for children of all ages, starting in preschool. These included after-school and summer camp programs, high school programs through graduation, and linkage to college. Children could grow up with us in a safe, supportive environment—with healthy meals provided, of course.

As we developed programs for children and youths of various ages, we learned what is needed to run high-quality programs. One key is having highly skilled staff, especially in leadership positions. For educational components, staff have to be able to develop a curriculum that is engaging and age appropriate and that builds on skills the children have. I remember one summer when children in our summer day camp studied baseball. They read biographies of famous players, enhancing their literacy skills. They learned about the "Negro leagues," the discrimination Jackie Robinson faced when he joined the Brooklyn Dodgers, and his many contributions to the civil rights movement. Using math, they learned how to understand batting averages. The dioramas they built to scale of many teams' stadiums required research, planning, math, and art. What a great project!

For social development, children need adults who care about them and listen to them. Friends and a sense of belonging and acceptance are crucial. Children need to be able to share their feelings, acknowledge when they are wrong, and problem-solve difficult situations, without fighting. Children should have time to play and have fun while gaining confidence in their own abilities. Staff have to be able to facilitate all this and more.

Ideally, programs for teens should offer educational support, athletics, art, a health component that includes sex education, counseling, life skills such as cooking classes and financial literacy, work experience and career exploration, and college guidance. SAT preparation classes are very helpful. We took high school students on college tours, including overnight trips to colleges out of state. Through a foundation-funded partnership with Fordham University, BronxWorks was able to offer a summer program called History Makers on the Bronx campus of Fordham, during which high school students studied aspects of Bronx history.

During the Bloomberg administration, CAB piloted many antipoverty projects emanating from the mayor's Council on Economic Opportunity. Each of these had a research component to measure their effectiveness. At times, we were involved with five of the programs and often hosted or attended press conferences with the mayor discussing the projects. If the projects proved effective, the aim was to replicate them in other places.

MORE RESOURCES FOR SOCIAL SERVICES

Real estate in the Bronx became an increasingly valuable commodity. The South Bronx was actually running out of vacant lots that could be built on. The price of remaining lots, used as inexpensive parking lots for decades, increased dramatically. The lots that remained sold for a million dollars or more, a far cry from when the city was giving them to nonprofits for a dollar. For-profit developers with deep pockets, available financing, and tax incentives could put together financial packages that allowed them to pay the steep purchase prices and construction costs.

Community development agencies were affected significantly by the lack of affordable building lots. Many became more deeply involved with providing needed human services. Mid-Bronx Senior Citizens Council, which owns over thirteen hundred units of housing, is a large provider of Head Start and child-care programs, along with other programs. New Settlement Apartments (NSA) offers high-quality youth programs as well as college guidance. Even SEBCO, with its six thousand units of housing in 450 buildings, runs two senior citizen centers and two homeless shelters. Banana Kelly has an after-school program, ESL classes, and social service assistance. Phipps Housing, a large, citywide nonprofit with significant holdings in the Bronx, created Phipps Neighborhoods as its social service arm.

Jack Doyle of NSA describes the importance of their youth programs and community organizing:

> The network of programs and services we developed over the years is a big deal. All the programs are focused in this neighborhood, but are not limited to residents of NSA. We have seven hundred children in after-school programs in several elementary, middle school, and community-center-based programs. The City keeps raising the bar in what happens in after-school, adding more focus on STEM subjects [science, technology, engineering, and math], which is fine.
>
> Hundreds of parents are involved with the Parent Action Committee, a restorative justice campaign in schools. We have worked with the Department of Education to get them to provide more support for teachers, including a new teacher center and mentoring for new teachers. We have also worked on issues of school safety.[22]

Maria Torres mentions some of the highlights of the Point's programs:

> SEBCO and Banana Kelly provided bricks-and-mortar and jobs. The Point gave the rest—recreation, arts, performances. We were key in bringing in the parks, which gave the community access to the water, making the water healthy, and increasing safety in the community. Tats Cru, one of the most successful graffiti crews, is housed with the Point. The artist Charlie Ahearn is giving workshops for kids here at the Point. You can see some of his figures on our walls. We are also working with Open Hydrant Theater

Company. Sharon De La Cruz, who spent time here, is a well-known artist. Some of our photography alumni are now professional photographers.[23]

In an effort to make child welfare services more responsive to people's needs, the City required the large foster care agencies, usually Manhattan based, to open offices in areas where the children and their families live. Staff from those agencies would work in the "outer boroughs," and hopefully learn more about neighborhoods and local resources. Families would not have to travel to Manhattan to get access to services.

Kathryn Speller, the neighborhood activist, sees the downside of social service and housing agencies when they are not community based:

> I don't like the new large agencies coming in from Manhattan that don't have roots in the community and don't really know the community. Their CEOs earn a lot of money and just care about the business. They lose their mission. They need to get out and walk the streets.[24]

Although I agree with Ms. Speller about the value of community-based agencies like settlement houses, the result of the child welfare agencies having a physical presence in the area was not, as we feared it might be for us, funding competition and loss of our existing funding. CAB's reputation and proposal-writing skills were strong enough to allow us to hold on to our financial support. And because there were more potential providers, the South Bronx received a slightly bigger piece of the citywide funding "pie." Indeed, being a community-based provider enabled CAB to receive funding for foster care prevention services, important work that supports families staying together safely. Children placed in foster care disproportionately drop out of high school, become teenage parents, enter the criminal justice system, and/or become homeless. Due to our staff's effective, intensive work with the families, very few of the children in CAB's prevention program had to enter foster care. Families were able to resolve their crises and stay together safely.

LESS DIRE WELFARE "REFORM"

As a country, the United States has always been ambivalent about poor people. Are they poor because of their personal failings, because they don't want to work? If we offer them assistance, will they take advantage of us? If others made it out of poverty, they can too if they try. This ambivalence plays out in America's policies for safety-net programs such as public assistance, food stamps, and Medicaid. Policy decisions about welfare are particularly important to the South Bronx with its high concentration of poverty. Unfortunately, these policy decisions often become highly politicized, causing people who are poor to lose help in crucial times of need. Kathryn Speller, Carmen Cordova, and many other people cited in this book were on public assistance for periods of time. Donnisha Wright, the community college student quoted earlier, states:

> Public assistance is very helpful. I couldn't go to college without it.[25]

When I spoke to Deon Shaw, she had been on public assistance for a year while living in a family shelter after being evicted. She was close to being able to move to her own apartment and discussed her plans:

> I will upgrade my license and work in a nursing home. I will have to take a refresher class. I have always worked.[26]

Welfare reform, a policy initiative of President Clinton, was passed by Congress in 1996. Its slogan was to end welfare as we know it, primarily through limiting the length of time a person could receive benefits. Many harbor myths about people on welfare, such as that poor people are lazy and providing benefits reinforces that tendency. Actually, one-third of families on welfare have an adult working, as is the case with close to two-thirds of families receiving Medicaid. The problem for these families is the low wages many companies pay.[27] Another myth is that people stay on welfare their whole lives. When welfare reform was passed, the average length of time a family was on welfare was two years, although many families need to stay on longer, often because of significant health issues. And, of course, most people on welfare are children who suffer the most when conditions are dire. Politicians claimed that ending welfare would actually be good for poor people because it would motivate them to work. As originally conceived, there were to be supports, such as child care for women working, job training, and help in finding a job. Systemic issues related to poverty, such as segregated schools, discrimination, lack of affordable housing, low-paid work without benefits, and predatory lending were not addressed.

I was worried about the implications for the thousands of people in the South Bronx on welfare. I decided it was fruitless to continue our welfare advocacy work. At times, working with others, CAB could influence NYC policy, but not federal policy. We needed to help people adjust to this new reality. We entered the field of employment services with support from foundations.

At first, much to my surprise, welfare reform did not seem to be causing many negative effects. The national economy was strong and people seemed to be getting jobs, although many of the jobs did not pay enough to get people out of poverty. I agreed that people were generally better off working if they were able to and if jobs were available to them. I knew from talking to welfare recipients required to work off the value of their checks at our senior centers that they liked having meaningful work to do.

CAB started a family child-care network that provided employment for women taking care of children in their homes. CAB provided the training for the child-care providers, helped them get their licenses, helped with recruitment of children, inspected homes on an ongoing basis, and provided ongoing support on the educational aspects of the child care. Women, including women transitioning from welfare to work, benefited because their children were in safe, educationally sound, licensed care.

A few of our offices were able to garner resources to hire job placement specialists. People in high areas of unemployment are at many disadvantages when it comes to locating job openings. Most jobs are found through word of mouth. If your friends and relatives are not working themselves, they can't help you find a job. Job developers fill this gap by helping people write résumés, by finding job openings and linking the job seeker to the employer. CAB's job placement services were welcomed by the community and heavily used by job seekers.

After getting several years' experience with job placements, CAB was awarded a large contract from the NYC Human Resources Administration (HRA) to provide job placements to welfare recipients referred to the program by HRA. This contract was part of the City's shift to performance-based contracts, when agencies would get paid only for results—in this case, job placements. These contracts proved to be risky for nonprofits.

Many of the variables were out of our control; we could not screen the people we were to help, nor could we control the job market. Thus, payments from placements were hard to predict accurately. Despite these challenges, CAB helped thousands of people find jobs and the program did not have a serious negative effect on our financial health, although it may have taken a toll in worry. Luckily, we had a very competent director running these programs, Karen Courtney.

CAB and other agencies actively helped people get benefits, including those known as work supports: food stamps, the earned income tax credit, the child-care tax credit, and government-supported health insurance, which act as supplements for low-income wage earners, benefits that help "make work pay." Although jobs should pay at least enough so that workers are not living in poverty, until that happens these income supports are an essential part of many people's income mix. However, what is still missing is a widely available rent supplement so that low-income workers can afford housing.

In New York State, as things turned out, welfare didn't necessarily end for recipients after five years. In addition to the federal welfare program, now called Temporary Assistance for Needy Families (TANF), New York State has a category of assistance called Safety Net. People without minor children and families who have received benefits for over five years may get help from the Safety Net category. Recipients are not without responsibilities, such as looking for work, attending school or a training program, or "volunteering" for the city or nonprofit. Unlike in many other states, the very poor are not left without any resources in New York. Hunger and homelessness are serious issues in NYC, issues that poor families should not have to endure, but people's absolute poverty is not comparable to that in other parts of the country.

Many states limit the lifetime receipt of benefits to less than five years, and some states limit it to just two years. Some states provide extremely low benefit amounts and make it very hard to receive benefits, resulting in only 25 percent of the people eligible actually receiving benefits. Some require drug tests, effectively treating applicants as criminals. Some states cap the family size to the number of people in the family when they applied. If additional children are born, the family receives no benefits for that child. Some states divert monies in the TANF block grant intended to help the poor to very different uses such as financial aid for middle-class students to attend college. Shamefully, estimates are that nineteen million people in the United States live in deep poverty, at 50 percent of the poverty line. A shocking one million children may live on less than two dollars a day. This extreme poverty has increased sixfold among households with children headed by single mothers since welfare reform was passed. These deplorable statistics have caused the United Nations Office on Human Rights to issue a report on extreme poverty and human rights in the United States.[28] Thankfully, New York does not believe that children (or adults) should live in grinding poverty.

COMMUNITY FIGHTS, BUT MONEY WINS

With great effort, local community groups may influence city government and even state government, but fighting directly against the interests of rich, powerful corporations can be even harder. The decision to build a new Yankee Stadium caused a lot of anger in the local district. The new stadium, completed in 2006, was hugely expensive, costing as much as $1.3–2.0 billion, with estimates of public subsidies up to $1 billion, depending on what is included.[29] And what was wrong with the old stadium? Many residents felt that the Yankees contributed little to the community except traffic jams. Tickets are too expensive for most residents to attend. The new stadium was built on twenty-five acres of heavily used parkland, including the baseball fields of Macombs Dam Park where thousands of other children played over the years. Four hundred large trees were destroyed to make room for the stadium. The proposed replacement parkland was not contiguous to the existing park, and the location was less convenient and less desirable. Some of the replacement park space was on top of one of four newly built, but underused, parking garages. Many residents were upset that the politicians pushed through the new stadium despite their strong objections. The local community board had voted overwhelmingly in a nonbinding vote to oppose the project. Many of the members who voted against the plan were not reappointed to the board by the borough president at the time, Adolfo Carrión Jr. The parking garages and lots built for the new stadium owe the City

$100 million in back taxes, rent, and interest. They are open only when there is a ball game.[30]

"Community benefits agreements" are sometimes offered to forestall community opposition to large-scale development projects. They have a very mixed record of effectiveness. Typically, community groups are offered a seat at the negotiating table, but when the groups start to fight for real givebacks to the local community, they may be excluded from key meetings, threatened with loss of funding, and/or forced to sign watered-down agreements. The promised benefits can include construction jobs for local residents, space to be used for community activities or programs, and donations to community groups. In the case of Yankee Stadium, community groups were not even involved in negotiating the community benefits agreement. It was negotiated by Borough President Carrión. As with other community benefits agreements in the South Bronx and elsewhere, the agreement for Yankee Stadium largely failed to deliver the benefits to the surrounding community, which suffered through years of construction noise, dust, and debris and will have to deal with the traffic jams forever. One key aspect of the agreement was $40 million to be distributed over forty years to community organizations. In 2017, groups in the area were disappointed but not surprised to learn that only 30 percent of the monies that had been distributed went to organizations in the four zip codes surrounding the stadium. Most of the rest had gone to more affluent areas.[31]

At the same time that the new Yankee Stadium was being built, rezoning in the area south of the stadium allowed for higher density—up to thirty stories for residential buildings. Almost thirty-four hundred units of new housing in a thirty-block area may be built as a result of the rezoning, as well as new retail and industrial space.[32] The Bronx Terminal Market mall, housing the first big box stores in the South Bronx, opened in this area in 2009—a million square feet of retail space built on a site that had been the Bronx House of Detention and a fruit and vegetable market. The community benefits agreement for this commercial development, negotiated mainly by the borough president with little substantive input from community groups, largely failed to deliver the promised benefits to residents. Several of the local groups refused to sign the agreement. A portion of funds for job training may have been diverted to other uses.[33] However, once the construction was finished, many people appreciated the local shopping opportunity the stores provide.

James Fairbanks, a senior staff person for Council Member Helen Diane Foster, whose district included Yankee Stadium during that time, recalls the unsatisfactory process:

> In the Bronx, community benefits agreements have had mixed to poor results. I represented Council Member Foster in the meetings related to the community benefits agreements for both Yankee Stadium and Gateway Mall [now called Bronx Terminal Market]. With Yankee Stadium, the animosity against the plan for the new stadium from the community, such as by Save Our Parks, resulted in BP [Borough President] Carrión ending community meetings and negotiating the community benefits himself. Council Member Foster was the only Bronx elected official to oppose taking parkland for private benefit, and as a result BP Carrión removed several members from Community Board 4 that she had recommended. It now appears the replacement parkland is four acres short of what was promised to the community.[34]

FISH PARADES, BOOGIE ON THE BOULEVARD, BACHATA, POLAR DIPS, KORAS, AND CARDI B

On a more positive note, Bronx arts and culture continued to flourish, as evidenced by the formation of new arts groups and the expansion of well-established organizations, including the Bronx Documentary Center, Bronx Music Heritage Center, Ghetto Film School, DreamYard, Bronx River Art Center, En Foco, Casita Maria, Hostos Center for the Arts and Culture, Andrew Freeman Home, Bronx Arts Space, and others. The Bronx Museum evolved into a substantial regional museum. Very significantly, the Bronx will soon have a Children's Museum near Yankee Stadium.

Under Bill Aguado's leadership, the Bronx Council on the Arts sought ways to support Bronx artists and artisans and bring attention to art being created in the Bronx. Bill established the Bronx Arts Trolley. The trolley runs one night a month, making stops at many locations. Bill also initiated significant grant programs that directly benefit artists and arts-related nonprofits. For several years, the Bronx Council held poetry writing classes for children in BronxWorks' shelters, which culminated in poetry slams.

Over the years, major events evolved that bring people together and help create a sense of community. These include a multitude of events during Bronx Week each May, culminating in a parade and a concert. Approximately six thousand cyclists choose between a twenty-five-mile and a forty-mile ride in the Tour de Bronx, the largest free cycling event in New York State.[35] The fun Fish Parade in Hunts Point, in which people dress up in costumes related to water and fish, promotes environmental awareness. The 2017 theme was "We are the roots of resiliency."

In 2018, the Bronx Zoo invited Grandmaster Caz, Grandmaster Melle Mel and Scorpio, street artists including Tats Cru, breakdancers, bomba, salsa, and mamba musicians, doo-wop singers, and others to perform at Boogie Down at the Bronx Zoo.

The Bronx Museum organizes Boogie on the Boulevard on several Sundays in the summer, during which the center lanes on the Grand Concourse are closed to cars. Music, activities, and programs provided by cultural and civic organizations and by artists are enjoyed by hundreds of neighborhood residents. Both the Bronx Puerto Rican Day parade and the Dominican Day parade are major festive events drawing thousands of participants and onlookers.

Three Bronx organizations—BronxWorks, the Bronx Polar Bear Club, and BronxNet—have joined forces to sponsor the annual Dip Against Homelessness at Orchard Beach each February. In 2018, the fourth year for the event, over fifty people either dipped or swam to raise awareness and resources to help people who are homeless. Several hundred cheered them on.

Artists continue to innovate, merging musical styles and influencing the world's music. Anthony (Romeo) Santos, a bachata superstar, was raised in the South Bronx in the 1980s and '90s, near Crotona Park. Of Dominican and Puerto Rican heritage, he grew up hearing the sounds of the South Bronx: salsa, hip hop, and merengue as well as a traditional Dominican music form, bachata. As part of a group of young Dominicans called Aventura, he created music that blended bachata with elements of hip hop and R&B. The group sold out Madison Square Garden four consecutive nights. Since Santos went solo in 2011, his music videos have had over a billion views. In July 2014, he sold out the fifty-thousand-seat

Yankee Stadium two nights, the first Latin performer to do so since the Fania All Stars in 1973. He continues to perform to huge crowds throughout the United States and abroad.[36]

Jennifer Lopez, one of the most successful and famous Latina performers ever, was born in 1969 in the Castle Hill area of the East Bronx—not the South Bronx. A singer, actress, dancer, and fashion designer, she is also socially active, speaking and providing financial support to causes such as the rebuilding of Puerto Rico after Hurricane Maria and health care for families. She was named the first-ever Global Advocate for Girls and Women by the United Nations Foundation.[37]

The rise of Cardi B (Belcalis Almanzar) to stardom as a rapper and songwriter was extremely rapid. Born in 1992, she is of Trinidadian and Dominican heritage. She grew up in Highbridge. After dropping out of Manhattan Community College, partly for financial reasons, she became a stripper. A large social media following from videos that went viral and popularity from reality shows convinced her to start singing professionally. Her hit song "Bodak Yellow" quickly moved to the top of the charts in 2017. A 2018 Super Bowl commercial in which she was featured increased her fame. She is known for her "unfiltered" style and lyrics.[38] Many see her brash style as Bronx moxie.

Some of the immigrants who come to the Bronx are skilled artists and musicians. As Bobby Sanabria, the talented percussionist and composer, states:

> All the new immigrant communities that are coming to the Bronx are bringing their cultures, customs, music with them. New forms of music will be created from the collision of cultures. It's the same thing that happened when Cubans and Puerto Ricans combined their cultures with jazz to create Latin jazz culture.[39]

Muhamadou Salieu Suso first came to New York in 1989 with plans to buy and export sneakers to his native Gambia. He was robbed in the taxi ride from the airport, effectively ending that plan. But Salieu is a skilled musician who plays the kora, a twenty-one-string traditional instrument made from a gourd. He met a Guinean drummer who asked him to join his band, Ballet Africa. His first performance was at the Bronx Zoo. Now he plays with several groups and formed his own group, called Jaliya Kafo

Muhamadou Salieu Suso, a skilled musician, emigrated from Gambia to the Bronx in 1989. As a kora player, he is an oral historian, telling stories through song. He plays both traditional and contemporary music. Photo credit: Elbert Mills.

Ensemble. He performs in the subway with the Music Under New York program. Salieu describes his music and his opportunities:

> When I came I played traditional music. With all the cultural diversity, I met many different people from many different cultures and bring their influence to my music. Spanish music, Indian music, Caribbean music. West Africa, South Africa, and East Africa each have their styles. I have been creating some of my own music. I am involved with a lot of contemporary jazz, with a band called African Rhythm.

Kora players are traditional oral historians. Salieu describes the relationship of oral histories, song, and migration. Clearly, knowing his family's long history gives him perspective and strength to deal with the challenges of being an immigrant:

> My great grandfather was from Mali. Another was from Timbuktu. Before that they came from Mecca, Egypt—a long family lineage. Telling history

through song. Not only ourselves, but other families. Where they come from, how they got there. And how they got to be a real family and how they got to inherit that particular area of the world. If you know the history of migration, you don't worry so much about being an immigrant. So in the tradition of Mande [referring to the region of West Africa where the Mandinka, or Mandingo, people live], many are immigrants. This is my country now.

He is grateful for the support he receives from Elena Martínez and the Bronx Music Heritage Center:

People don't know about the musicians in the Bronx. Bronx Music Heritage Center brings us together. It has been a real help for me. The Bronx is a city of artists. I love the Bronx.[40]

Bobby Sanabria sums up his own relationship to the Bronx this way:

I was nominated for seven Grammys but my greatest accolade was being inducted into the Bronx Walk of Fame in 2006. I said, "Are you sure you got the right person?" June 24, 2006. Everyone has a street sign. I am so popular, they stole my street sign, also Eddie Palmieri's. Not even in my wildest dreams did I think I would go full circle, come back to live in the Bronx, and contribute to the recognition this borough so much deserves. Ain't this a bitch. When I was a kid, I just wanted to get the hell out of here.[41]

BUYING A FUNERAL HOME AND CHANGING NAMES

As CAB grew, we needed more space for both administration and programs. The area of the West Bronx where we were headquartered has little office space. At various times, we had rented the basement of an old church, space above a store, a professional office on the Grand Concourse. The four-story Girls Club building had become overflowing with programs. I was delighted at our success in turning it into a very busy community center, but soon there was no room for expansion there.

So, on the recommendation of our controller Carmen Hernandez, we bought an old funeral home. I must say the board was surprised when I first suggested it—they feared it might be a program expansion into the undertaking business. It took us a while to borrow the money to buy the property and several years to develop the plans and finance the construction, which included adding a floor. I wasn't thrilled about taking on substantial debt, but the building was a separate property that could be sold if agency finances took a turn for the worse in the future. There were environmental concerns—had embalming fluid been dumped in the backyard? Soil tests were ordered. We had to insist that the owner get rid of the bucket of blood in the basement before too many people saw it. The deed was to have a restriction that the property could not be used as a funeral home in the future. The seller owned most of the funeral homes in the Bronx and wanted to prevent any future competition. Once rebuilt, very little of the original structure remained and nothing that would indicate its previous use. We added a floor and used the three-story building for administration, including our fiscal, human resources, fund-raising, and training departments, and as office space for the Homeless Outreach Team (HOT). It was a big, complicated undertaking and all the board members were very helpful. Marc Kemeny, an architect, was invaluable.

The same day we had the formal ribbon cutting for the new building, we publicly announced our new name. The name Citizens Advice Bureau seemed out of date—so many of the people in the Bronx were not citizens, but all were certainly very welcome at our programs; we did a lot more than give out advice; and "bureau" sounded too much like a government agency. For years I had fiddled with our initials while riding the subway. Since most people knew us as CAB, I thought another name with the same initials would be great, but I couldn't come up with one. We hired a consultant, actively involved board and senior staff, and decided to select the name we were using for our employment programs, BronxWorks. On reflection, it did seem like a good name: it presents a positive view of the Bronx, our staff work hard on behalf of the clients, and our programs are effective (they work) and comprehensive (like pizza with "the works"). We also changed our logo and tagline to indicate that "we feed, shelter, teach, and support our neighbors to build a strong community."

But how to present the new name to our six hundred staff members so they would embrace our change? Elisa Istueta, then the director of children and youth programs, came up with a creative idea: present it as a game show with teams of staff guessing letters and the rest of the staff watching. When all letters were revealed and a team guessed the name,

Deputy Borough President Aurelia Greene and Congressman
José Serrano join Carolyn McLaughlin in celebrating the
Citizens Advice Bureau's change of name to BronxWorks and
cutting the ribbon for the new building at 60 East Tremont in
2009. Both Serrano and Greene grew up in the South Bronx and
have long, distinguished records of public service. Photo credit:
Dan Senes, BronxWorks.

staff were stunned and wondered if everyone would now become employment counselors. But we played triumphant music, danced around, blew
horns, and celebrated. The new name was accepted by staff and eventually
by the community. The programs did not change.

HOMELESSNESS CONTINUES TO INCREASE, AND HELP EXPANDS

New York City has been searching for solutions to homelessness among
families since the 1980s. In earlier centuries, the response was the dreaded
workhouse or sending children of the destitute to live with farm families
in the Midwest. When Mayor Bloomberg appointed Linda Gibbs (later
promoted to deputy mayor for human services) to be the commissioner of
the Department of Homeless Services in 2002, I gave her a present. Since

the days of Mayor Dinkins, I had been putting all the City's five- and ten-year plans to end homelessness in a cardboard box in my closet. The Bloomberg administration should see what other administrations had tried, so I presented Gibbs with my heavy cardboard box full of plans to end homelessness. After consultation with providers and experts in the field, she set and tracked targets for decreasing homelessness. Her department tightened eligibility at the "front door," making sure families had no other viable options before approving them for entrance into the shelter system. They set move-out targets for shelter providers, experimenting with financial rewards or penalties for meeting or failing to meet the set goal for the number of families moving out each month. They tried providing various time-limited rent supplements to landlords to encourage them to accept the families—an effort to close the affordability gap between what lower-income people could afford to pay and what landlords were charging. Out of necessity, the city asked providers to open more shelters. BronxWorks responded by opening a third large shelter, Willow Avenue Family Residence. With the other two-family shelters opened in the '90s, BronxWorks could now house over 270 families at a time.

When I met her, Deon Shaw was living at our Willow Avenue shelter. She and her twelve-year-old son were moving in a week into a new building near the Bronx Zoo with a subsidy that would help her afford the rent. Her son was very excited that he would have his own room, because for the past year they had been living in one room (with a kitchen area and bathroom) in the shelter. Deon is very proud of her two grown sons. The oldest is a graduate of Columbia University and is now a lieutenant in the Marines. He is married to a woman who also graduated from Columbia and they have a young son. Her middle son works in the newsroom of the *New Yorker* magazine and has started college. Her problems with homelessness had started several years earlier when her partner was arrested:

> In 2007, I was evicted. We were both working until he got arrested. I couldn't afford the rent by myself. That is how it started with me being in a shelter. I was in the shelter for two years. I was placed into housing, into a three-story house with a backyard. It was nice. I was working as a security guard. I had FEPS, a rent subsidy.

But Deon was evicted again when the building owner went to jail and the building was sold. The new owner did not want to accept rent subsidies, and since it was a private house, he did not have to accept the subsidy or renew her lease. Deon recalls:

> The landlord was put in jail and the bank took the property. A new landlord bought the property. I was working in a nursing home. He didn't want any programs [such as FEPS]. He took me to court. We were in court for six months. The judge was sympathetic and said I will give you time to move. I left my apartment last November. I have been here in the shelter for a year.[42]

The basic cause of homelessness is a lack of affordable housing for low- and moderate-income people, aggravated by the federal government drastically decreasing its support for housing subsidies, both by failing to adequately support public housing projects and by severely limiting the number of Section 8 rent vouchers issued. The issue is compounded by the shortage of housing, which has the effect of rapidly increasing rents despite rent stabilization laws. And of course, NYC's vast income disparity between the rich and those with limited incomes also plays a role.

Besides family shelters, NYC also has shelters for men and women who do not have children living with them. BronxWorks was asked by the City to open shelters for homeless men, but I declined, not liking either the proposed locations or the buildings.

New York City recognizes a right to shelter for both families and individuals, so individuals who live on the street rather than in a shelter are often those who can't conform to the rules or conditions in the shelters, usually because of mental illness and/or substance abuse. BronxWorks continued to be the agency in the Bronx responsible for helping this population.

Whenever I saw a person who might be homeless in an unusual location, I would make sure to stop into our HOT office and give them the location. Once, while canoeing down the Bronx River with the Bronx River Alliance, I saw a man living along the riverbank under a bridge. Ralph Acevedo, the HOT director (who as a teenager had worked in the gardening project in Hunts Point described in chapter 5), said they would find him. A few months later, Eileen Torres (our general counsel) and I had an unexpected visit from four detectives who said an agency van may have been involved in a hit-and-run that killed a policeman in Brooklyn. They had a partial license plate and said our van was the only one in the state of New York to fit the description. We called staff to bring the van in question to the office. While waiting on the sidewalk for the van to arrive, a HOT car pulled up to take the man whom I had seen under the bridge to an apartment. The staff had found him, applied for supportive housing for him, and he had been accepted! I was delighted. The detectives later determined that our van was not the van from the hit-and-run, because of its signage and a GPS reading that confirmed it had not been out of the Bronx on the night in question. Eileen and I were greatly relieved.

The City wisely instituted "Code Blue." This policy requires that HOT staff check on people living outdoors in the Bronx every few hours, all day and all night, when the temperature is below freezing. If the person is deemed at risk and if staff are unsuccessful in convincing the person to go to a place with heat, there is a procedure in which the police can be involved to prevent a death from freezing. In these situations, usually the person will let HOT help them. Other agencies have this responsibility in other boroughs. Scott Auwarter was instrumental in getting the City to separately track deaths of homeless people, to learn more about the causes and how deaths could be prevented. Another important step the City took was the implementation of the 311 phone system, in which residents can call the City with requests or questions. The 311 calls about people living on the streets in the Bronx are forwarded to BronxWorks. Staff are expected to go to the location provided by the caller quickly and assess the situation. The City also selects one night in January to count, as accurately as possible, the number of people living on the streets. Although weather can affect the results, because very cold nights decrease the number of people found, the count does give an indication of the effectiveness of the work.

BronxWorks continued to have remarkable success in decreasing the numbers of people living on the streets of the Bronx. One commissioner told me that if the Bronx were a separate city, it would have the lowest percentage, among major cities, of people living on the street. BronxWorks was able to add beds in little "roomlets" to our Living Room drop-in center and at another location. These "Safe Haven" beds allow more stability for medically frail clients as they apply for and await placement in permanent housing.

Housing for this population became more available when the City sensibly adopted a "housing first" policy. No longer did clients have to be "clean and sober" or have mental illness issues under control before being placed in housing. Now clients could be placed in housing, have some stability in their lives, and then start to work on their other problems. In 2010, Manny (see chapter 6), who had been homeless for years and had been staying off and on at the Living Room, had the opportunity to move into permanent housing, while keeping the support he valued from BronxWorks. BronxWorks was asked by Breaking Ground, a nonprofit housing developer, to provide the social services at the Brook, a brand-new, six-story supportive housing project in the South Bronx. Manny recalls:

> I was one of the first fifteen people who moved in here at the Brook. It was great sleeping in my own bed. I am happy. I cook my own meals. If you would taste my cooking—rice and beans, fried chicken, my favorites. It is the best thing that happened to me. I have made six years in my own apartment.[43]

BronxWorks offers money management assistance for the tenants of the Brook, as well as case management and medical and psychiatric services. This has resulted in the tenants retaining their housing, with less than a 2 percent eviction rate.

The continuum for street homeless that BronxWorks developed—HOT, the Living Room, Safe Haven beds, and permanent supportive housing, all with medical, psychiatric, and social service assistance—has caused a decrease of over 90 percent in the number of people living on the street in the Bronx. It has helped that all the pieces of the continuum are with one agency, so people can move smoothly from one step to the next. BronxWorks' success in this area demonstrates that difficult social problems can be solved. This model was replicated in other places.

FACES OF SUCCESS

On August 17, 2011, staff of HOT and the Living Room put together the most extraordinary event, certainly a highlight of my thirty-four years at BronxWorks. Staff reached out to the approximately two hundred

previously long-term homeless people BronxWorks had placed in permanent housing in the past few years. Some of the men and women had lived
on the street for more than ten years. Staff invited them to a special ban-
quet in their honor at the Bronx campus of Fordham University. Called
"Faces of Success," the event acknowledged the clients' hard work at successfully overcoming homelessness.

Over a hundred guests attended. Staff had provided suits to those who
did not have dress clothing. Every HOT vehicle was used to pick up people
from their residences and get them to the right building on the beautiful
but expansive campus. Set with tablecloths, china, and silverware, not
plastic, the tables looked beautiful. Photographs were taken of all the
guests in their dress clothing and provided to them in a frame before the
event was over. Scott Auwarter explained to me that most people who were
homeless did not have any pictures of themselves, all their personal belong-
ings having been lost over the years. Ralph Acevedo remembers the night:

> The waiter service and getting clients appropriate clothing who needed it
> provided the night with the appropriate dignity and environment of respect.
> These men and women had turned their lives around.[44]

And Manny says:

> Faces of Success, it was so beautiful. It was at Fordham College, I was never
> at Fordham College before. The people there were nice. I took pictures. I
> had a beautiful time. The video was nice. I had so much fun that night. I was
> living here already. Doug, the HOT director at the time, got me a suit to
> wear. I was blown away by that.[45]

The excitement and positive feeling was incredible—it was through the
roof. The food was of gourmet quality. Fordham students waited tables.
One of the speakers was Iran (The Blade) Barkley, a three-time middle-
weight and light heavyweight boxing champion and a Bronx native. He
had been homeless and we had helped him get disability income and
placed him in housing.[46] Another speaker was Marvin Shepard, an ex-
Marine who had been on the streets for ten years and had been housed for
two years. But the highlight was a video that showed the stories of four of
the guests. At one point in the video, Donald, who had been homeless for
many years, talks about what it means to have your own place to live, and

holds up his keys and jiggles them in the air. During the screening of the video at the dinner, Donald again held up his keys, shaking them. Other guests instantly did the same, laughing and clapping. The joy and pride were wonderful, inspiring, tear-jerking, exhilarating.

A front-page article in the *New York Times* described the evening: "The event had the air of a class reunion, but the attendees shared memories of shelters rather than of schools, of recovery rather than of careers."[47] The *Times* article also describes Mr. Shepard's journey overcoming homelessness. An October 5, 2011, *Times* video features Mr. Shepard and Bronx-Works' successful efforts to help him.

HEALTHY EATING AND COMMUNITY HEALTH

A few years before I retired, the board and senior staff went through a strategic planning process to set goals for the next several years. Given that the Bronx has the worst health indicators in New York State (although above par nationally, compared with other low-income areas), the one new programmatic area I wanted us to concentrate on was health, wellness, and nutrition. Providing food had been a significant part of our work for many years. In fact, our kitchens produced four hundred thousand meals a year. These included meals eaten by senior citizens at our four senior centers, by children in the two early-learning centers and in four after-school programs, by clients in our HIV/AIDS programs, and by people in the Living Room and Safe Haven homeless programs.

BronxWorks had developed close working relationships with Food Bank For New York City, which had supplied our kitchens with food at low cost to supplement what we purchased. For several years, Food Bank sponsored a healthy-eating program for children in our community center's after-school program. We actually had videos of children saying how much they liked vegetables and why they didn't eat junk food anymore! Staff held excellent cooking classes for the teens in our large kitchen. Often, I was invited to taste some wonderful vegetarian dish they had prepared. We worked with Food Bank and other organizations in coordinating food stamp outreach in the South Bronx. Statistics showed that only about half the people eligible for food stamps were receiving them. Any household that is eligible for food stamps clearly needs them, because a family's income has to be very low to qualify. We helped thousands of families receive this important benefit.

But we needed to do more. Several times I invited the head of the Bronx office of the New York City Department of Health to speak to program directors about the epidemic of diabetes in the Bronx. I worried about staff and community residents in their thirties and older who had diabetes and were struggling to control it. We had always made affordable health insurance available to salaried staff and their families, but just having health insurance wasn't enough.

At one all-staff meeting, held at the Lincoln Hospital auditorium in two sessions because the staff had grown to six hundred members, I spontaneously announced that I was banning the use of agency money for the purchase of sugary drinks. I was asked what teens on field trips would drink. Easy answer—water. That announcement did mean I had to scrutinize invoices when signing checks to make sure no purchases of soda or sweet tea were slipping through.

The agency was fortunate enough to receive enhanced funding that allowed us to add gyms at two of our senior centers. Seniors in their sixties, seventies, and eighties worked out on equipment with a personal trainer. We also tried to motivate people to walk, by setting up walking clubs at the senior centers, encouraging people to take the stairs rather than an elevator, and taking walks at lunch hour.

Seniors and staff surveyed the availability of fresh fruits and vegetables in grocery stores in the community. Despite the location of the huge Hunts Point Produce Market in the Bronx, grocery stores were few and far between, with very little in the way of fresh food. Clearly our area of the South Bronx was a "food desert." John Weed and his staff made arrangements and got permits to open a farmers market to provide healthy, locally grown food to area residents. BronxWorks processed the food stamp payments for the vegetables, saving the farmers paperwork and payment delays.

Children's and seniors' programs expanded gardening projects. The children used planters on the roof of the community center. The seniors were able to secure space in a local community garden. Although it was not possible to grow large amounts of food, children could plant some vegetables and seniors could once again experience gardening.

Additionally, we were able to patch together funding from a number of sources to hire a wonderful part-time medical director, Dr. Andrea Littleton. She oversaw the medical services provided in our homelessness programs, helped set the direction of the HIV/AIDS programs, reviewed senior citizen's medications to make sure none were incompatible with others, and helped oversee the wellness component. Funding for our HIV/AIDS programs expanded to encompass people with other serious, chronic illnesses.

APPROACHING RETIREMENT

Shortly before I retired in 2013, we had amazing experiences with three real estate firms that demonstrated how organizations with very different objectives can work together to benefit the community. The office that John Weed and Carolyn Pelzer helped start in 1990 was in danger of closing because of a lack of funding. Many people depended on it for help with their housing and other problems. The office's landlord offered to waive most of the rent in order to keep the service in the community. Another owner offered us free space and half the cost of running an after-school program in one of his buildings if we raised the other half.

A third, Peter Magistro of Bronx Pro Realty Group, was extremely generous. Peter, a Fordham University graduate, was born and raised in the Bronx. He bought his first building with his dad when he was only twenty-four. Now, his firm manages over eighteen hundred units of housing. The buildings he owns all have "Statue of Liberty green" fire escapes. Working closely with the art group DreamYard, he turned a vacant lot into a beautiful park, decorated with mosaics. In one of his recently rehabbed buildings, he built out the ground floor so that it could be used by BronxWorks as a child-care center with three classrooms. Since it was as large as the child-care center in our community center, we were able to double the number of children and families benefiting. I was very impressed by this significant philanthropic support from the for-profit real estate sector in the Bronx.

The City Council and Borough President Rubén Díaz Jr. allocated significant funds toward badly needed renovations to the community center on the Grand Concourse, including a new play roof, a new boiler, a new elevator, and upgrades to the swimming pool. More funds were allocated for these projects after I left. This important building, a true community resource now over ninety years old, will continually need repairs, but it was in better shape than it had been in forty years.

We had made a lot of progress in going to scale. BronxWorks was helping over thirty-five thousand people a year through the various programs. We had become proficient at tracking outcomes—from the educational and social gains of the children in the early-childhood programs, to the passing rates of young people taking the high school equivalency exam and their matriculation into college, to the numbers of jobs secured and their pay rates—for the employment programs. Almost all of the agency's funding for the foreseeable future was secure, or at least as secure as it ever can be, given the nature of the work. Foundations were willing to continue their support, despite a change in leadership. Most of the government funding was locked in with multiyear contracts. Given the large percentage of low-income people in the South Bronx, we worked hard to obtain a grant to help people enroll for health insurance through the Affordable Care Act, known as Obamacare.

On a personal level, although it was very hard to leave an organization that was my life's work and people I love and respect, I knew that BronxWorks was in good shape with a great staff and board. Eileen Torres, in particular, was very strong. I had worked hard for thirty-four years and felt that I couldn't keep up the pace indefinitely, being too set in my ways to change my work habits. I had developed a health issue. My husband had retired years earlier and I wanted to spend time with him. New leadership and energy would be helpful to the agency. I had been blessed to have this wonderful job for thirty-four years, but it was time to go.

It was gratifying that people thought highly of BronxWorks. Recognizing successful collaborations, Food Bank For New York City and the Bronx Council on the Arts honored our work at special events. Also honored at the Food Bank event was Dr. Lucy Cabrera, the retiring CEO and a valued colleague. (John Weed, Maria Rivera, and Jeanne Tibbets had worked closely with Food Bank for years, as had Marjorie Jeannot and Wanda Cruz with the Bronx Council on the Arts.) The BronxWorks board of directors decided to name the large community center on the Grand Concourse the Carolyn McLaughlin Community Center—what a huge honor! I also received many citations from elected officials. The staff threw me the most wonderful party, which my children, their spouses, and my grandchildren attended. But for me, it was also a sad time.

While I was working on this book, Gladys Carrión—who served as a commissioner of children's and family services for both New York State and NYC and whom I have always admired for her strong and brave positions—gave me a compliment that I hesitantly include in this book for fear of appearing boastful. But I do think the points she makes about the characteristics of BronxWorks that helped make the agency successful are correct, and she emphasizes the important role human services can play in a community:

> When I was at legal services, we referred families, did workshops for your staff and with your staff for other groups. You were a real anchor in that community. Hundreds of thousands of people benefited from your work. I remember you building that organization for years. To your credit, I think you need sustained leadership for an organization to thrive. I always admired how you were able to understand what the needs of the community were and you sought community input. You took risks. Always good services—you valued not having just a program, but made sure they were of good quality. You brought in people from the community to work there, and that strengthened the community.[48]

Gladys's kind words are much appreciated, and I did try hard to keep a focus on the quality of our programs. We took significant risks and also tried not to compete for funding against other Bronx organizations. The vast majority of the staff were from the Bronx. We were often able to identify emerging issues, such as services needed to help people who were homeless, people with HIV, immigrants, and housing and educational trends. As our capacity grew, we made significant progress in improving educational opportunities for children, preventing evictions, decreasing street homelessness, sheltering homeless families, providing hundreds of thousands of healthful meals, expanding employment opportunities, aiding immigrants, and improving the quality of life for senior citizens. Change doesn't happen easily. It can take decades of hard work. As Evelina

Antonetty illustrated, it is important to hold on to one's values. Many other fine nonprofits, some of which are noted in this book, contribute greatly to improving the quality of life and the opportunities for people in the Bronx.

WHAT I DID RIGHT: HIRING EXCELLENT STAFF

I honestly think the main thing I did right was hiring dedicated people early in their careers and including them as partners in the growth of the agency. As we moved into new programmatic areas, senior staff stepped up and developed the knowledge base and skills needed to run high-quality services. Staff stability helped; many members have worked at the agency for more than twenty-five years.

Eileen Torres had developed professional human resources and training departments. Over the years, her legal expertise was invaluable to the agency and I learned a great deal from her. Eileen is smart, principled, and hardworking. I am very thankful that she is the executive director. John Weed, assistant director, developed strong community-based programs and did an expert job in budgeting and contract management. Scott Auwarter, assistant director, created many of the programs for people who are homeless and has expertise in helping people living on the street move into housing. Ken Small, the director of development, raised many millions of dollars to support the programs. Vivian Vázquez developed many of the children's and youth programs. Maria Rivera, a passionate advocate for the elderly, led the senior citizen programs. Julie Belizaire Spitzer excelled at housing, eviction prevention, and program management. Bibi Karim ran excellent AIDS and child-welfare programs. Karen Courtney developed high-quality workforce development programs and worked on long-term planning issues. Carmen Hernandez kept our finances on the straight and narrow, managing hundreds of audits without major deficiencies. Noel Conception competently and compassionately managed the programs for single people who are homeless. Marjorie Jeannot, Wanda Cruz, and Crosby Inman were the mainstays of the family shelters, providing help to hundreds of families. Yonnel Olivio and Igor Zektser managed BronxWorks' ever-expanding information technology requirements. Alex Soto trained staff and others on technology and other issues. Other staff, too many to list, also made important and impressive contributions. Although Vivian, Karen, and Crosby left the agency prior to my departure, their contributions remain part of the fabric of BronxWorks. Sadly, Carmen died in 2016. Newer staff in leadership positions, hired or promoted during Eileen's tenure, are making their mark on the agency and the Bronx, along with the long-term leaders. The work continues.

8 "The Bronx Was the Last Place"

REFLECTIONS ON DISPLACEMENT AND
GENTRIFICATION

Years ago at the Point, people talked about gentrification
and I saw it as very far away. Now, in the last few years, for
economic reasons, the Bronx is seen as the last frontier. I
hope we are prepared for it. People are working to have it
happen in a way that we are not damaged by it, so that we
still are who we are. So that people are not pushed out.

Elena Martínez, cofounder, the Bronx Music Heritage Center

One of the challenges now is to stop the brain drain, young
people leaving the community. Hunts Point is on a preci-
pice of gentrification. It could become gentrified quickly.
Our mission is for people to build the neighborhood they
want and to hang on to it. The people who worked so hard
for the parks shouldn't be pushed out. The issue is what is
affordable. We define it differently than does the City.
Affordable is not affordable if the teachers in local schools
couldn't afford to live here.

Maria Torres, president of the Point Community Development

I took the subway to Frederick Douglass Boulevard in
Harlem, walked up the stairs, and thought I must have
taken the wrong train. Women with baby carriages going
into coffee shops. I didn't see a black figure. They say we are
eliminating poverty. How? By driving people out. I am
against people moving in and reinventing the neighborhood. I have seen it in other places. One person moves in

and they fit into the community. Other upper-middle-class people move in and they form their own group. Soon they dominate the area. We have Mexicans, Central Americans, West Africans, struggling to make ends meet, struggling to open small businesses. They become strangers in their own neighborhood.

Bill Aguado, now executive director of En Foco

People in the Bronx have been struggling for years with the rent affordability gap. CAB documented this as far back as 1986 by publishing a report, "Tenants of the West Bronx on Their Way Out, but No Place to Go." Now the situation is worse. A 2017 study by the Regional Plan Association showed that residents of the Bronx are at a higher risk of displacement than anywhere else in the metropolitan region. Factors include households paying over 30 percent of their income in rent (56 percent of households in the Bronx) and households having income under $25,000 a year and not receiving a rent subsidy such as Section 8 or public housing (36 percent of Bronx households). Many families pay over half of their income in rent.[1] An additional risk factor is that 75 percent of South Bronx residents lack savings that could be used to pay rent in case of a short-term emergency.[2] According to the Regional Plan study, characteristics that make an area desirable and thus ripe for gentrification include walkable neighborhoods, good transportation, access to jobs, good housing stock, and a comparatively low crime rate.[3] These attributes describe much of the South Bronx. No wonder people are worried.

In gentrifying areas, as rents increase and become out of reach for working families, apartments are likely to be rented jointly to several young adults in their twenties. For example, a working family cannot afford to pay $3,000 a month but three young people can each chip in $1,000 to cover the rent. Single and young, they are less likely to become involved in the neighborhood, shop locally, attend local churches, use local schools. They are less likely to stay long term and contribute to the community.

GENTRIFICATION VIA LARGE-SCALE
DEVELOPMENT IN MOTT HAVEN

Over twenty-five hundred wealthy individuals partied lavishly on October 29, 2015, to celebrate the purchase of land where luxury housing will be built in Mott Haven along the Harlem River waterfront. Neighborhood residents were insulted when they learned that the party's decorations featured fires burning in trash cans and wrecked cars riddled with bullet holes. They were further offended when the developers tried to rebrand the area as the "piano district." Others loudly voiced fears of gentrification and displacement.[4] Photojournalist Ricky Flores shares the community reaction:

> The bussing in of an elite group of people that held the party seemed to mock the South Bronx of the fire years. The event included an abandoned car installation, fires in oil drum cans, and the promise that they would be bringing the Bronx back, ignoring a vibrant community that already lives there. It was a tone-deaf event that attempted to ridicule the history of the South Bronx and dismiss what has been built since the fire years.[5]

The developers, Joseph Chetrit and Keith Rubenstein, planned for thirteen hundred market-rate apartments for two sites along the Harlem River. The twenty-five-story buildings on a six-story base would include pools, gyms, pet-care facilities, a cafe, a library, and a screening room. Apartments would rent for around $3,500 per month. The developers expected to borrow $500 million of the $600 million projected cost—significantly more than had ever been borrowed for a project in the Bronx. There are no other buildings like this in the Bronx, and they certainly would quickly change the area. The *Village Voice* newspaper dubbed it "the South Bronx's 1,300-unit gentrification Death Star."[6] In 2018, the developers sold the property, for which they had paid $58 million, to another developer, Brookfield Property Partners, for $165 million.[7]

A walking tour of the most southern tip of the Mott Haven neighborhood in May 2017, led by Mychal Johnson and Monxo López of South Bronx Unite, poignantly illustrated the difficult situations current residents face. Daily, a hundred thousand vehicles speed through the highways and bridges. A waste transfer station that handles one-quarter of

Manhattan's garbage draws a steady stream of garbage trucks. Trucks coming from upstate New York exit the Major Deegan Expressway and travel three miles on local streets to Hunts Point Produce Market. Despite strong community opposition, FreshDirect opened an eight-hundred-thousand-square-foot headquarters in Mott Haven, adding another thousand trucks a day.[8] The air pollution from black carbon emitted by the diesel trucks is the major contributor to the very high asthma rates in the area. Pregnant women's exposure to air pollution has been linked to low birth weights of babies.[9] The area's few parks lie alongside the highways, making exercising an unhealthy endeavor. Residents have virtually no access to the Harlem River that borders the area, even though much of the land along the riverbank is publicly owned.

Yet despite all the existing problems Mott Haven residents face—the severe air pollution, poor health, lack of parks, low-performing schools, lack of waterfront access, and a median income of under $20,000—the biggest challenge is the impending gentrification. About two thousand units of market-rate, luxury housing spread throughout nine buildings are are planned for the immediate area.[10] South Bronx Unite has been working for years to get waterfront access for the community. Indications are that improvements will be made to public spaces, such as constructing a park along the river, but the timing is suspicious. Are the improvements coming because of the community's efforts to improve the area or are the improvements for the newcomers?

For years, the area has been home to a number of artists from the Bronx and artists who have been priced out of other areas. The cost of studio space has been relatively manageable. There are now three galleries in the area. Artists are often seen as harbingers of gentrification, but they can also be victims of gentrification.

Proponents of development argue that since existing housing is not being torn down to make way for these luxury buildings, how could there be displacement and job loss? But this has happened before in other parts of the city. New businesses open to take advantage of an affluent customer base moving into the area. Sensing the changing market, commercial landlords raise rents significantly, driving out the mom-and-pop businesses that, collectively, are currently the second-largest employer in the Bronx (next to the health-care industry), employing over forty-four thousand people who earn an average of $2,600 a month.[11] New upscale businesses are less likely to hire community residents, preferring salespeople and wait staff that are more closely aligned to their customer base. With the new luxury housing and stores, neighboring residential properties also become more valuable. Owners spruce up their buildings and rent to higher-income tenants. The change can happen quickly, in the span of just a few years. People who have lived in the neighborhood for twenty or thirty years disappear—some turn to the City's shelter system, some double and triple up with their families, and others go to God knows where.

Jeniffer Montaño, the young woman quoted in chapter 7 who graduated from BronxWorks' transfer school and is now a teacher, shares her thoughts on what is happening to her Mott Haven community:

> Honestly, when you drive up the highway, towards 161st Street, it is so different. I was driving through it my whole life, since I was three. I have never seen all those huge stores. They get built but it takes forever for streets to get repaired.
>
> No one ever wanted to come to the Bronx. People wouldn't even want to walk around here. They took over Harlem and Brooklyn. Now we have to deal with our land, our homes being taken over. If you are a person of color, no one cares about you. People live in apartments with rats and roaches. Many apartments would be much better if just some work was done on them, if the holes were patched and with a new paint job. But that doesn't happen. So many people struggling, students just struggling to survive. Where will we go? You can't live in Brooklyn, Queens, Manhattan, it is too expensive. The Bronx was the last place. Now families are losing their homes here. People want to take over our culture now too.[12]

DISPLACEMENT FROM PREDATORY INVESTMENT ON THE GRAND CONCOURSE AND OTHER AREAS

In addition to Mott Haven, another geographic area of concern for displacement in the South Bronx is along the Grand Concourse and neighboring streets in the West Bronx and in other areas. The cause is not new luxury development as on the Mott Haven waterfront, but landlords buying buildings to take advantage of a tight housing market to maximize profits. Advertised rents in 2018 range from $1,800 to $2,600 for a two-bedroom apartment. At 30 percent of income for rent, a family needs an annual income of $64,000 to $100,000 to afford these rents.[13] The average income in Community Boards 4 and 5 is $31,500 and $26,000, respectively.[14]

New York City has regulations designed to prevent rapid rent increases in multiple dwellings as a way of protecting tenants in a tight housing market. These rent stabilization regulations determine how much landlords can increase rents in most apartments that rent for less than $2,700. Management firms are becoming proficient at manipulating the system to increase rents as much as possible. Kenisa, a young woman with a small child, lives in a desirable building on the Grand Concourse and worries about the changes happening in her building:

> I grew up in this building. I have lived here for almost twenty years. Throughout the years, all the tenants used to be very close to each other. Everyone knew each other, we all grew up together. We were very close to the people who worked in the building.
>
> Ever since this new company took over, about four years ago, everything changed. The first thing they did, they took all the employees out and brought in different people, management, the door man. Then they started going after the tenants, those whose apartments were not in their names. They kicked a lot of people out.

The lease on Kenisa's apartment was in her mother's name, but Kenisa had a background in tenants' rights and was able to fight to maintain her tenancy. Many others were less fortunate.

Landlords buy buildings at prices that current rent-rolls cannot support, with a plan to change the economics of the building by forcing out long-term tenants and bringing in higher-income renters. The investors who finance the purchase, both major banks and private equity firms, are complicit in this plan. Each time the owners turn over an apartment and re-rent it, they can raise the rent. The owners also make major capital improvements in the building that allow them to raise rents significantly. The rent increases from major capital improvements do not end when the cost of the work has been covered but stay as part of the rent indefinitely. It is not uncommon, in a building that has stable tenants for many years, to have a 50 percent turnover within a few years of the building being sold. Kenisa continues:

> Many of the new tenants are strangers. Most are doctors at the local hospital. You have to make more than $80,000 to rent here now. I have a friend who earns good money, she earns about $50,000. She didn't qualify for an apartment. A lot of the old tenants were evicted. Others decided to go because of the pressure. Management has been coming up with "rules." They started taking people to court for anything but not everyone is willing to fight.[15]

In some buildings, unscrupulous landlords harass long-term tenants by withholding services to force them to leave, so they can raise rents. This takes the form of refusing to make essential repairs, such as fixing leaks that cause ceilings to fall or patching holes in walls or ceilings. Landlords add unwarranted extra charges to rent bills that tenants, after futilely trying to contact the landlord, refuse to pay—and then are taken to housing court by the owner. Housing court can be an unnerving, intimidating experience for tenants, as virtually all landlords are represented by lawyers.[16] Historically, less than 10 percent of tenants have had lawyers. Tenants often feel coerced to sign agreements that are unfair to them, which can have disastrous results, perhaps even ending up in their eviction.

A 2018 report by the Regional Plan Association looks at the effect that bad landlords have on both the city as a whole and on their tenants. Bad landlords bring twice as many eviction cases as other landlords, and their buildings get issued at least ten new code violations a year, with an average of sixty-three recorded violations per building. The report states that bad landlords, although a small percentage of all landlords, cost the City over $300 million for Legal Aid, housing court, shelters, emergency repairs, and code enforcement expenses. The tenants suffer from lack of heat, mold, roach and rodent infestation, and harassment. For the tenant, the results are often disastrous, with out-of-pocket costs in excess of $1,000, lost days from work, children's health problems, eviction proceedings, and higher rates of homelessness. Tenants in the Bronx are twice as likely to have a bad landlord as those who live in other parts of the city, and low-income tenants are, of course, more likely to have a bad landlord than other tenants.[17]

THREAT OF DISPLACEMENT FROM PUBLIC POLICY
INITIATIVES ALONG JEROME AVENUE

A third example of how displacement can occur is through well-intended government initiatives. The lack of affordable housing is an issue citywide, not just in the Bronx. It is more acute in the Bronx because of residents' low income. As one of his major initiatives, Mayor Bill de Blasio promised to build or preserve two hundred thousand units of affordable housing at a cost of $4 billion, and he is making progress toward that goal.[18] Large areas are being rezoned to allow the construction of the taller buildings and denser neighborhoods. Mandatory Inclusionary Housing (MIH) requires developers to include a percentage of permanently affordable housing units in any building constructed in an area that is rezoned. The City believes that besides fostering economic integration, rezoning and MIH will help ease the chronic housing shortage.[19] MIH is a tool to force developers to build some low- and moderate-income housing, but in a global city like New York, it remains to be seen if building more housing will bring down rent levels. The mayor argues that rezoning gives the City some measure of control over new development. At least not all of the new housing will be market rate. He states that the City does not have the funds for the level of subsidies that deeply affordable units require.

The proposed up-zoning in the West Bronx is for ninety-two blocks of Jerome Avenue and the surrounding area. Jerome is a commercial street that runs parallel to the Grand Concourse a few short blocks to the west. It has a subway too, but unlike the Grand Concourse, whose subway is below ground, Jerome's is elevated. The elevated train makes the street dark and noisy, and its metal supporting columns impede the flow of traffic. The dominant businesses have been modest auto repair shops. Hawkers stand in the middle of the street under the elevated subway, attempting to wave customers in. Inexpensive stores and restaurants serving local workers and residents mingle with the auto repair shops.

The rezoning allows the construction of forty-six hundred units of new housing. To make space for all these units, the rezoning permits taller buildings.[20] The majority of the auto repair shops will be rezoned out, and the other small businesses will be priced out. Land values increase as developers offer to buy one-story business properties to knock them down to build large, multiple-dwelling buildings. Many developers are likely to choose to build 100 percent "affordable" housing so that they can take advantage of available subsidies and tax benefits.

The proposed construction of thousands of units of "affordable" housing caused alarm among many residents. Through an organization called Community Action for Safe Apartments (CASA) and a related group, Bronx Coalition for Community Vision, tenants organized for two years around the planned rezoning of the ninety-two-block Jerome Avenue corridor. Residents of the area, with an average median family income of $25,000, posed the key question about "affordable" housing: The new apartments will be affordable for whom? They knew from the City's original proposal that only 10 percent of the new apartments would rent to families in their income level. If new housing is going to be built in their neighborhood, why shouldn't they be able to rent it? They felt they held the area together during bad times, and they should be able to benefit, not be hurt, if new housing is built.

There are multiple factors used to determine income levels and rents in newly constructed "affordable" housing, including the type of subsidy or tax breaks the developer used and the program the building falls under. In some developments, households earning up to $111,000 may qualify for affordable housing. For the housing program that will likely be used in the Jerome Avenue area, families with incomes up to $56,000 would qualify. This figure is still more than double the median income of current residents of the area.[21] The City's plan calling for only 10 percent of new apartments actually being affordable for current residents was seen as very unfair. And there is concern that those truly affordable apartments may be mostly studios and one-bedroom units, inadequate for families.

Fitzroy Christian, who became involved in housing issues as a result of long-term repair problems in his building, says:

> What we have is a mixture of cultures and ethnicities that is unique. If we are not careful, the up-zoning could lead to wholesale gentrification, which would drive away many people.[22]

Vivian Vázquez understands the issue. She now works with three schools and a community center at the New Settlement Apartments (NSA) Community Campus building:

With the rezoning of the Jerome Avenue corridor, most of the auto repair businesses will be demolished and the sites used for housing and stores. CASA pushed for an expansion of the area that would allow the existing businesses to remain. The auto businesses are a major source of employment for many immigrants in the area. Note the elevated subway overhead. Photo by author.

With the proposed rezoning of the Jerome Avenue area, what will happen to the African Americans, the Dominicans and Mexicans, especially the undocumented, who live there? It seems like the same pattern as the '60s and '70s, when people living in the area that is now Lincoln Center and Columbia University in Manhattan were displaced and had to find some sort of housing in the Bronx. The Dominicans and Mexicans in our area will be displaced, but to where? And now the private-sector money is in control, not government money, like in the '80s.[23]

Residents are also genuinely concerned about the fate of the businesses and workers on Jerome Avenue. The minority- and/or women-owned businesses employ mainly middle-aged skilled immigrants who are able to make a good living working on Jerome. A beautiful book of photographs documenting the workers and their livelihood has been published by the Bronx Photo League of the Bronx Documentary Center. Besides pictures of autoworkers who can fix a flat in five minutes or replace a cracked windshield, there are photos of women selling food and frozen carbonated beverages; men selling bottles of water and peeled oranges; workers in hair and nail salons, "99 cent" stores, and small restaurants; and an auto shop that is converted to a church in the evenings.[24] Some of the businesses are light manufacturing. All the workers take pride in their work, and all have very limited options when they are forced out.

Residents believe that as property values rise, landlords of existing residential buildings on blocks near the rezoned area will try to raise rents and bring in higher-income tenants. Residents fear they will lose their homes. Similarly, they fear that the rezoning will cause commercial rents to rise and existing businesses to close. Soon after the rezoning plan was announced, residential rents started to increase significantly,[25] and some businesses have been torn down to make way for high-rise buildings. Jack Doyle, the executive director of NSA and the major sponsor of CASA, has been witnessing the speculation that the hot real estate market, fueled by the rezoning of the Jerome Avenue corridor, is causing:

> The Bronx has been seen as the only place with reasonably affordable land. I get lots of calls from real estate people. A lot near here recently sold for $3.5 million and is back on the market for $6 million.[26]

Maria Rivera, BronxWorks' director of senior services, told me that shortly after news of the rezoning became public, local homeowners were offered large sums to sell their houses. These would become building lots for large apartment buildings. Land speculation happens quickly. Thankfully, BronxWorks bought the property with the old funeral home for its administrative and homeless outreach office when it did, before speculation in the rezoning area drove prices sky high.

The changes that caused the destruction of so much of the South Bronx in the 1970s and '80s, the fleeing of the middle class, and the reduction of basic services described earlier in this book happened very rapidly. Some neighborhoods changed within a few years. People who were poor, primarily people of color, were the ones who were left to live in extremely difficult conditions. The toll it took on families cannot be overstated. Most survived, suffering through the fires and the twin epidemics of drugs and AIDS, and helped create the new South Bronx.

The rezoning ushers in another period of very rapid, and some feel risky, change for a stated good cause: creating more "affordable" housing, urgently needed in NYC. But the rezoning primarily targets low-income areas, and residents wonder why poor areas are the ones forced to take things that other areas resist, like waste treatment plants, highways, and now rezoning. Despite the City's pledge to protect tenants with anti-eviction and anti-harassment services, the rezoning may unleash market forces that will upend neighborhoods like the Jerome Avenue corridor. Rezoning is now being proposed for an even larger area in the South Bronx around Southern Boulevard in Longwood.

So far, a proportionate share of the large-scale rezoning has not been proposed for higher-income residential areas of New York City, where MIH would bring in low-income tenants. Why not rezone more affluent, primarily white, neighborhoods where good schools, parks, and other infrastructure can more easily sustain new growth? Doing so would expand housing opportunities for people who are low-income rather than contract them. Why not use this opportunity to integrate NYC by bringing people who are poor into affluent areas?[27]

Unlike the waterfront area of Mott Haven, the new construction in the Jerome Avenue area is less likely to cause what is typically thought of as gentrification: high-income white people descending upon a poor area and taking over. If developers decide to accept construction subsidies, the new housing will be categorized as affordable, with upper income limits as to who can qualify. The people who would move in are likely to be predominantly people of color with moderate incomes. However, displacement of current low-income tenants is feared.

The vast scope of the new housing being built in the Bronx is truly impressive. Many of the developments have hundreds of units, and at least one will have over a thousand. With names like Crossroads Plaza, Elton Crossing, La Central, the Peninsula, and Bronx Point, these buildings are changing Bronx neighborhoods. Crossroads Plaza has three buildings, totaling 425 units. Building 3 of the development is for people with incomes 50–100 percent of metropolitan New York's median income, or between $45,300 and $99,600.[28] The area's median household income is under $20,000.

Within NYC, the South Bronx has been the area with the most reasonably priced housing. It has been the place to which people who were displaced from other areas moved. As this changes, what housing options will there be for people living in or near poverty—endless waits for public housing or Section 8 vouchers that never materialize, the City's shelter system (with possibly a subsidy when placed into an apartment), or exiting NYC altogether? What will NYC be like if it loses so many of its poor residents? What if it becomes a less diverse city? What if the energy, talents, and creativity of low-income families are depleted?

COMMERCIAL REAL ESTATE GOES THROUGH THE ROOF, TOO

Commercial real estate is going upscale as rapidly as residential real estate. The editors of the *Commercial Observer*, an online real estate newsletter, stated in 2015 that they love the Bronx, comparing it to pre-gentrification Brooklyn. Attractive features include good transportation and low land prices. The article goes on to say that "the Bronx is ripe for picking."[29]

The recent history of the BankNote Building in Hunts Point (described in chapter 6) illustrates how wealthy developers are venturing into the Bronx's commercial real estate. Occupying a full block, with four hundred thousand square feet of space, this landmarked, huge brick building once printed foreign currencies and stock certificates, and later housed other manufacturing operations. It was owned by a wonderful man, Max Blauner. Welcomed by the Blauners and, after a series of meetings, by many of the neighbors, BronxWorks opened a drop-in center for chronically homeless people in the building in 1997. The Blauners rented to other nonprofits and to a second-chance school. Some long-term tenants were small businesses, manufacturers, and artists like Arthur Aviles and his dance company. In 2007, Taconic Real Estate purchased the building for $32.5 million[30] and initiated eviction proceedings against CAB, stating that homeless people were not part of their vision for the building. Taconic renovated the building and planned to make it into an art center. The endeavor failed, but Taconic did force out CAB and other long-term tenants and upgraded the building.[31] Luckily for CAB, the Blauners still owned another building in the area that was suitable for a drop-in center. We were able to hold off the eviction for two years while we raised funds and renovated the new space.

When Taconic found they had over two hundred thousand square feet of unrented space on their hands as the art center concept failed, they rented space to the City to house several welfare and food stamp centers.[32] But LightBox-NY, a studio that films celebrities like Lady Gaga and Mary J. Blige, also has space in the building, illustrating the dynamic between the still prevalent poverty of the Bronx and the prospect of fame and big money. Taconic sold the building in 2014 for $114 million.[33] They had made tons of money, setting an example of one type of venture that will continue to lure well-heeled developers into the South Bronx.

An interesting footnote: Vivian Vázquez's son was invited to a high school party given by a wealthy family in 2012. The party was held in renovated space in the BankNote Building. Private security lined the perimeter of the building. When neighborhood kids asked what was going on, they were told to "go away, you don't belong here." Sadly, gentrification makes people feel they don't belong in their own neighborhoods.

Further evidence of the desirability of commercial real estate is that two other studios recently moved to the Bronx. Silvercup Studios purchased an old warehouse in Port Morris and converted it into four large studios. The large film and television production facility, which cost $40 million, opened in 2016. In 2017, York Studios broke ground on a ten-acre, $100 million facility in the Soundview section of the Bronx that will host eight film stages.[34] Hopefully a large percentage of the employees will be from the Bronx.

CONSEQUENCES OF GENTRIFICATION AND DISPLACEMENT

Bill Aguado, Jeniffer Montaño, Fitzroy Christian, and CASA members base their concern for the South Bronx on what is happening in areas of Brooklyn and Manhattan, such as Harlem. In popular usage, the term *gentrification* is used to describe displacement of low- and moderate-income residents from a geographic area. The people who are displaced generally are people of color and the displacers higher-income people, usually white people. Areas of the city that have undergone gentrification show an increase in the number of households with incomes over $100,000 and a decrease in low-income households. This is accompanied by an increase in the percentage of people with a college degree.

A 2016 study by the Furman Center at New York University, called "Focus on Gentrification," documents the rapid demographic changes that gentrifying areas of Brooklyn are undergoing. The changes show up in descriptions of characteristics of the population over time. The data compare 2014 to 2000, in constant dollars. In the Williamsburg-Greenpoint section, rents went up by 58 percent, income rose by 41 percent, and the percentage of residents with college degrees rose to 44 percent of the population from 18 percent. There was a decrease in the Hispanic population. In Bedford-Stuyvesant, rents increased by 36 percent, income rose by 12 percent, and the percentage of adults with a college degree increased to 25 percent from 11 percent. There was a loss of African Americans, from 75 percent to 60 percent of the population. Citywide during this time, rents rose by 19 percent, there was no increase in income, and college attainment rose to 34 percent from 26 percent.[35] Additionally, there is evidence of a dramatic drop in the number of black-owned businesses in NYC because of gentrification, despite an increase in the number of businesses overall and an increase in black-owned businesses in many other major cities. From 2007 to 2012, the number of black-owned businesses in NYC decreased by 30 percent, according to a study by the NYC comptroller.[36]

For a family, displacement means the loss of their housing, their children's school, and their social networks, such as family and friends, and loss of support systems such as churches and social service and medical providers. It is a traumatic event. There is no comprehensive study, that I could find, that tracks people after they are displaced.[37] Many may move in with family or friends, but these seriously overcrowded arrangements quickly become untenable. They then apply to the NYC shelter system, an expensive but essential safety net.

A disproportionate share of families in NYC's shelter system come from the Bronx. (But the South Bronx also shelters more homeless people than became homeless in the South Bronx. This is because shelters tend to be put in areas that are poor.)[38] The Bronx has the highest number of evictions of any borough, even with BronxWorks, Legal Aid, Legal Services, and other groups' often successful efforts to prevent the eviction of their clients.[39] The numbers of people needing help are staggering, and there are not always answers to the question of where the rent money will come from. Despite Herculean prevention efforts, the number of people NYC is sheltering keeps increasing. In December 2017, NYC was providing shelter for over 60,400 people, including 12,800 families with 23,000 children.[40]

Due to frequent moves and high levels of stress, children in families who are homeless suffer significant educational losses. With an absenteeism rate approaching 50 percent, they lag behind their peers in standardized English and math test measures and are twice as likely to be held back or suspended. Some school districts in the Bronx have between four thousand and ten thousand students who are homeless, representing 11–20 percent of the student population! This includes children in families living doubled up with another family as well as in shelters. Many of these children never catch up.[41] These figures demonstrate that the displacement crisis is already here. All possible efforts need to be made to keep it from getting worse.

Some people who are displaced may move out of NYC. The cities and towns of the surrounding areas tend to be segregated. Low-income people are just as unlikely to be able to afford to move into an area with good, affordable housing and schools outside the City as they are in NYC. There is evidence that eviction rates and homelessness are rising significantly in those outlying areas too.[42] Moreover, those towns are less likely to have good transportation or the availability of jobs that NYC has.[43] For example, 47 percent of children in Newburgh, New York, live in poverty.[44] Some buses run every two hours, some hourly—whereas most NYC subways run every ten to fifteen minutes. Some advocates see gentrification as a human rights violation.[45]

When an area gentrifies, some households are able to stay—but those who stay face rapid changes. They are likely to be heavily rent burdened, paying over half their incomes in rent, leaving little money for food and other necessities. They cannot afford to shop at the new stores. The power structure, institutions, and human services adapt to meet the needs of the newer, more influential groups.[46] Some benefits of gentrification that are often cited include more police protection and cleaner streets and parks.

However, increased police presence can have harmful effects on long-term residents, causing more life-altering arrests, often for incidents that previously would not have led to an arrest.[47] Schools generally do not integrate, because the higher-income families send their children to private schools or find ways to get them into high-performing public schools.[48]

OTHER THREATS

Besides displacement and gentrification, other significant challenges exist to maintaining housing for people with low and moderate incomes. The Bronx has over forty-four thousand units of public housing spread over eighty-nine developments. Public housing, historically supported significantly by the federal government, has not had sufficient funds to make necessary repairs. It is estimated that $17 billion in capital funding would be needed to bring NYC's public housing projects up to standards and keep them there. Now NYCHA gets only $300 million a year from the federal government for capital repairs, a far cry from what it needs.[49] In June 2018, partly as a result of a lead paint scandal, the City agreed to federal oversight and to fund $1 billion in repairs.[50]

Many of the buildings that were rehabbed in the Bronx in the past fifteen to twenty years used government subsidies as part of the funding package. In exchange, the owners agreed to keep the rents below market for a number of years, most often thirty years. Many of these agreements will expire before 2030. When they do, if other subsidy agreements are not put in place, rents can rise to market rate. This loss of affordable units will decrease the pool of apartments available to families with limited means.[51]

Some experts see the risk to housing stability as coming not from gentrification but from a different direction. They think the likelihood of the South Bronx gentrifying is being oversold to investors and that the result could be another cycle of disinvestment in the upkeep of apartment buildings, such as happened in past decades. Bill Frey of Enterprise Community Partners states:

> Investors are seeing the Bronx as the new Brooklyn. They are being unrealistic. Buildings are selling for much more than their value. There is a danger

that if investors overpay and the building cannot support the mortgage and operating expenses, we will go back to the old days. Part of the problem of overpaying is with funds coming from equity investors. The banks at least do appraisals.[52]

Another threat to stability in the South Bronx is the rise of heroin laced with fentanyl, which started showing up in 2015–16. The synthetic painkiller makes heroin cheaper, more profitable, and much more dangerous. The number of overdoses is rapidly increasing. Although naloxone can still prevent deaths from fentanyl, often it is less effective and several doses may be needed. Heroin laced with fentanyl is causing deaths among people living on the streets as well as those in housing. Fortunately, as of 2018, crime had not increased in the Bronx or in New York City as a whole.

Since 2017, the stability of undocumented immigrants and those living under DACA is increasingly threatened with the heightened possibility of deportation. People are still going about their lives, but this kind of intense worry and uncertainty takes a toll on families. Nonprofits and colleges offer workshops that provide advice, and limited legal help is available. Since its inception, BronxWorks has helped low-income people, including immigrants, apply for food stamps, medical assistance, and housing. At the time of this writing, a policy change in Washington is being considered that would cause immigrants who use public benefits, even temporarily, to become ineligible for a path to citizenship. What a terrible choice for families—face hunger, homelessness, and illness or risk never becoming a citizen. How does society benefit if people are malnourished, ill, and/or homeless?

LOOKING FOR SOLUTIONS

The Bronx is a tipping point for our city: a measure of how we succeed and whose lives we value. If we cannot figure out how to bring in investment in the Southwest Bronx without displacing thousands of tenants, without repeating our past, then we can't do it anywhere. But if we can do it here, we can do it everywhere.

CASA white paper[53]

Employment

The Bronx is diverse in its people and also in residents' views about new development. Many see the massive investment occurring in the Bronx as a good thing. Borough President Rubén Díaz Jr. welcomes businesses moving in for the jobs they bring, as well as new housing for people of varying income levels. Marlene Cintron is president of the Bronx Overall Economic Development Corporation, an arm of the borough president's office. A lifetime resident who was born on Kelly Street (and a former member of the Young Lords), Marlene has worked for elected officials, in banking, and for nonprofits. She is pleased with the new business and residential development:

> When Rubén interviewed me, he gave me a goal of getting the Bronx off the rank of number one as the county in New York State with the highest unemployment rate. To do that, we needed to get 11,000 people employed. At that time, we were at 14.1 percent unemployment, now in 2017 we are at 5.9 percent. No other borough has gone down that much—117,000 more Bronx residents are working today than when Rubén took office in 2009.

Clearly her first priority is jobs:

> If a building is a warehouse, it will stay a warehouse. We need the jobs. We have been asked if we would change zoning for affordable housing. Although we support affordable housing, we are going to protect the manufacturing zones. You cannot have affordable housing if the tenant cannot find a place to work.

She values the range of income levels of tenants that the new housing brings:

> The affordable housing has bands for income eligibility. There are no poor buildings. They have people of different incomes up to 80 percent of AMI [average median income]. We can encourage the sons and daughters from the Bronx to come back once they graduate from college.
>   This should be a borough where everyone can afford to live. When people say they don't want gentrification, they mean we don't want any white people. We want a diverse borough that includes everyone. Many of our new immigrant neighbors are in business.[54]

In addition to more availability of jobs from the movie studios and other businesses moving to the Bronx, another positive economic factor is the increase of the minimum wage in NYC to $15 an hour in 2019. Even with this increase, however, families earning minimum wage, many of which are headed by single women, will still earn an annual income of only $26,000 to $27,000. With NYCHA projects having waiting lists of 250,000 families, there is little reason for other families to even apply.[55] If only 10–15 percent of the mayor's pledged eighty thousand units of new housing are deeply affordable, the low-income housing shortage crisis will likely continue to worsen.

Workforce development programs and higher education have a role to play in increasing wage earners' ability to afford housing. The workforce development field talks about "career ladders" that create a path for people to move to higher-paying positions. So far, career ladders have met with mixed results. One type of career ladder that has had some success is technology. Public colleges, including community colleges, play an important role in helping low-wage earners advance. A 2017 study on the effects of college education on income, based on millions of tax filings and financial aid forms, showed the value of the City University of New York system. Lehman College ranked fourth nationally, and Hostos Community College and Bronx Community College ranked sixteenth and seventeenth, respectively, on the mobility rate of students moving from the bottom 40 percent of income to the top 40 percent.[56] But even with some people benefiting from youth and workforce development programs, public colleges, and the availability of more jobs, still many people will not be able to afford housing and will need deep subsidies to prevent them from becoming homeless.

Preserving Existing Housing for Current Tenants

Residential real estate speculation threatens the viability of privately owned buildings. Peter Magistro of the Bronx Pro Group, a developer and manager of affordable housing, explains how rampant speculation affected tenants in buildings they were asked to save:

> We have been active on the rescue and preservation side of development. We have just completed over five hundred units of distressed properties. These

units were owned by irresponsible firms that purchased at inflated prices, subsequently pushing up rents aggressively and cutting services to cover their bottom lines. This behavior has proven to be very difficult for tenants and the cause of rapid deterioration to these properties. Unbelievable as it may sound, literally there were bathrooms and kitchens that were moments from collapsing, presenting very dangerous conditions to their inhabitants and subsequently to our construction team during renovations.

We had to relocate five hundred families from their apartments in order to do the required renovations. It took an inordinate amount of work, convincing and calming down tenants in order to conduct the renovations. This preservation work makes our new construction projects seem relatively easy.[57]

Also concerned with preserving existing housing for current residents, Jack Doyle has taken proactive steps to make sure that the sixteen buildings NSA owns remain in good condition and affordable for the foreseeable future:

Our biggest accomplishment has been maintaining decent, stable housing for over three thousand people. New financing will maintain the buildings and the affordability for another fifty years. With the $45 million renovation we are now undergoing, all the apartments are getting new kitchens, bathrooms, and windows. We are replacing the roofs and putting in solar panels.[58]

Another tool to fight displacement is tenant organizing. CASA, NWBCCC, Banana Kelly, and others help form tenant associations when landlords are withholding services, such as heat and essential repairs. CASA has weekly housing clinics to inform tenants of their rights and provides support to many tenant associations. Nancy Biberman of WHEDco notes:

There are two parts to keeping a neighborhood affordable: preserving what is affordable and building for who lives there now. Studies show that you can't build your way out of a lack of affordable housing, you can't build fast enough. For aggressive preservation of housing for poor people, they need to have lawyers. And new construction needs to come with deep subsidies.

NYC took a big step by adding more legal protections for low-income tenants threatened with eviction or harassment by landlords who want them to move out so that rents can be raised. Such harassment can include withholding of services, as described above by Peter Magistro, or threatening tenants with eviction, as described by Kenisa. Nancy describes the importance of the right to counsel in holdover cases in which the landlord alleges that the tenant is violating aspects of the lease:

> It is very significant that the City will now provide lawyers for people in housing court. You need a lawyer for holdovers. To bring an eviction proceeding, the owner can make a million allegations against a tenant that on the face of it could be true. The owner doesn't have to prove it up front. For example, he can state that the apartment is being used for immoral or illegal purposes or that the tenants are a nuisance. Tenants have to be able to defend themselves. Civil cases are subjective. It is not the same level of proof as in criminal cases.[59]

CASA and other groups had been advocating for a right to counsel for tenants in housing court for years. Although nationally there is a right to counsel in criminal cases, there is no right to counsel in civil cases. The vast majority of landlords (98 percent) hire lawyers to represent them in housing court, but in 2013 less than 20 percent and maybe as little as 1 percent of tenants had lawyers.[60] In a *Daily News* article, tenant leaders Carmen Vega Rivera and Fitzroy Christian explain how tenants often don't know their rights and feel coerced into signing stipulations that are not in their best interests.[61] (For thirty years, BronxWorks paralegals helped tenants with housing court cases but could not officially represent them.) City Council Member Vanessa Gibson, whose district covers CASA and many of BronxWorks' offices, cosponsored the right-to-counsel legislation in NYC, which passed in August 2017.[62] CASA is widely credited with spearheading this initiative. Eviction rates have already started to fall. Other major cities and some states may implement a similar housing-court right-to-counsel if it proves successful in reducing homelessness in NYC.[63]

CASA and others also pushed for legislation that would require landlords to obtain a Certificate of No Harassment prior to obtaining City approval for undertaking major work in apartments or entire buildings. This legislation also passed in 2017. A recommendation on harassment in a CASA white paper reads as follows:

> *Pass and Implement Citywide "Certificate of No Harassment" Legislation.* Renovations are one of the key tools landlords use to raise rents through Individual Apartment Increases and Major Capital Improvements, and, more generally, are often needed to attract higher-paying tenants.

Renovations also represent a moment in the cycle of displacement where the City has a real ability to intervene because of the need for Department of Buildings permits for most major work in both individual apartments and building-wide.[64]

Thus, if the landlord can't get the certificate, then he can't get approval to make renovations that allow him to increase rents. CASA has started to advocate for ending rent increases for capital repairs, arguing that it is the landlords' responsibility to maintain their buildings. CASA has other recommendations that can be viewed on their website.

Other progressive laws and policies are in place to help the economic situation of low-income families. CASA lobbied for legislation, which passed, to increase construction workers' training and safety. Laws have been passed mandating that employers provide sick leave, raise the minimum wage, pay family leave for employees of private employers, provide protections for LGBT people and immigrants, and require that employers not ask about criminal backgrounds until after a job offer has been made. Fair Fare provides half-price subway MetroCards to low-income New Yorkers. Some City and State policies seek to make the lives of shift workers more predictable. NYC also funds groups to provide easier access to work supplements such as SNAP (food stamps), earned income tax credits, government-subsidized health care, and other benefits. City funding provides immigrants with ESL classes and adults with basic adult education. In July 2018, a waste equity law was passed that reduces the permitting capacity of waste facilities in oversaturated neighborhoods in the South Bronx and other areas. Many of these progressive policies have been lobbied for by community-based organizations. Started under Mayor Bloomberg and expanded under Mayor de Blasio, "Universal Pre-K" for four-year-olds and "3–K for All" for three-year-olds are providing free, full-school-day education to growing numbers of young children.

Deeply Subsidized Units in Affordable Housing

Initially, CASA leaders Fitzroy Christian and Carmen Vega Rivera both became involved with CASA because of their own housing problems. The two have worked hard to make the rezoning benefit and not hurt people in the area. Fitzroy says:

Fitzroy Christian and Carmen Vega Rivera, two long-term, volunteer leaders of CASA, work to prevent displacement of low-income tenants. Serious repair needs in their respective buildings led to their involvement in a broad range of housing stability issues. Photo by author.

We are fighting to make sure housing remains affordable for people to be able to stay in their homes. As an organizer, it is to bring a sense of hope, to show them something else is possible. We are building this community for us. We don't just work here, we are saving the community for us, for me, my family and the next generation behind us.[65]

CASA organized tenants to fight the threatened displacement they fear will come with the rezoning. They pushed for much deeper subsidies so that half of the new units could be rented to people with lower incomes. They wanted 25 percent of the apartments to be available to families with annual incomes under $27,000 (not the 10 percent the City proposed) and another 25 percent under $36,000. The remaining 50 percent would rent to families with incomes up to $56,000. The City's obvious concern was that as the cost goes up with deeper subsidies of rents, the fewer the number of units the City can afford to build. Mayor de Blasio had initially pledged to build or preserve two hundred thousand units of affordable housing, eighty thousand of which would be new construction. He raised

Members of CASA marching down the Grand Concourse to a Rent Guidelines Board
public hearing in June 2017. CASA played a key role in the passage of progressive
legislation, including the right to counsel for tenants in housing court, which benefits
low-income tenants citywide. Photo credit: CASA.

the number to three hundred thousand in 2017. If units are more expensive because of deeper subsidies, the City might not meet his goal.
Sophisticated housing and organizing nonprofits such as Banana Kelly,
NSA, and NWBCCC lent their expertise to CASA to come up with alternative deep-affordability models, but the City did not accept those models.

CASA's monthly meetings at NSA's Community Center were usually
attended by upwards of a hundred people. Used to educate community
residents about the issues, the meetings provided updates on the City's
response to CASA proposals, strategizing of options, and conversations
with potential allies, such as unions, elected officials, and groups in other
boroughs. Simultaneous English-to-Spanish and Spanish-to-English
translation was provided. Meetings often included a chant, "Whose
Bronx? Our Bronx!" and "Nothing about us, without us, is for us."

Thousands of people were involved, speaking out in public hearings and protesting the plan for the Jerome Avenue rezoning. City Council members who have a key vote on the rezoning were publicly asked to commit to supporting CASA's proposals at community forums. CASA developed position papers and a white paper that explained options that would allow for truly affordable housing. These options included a larger role for nonprofit housing developers.

Probably as a result of the critical publicity and pressure from groups such as CASA, the City has made some changes to the term sheet for the affordable housing developments in areas such as Jerome Avenue that will make more units available to those with very low incomes and to the elderly.[66] The funding that many developers will use in the South Bronx will likely require a 10 percent set-aside for families who are homeless. The City has budgeted an additional $1.9 billion to increase the number of units and to deepen affordability citywide.[67] These changes were still a far cry from what CASA felt was needed. CASA rejected the City's position that it can't afford to give deep subsidies to a significantly larger percentage of apartments to make them available to very low-income people. Let the City build fewer units and give them to people who need them the most, advocates argue.

Although the deal the City Council passed did not include some of CASA's key demands (such as a smaller area subject to rezoning, a larger percentage of deeply subsidized units, and a larger area for auto-related businesses), CASA did influence the outcome for tenants citywide through the right to counsel, the Certificate of No Harassment, and important safety training for new construction workers. Included in the overall agreement will be funding for two new schools, money for parks, and funds for preservation of existing affordable housing. CASA is monitoring the implementation of the rezoning and the community benefits. Bill Frey of Enterprise Community Partners comments:

> There are lessons to be learned from the past. Lots of things repeat themselves. I am glad organizing is happening with the NWBCCC and CASA. When Roger Starr [New York City's housing and development commissioner] was talking about planned shrinkage, there was no representation of the people from the community. The housing industry is very strong. Developers and city officials think they know what is best with the

up-zoning, but they are not talking to people in the community. If the rezoning has to happen because the city has to grow, they need to make sure they
are listening to and working with people in the affected communities. The
United States has done a bad job housing poor people.[68]

At the time of this writing, in order to address the crisis of sixty thousand people in the city being homeless, a bill was introduced by a City
Council member from the Bronx, Ralph Salamanca Jr., that would increase
the set-aside for homeless units to 15 percent in any rental housing project
that receives government subsidies for new construction or preservation.
The mayor is not in favor of the bill, arguing that this approach is more
expensive and slower than providing rental assistance.[69] While it is significant that elected officials are actively considering additional steps to provide housing for those most in need, the housing affordability crisis affects
a great many more low- and moderate-income families

New Housing Models

Interest in community land trusts as a way to ensure permanently affordable low-income housing and public space is growing in the Bronx. In this
model, the government transfers ownership in real property over to a
community land trust, which preserves affordability in perpetuity. Either
a nonprofit or for-profit developer can develop the property, but they have
no ownership. Real estate speculation in areas of rising land values is not
a factor in the cost of the project because the land is taken out of the spec-
ulative market and leased directly by the land trust. A governing board—
often composed of government officials, community members, and tenants—manages the use of the housing or other real property. Studies have
shown that subsidies have more impact in the land trust model than in
traditional government-subsidized affordable housing. South Bronx
Unite, Nos Quedamos, Mary Mitchell Center, and NWBCCC are exploring
using a land trust model to create permanently affordable low-income
housing. South Bronx Unite hopes to gain ownership of the old Lincoln
Hospital detox site through its land trust for use as a community center
with a focus on health, education, culture, and the arts in Mott Haven.
Mychal Johnson, cofounder of Mott Haven-Port Morris Community Land

Stewards and a leader of South Bronx Unite, describes why the organization decided to use the land trust model:

> Our community land trust in the South Bronx was born out of decades of struggle against social, economic, and environmental injustice. Now faced with an unprecedented land grab following a half century of planned shrinkage, our community land trust is one of the most viable avenues of taking our public land out of the speculative real estate market and preserving it for the benefit of the community.[70]

Spofford Juvenile Detention Center was a notorious jail for teens and young adults in Hunts Point. Closed in 2011 in response to community pressure and a widespread realization that this facility was inappropriate for young people, the building will be torn down and the large site used for mixed-use housing: 740 units plus light industrial, commercial, and community facility space. Eighty percent of the housing will be for people who earn less than 60 percent of the area median income. Current community residents will have priority for half of the units. Some units will be set aside for people who are homeless. The community facility space will include a health and wellness center operated by Urban Health Plan, a Head Start center, as well as spaces for arts groups including the Point and the Bronx Academy of Art and Dance. A community bank and a grocery store will occupy commercial space. A bakery, a catering service, and Hunts Point Brewery plan to use the industrial space. It is anticipated that 175 permanent jobs will be created. Five nonprofits are community partners. The goal is to create a community with housing, jobs, recreation, and services. Maria Torres explains why the Point is supporting the project:

> What is exciting is that the businesses that are coming to the site are already based here, in Hunts Point or nearby. They are looking to expand. They have been here for years and will hire local people. It is good that local businesses are deepening their commitments to our community.
>
> For us, keeping the housing at 100 percent of affordability was important. We want all the people who live in the area to feel that this is their space too, whether or not they actually live in the new apartments.
>
> What we fear is the speculation that may come with new projects. Already a long-term business has been told his rent will be raised. There are residential buildings across the street. Hopefully these landlords will not take advantage of the situation and displace people.[71]

There is no question that rapid change is coming to the Bronx. The construction of huge new apartment buildings, big box stores, and production studios show that the transformation is well underway. The booming real estate market may present opportunities. But questions remain. Will residents with low incomes share in the wealth being generated? How much will displacement increase? Most New Yorkers would agree that the city should continue to be home to those who are poor as a matter of social justice, as well as for practical reasons. With their energy and entrepreneurial skills, low-income people have an important role to play in the workforce. Their children will be tomorrow's City workers and leaders. Their contributions keep refreshing the culture. The South Bronx has been the place where people who were poor moved when they were forced out of their homes in other boroughs, and it is essential that people of modest means are not priced out of the city. Poor communities need an influx of resources to improve, but not a large influx of high-income people that will displace them. As Jeniffer Montaño said, "The Bronx was the last place."

Will the NYC government take the necessary steps to protect people with low and moderate incomes from the powerful housing industry? To do this, officials need to truly listen to residents and include them as full partners in the planning for the future of their communities. Developments on public land should benefit low-income people and should be truly affordable permanently. Rezoning should not be concentrated in just low-income areas and must come with restrictions requiring that a significant percentage of new apartments be rented to people with very low incomes. To foster economic integration, the City should have affordable housing built in middle- and high-income areas, even if the City has to subsidize the high cost of purchasing the land. Rent stabilization laws and enforcement should be strengthened to prevent apartments falling out of this protection, given that the City will never be able to supplement the rent for all who cannot afford marketplace rents. Historically the federal government played a major role in funding low-income housing through a variety of programs, including Section 8, support of public housing, and a range of funding streams and tax credits for developers. These programs have been steadily reduced, contributing to the rise of homelessness nationally. We should not give up on advocating that decent housing is a human right, as are food and medical care.

Here is my wish. I hope to see the South Bronx emerge from this period of change as a stable home to families who have very low to moderate and middle incomes, with well-managed, truly affordable housing; stable businesses run by local residents; good schools; effective social services for those who need help; employment opportunities that pay a livable wage; quality preschool, after-school, and summer programs for all children; affordable and healthful food; new parks and open space; clean air; a flourishing arts and culture scene; and activist community groups. The South Bronx could be a place that becomes even better at helping low-income people move out of poverty, rather than, as feared, being pushed out of the area. Surely neighborhoods with a high percentage of people who are poor can be more than "not bad"—they can be truly good neighborhoods. Surely children who are poor deserve a fair chance.

We need to ask ourselves what prevents this vision from fully materializing. Is it the same stereotypes that poor people have been facing for centuries—that poor people and poor communities are not really worth investing in? People of the South Bronx are doing a lot of heavy lifting to preserve and improve their communities, but they have been shortchanged for years. Can a consensus arise that low-income communities play an essential role in our social fabric, that discriminatory practices need to be faced head-on, that public education, health care, government-supported housing, and the environment need to be protected and strengthened?

One thing is certain: the future will be one of rapid change, of threats and possibilities. The South Bronx has presented a model for the rest of the world of an amazing comeback from terrible devastation. Can it now develop a model that effectively protects low-income tenants from displacement while large numbers of higher-income people move in? I do know that the people of the South Bronx will seize whatever opportunities exist to continue the work of building strong communities for their families.

9 Lessons Learned

I approached my work at BronxWorks from a social justice viewpoint. Despite a few rocky times, my life was comparatively smooth. I always had food, and, except for a few months during my divorce, a stable place to live. I received an adequate education and was able to educate my children. Finding a job was not hard. I felt that families in the South Bronx should have the same opportunities as my family, and clearly that was not the case. Stemming from my college experiences as an exchange student at Fisk University, I valued racial diversity—a commitment strengthened by the racial backgrounds of our children. I also valued hard work and high standards.

Thus, I began my adult life with certain values, but then I learned, or tried to learn, additional values. The generosity of the people I worked with is something I am still trying to emulate. Their warm friendliness was different from my staid upbringing. We built a community at the agency when we were small and tried, with some success, to maintain that feeling as we grew. The traits of generosity and acceptance of others' differences that I saw at BronxWorks are some of the same qualities that contributed to the South Bronx's revival. In retrospect, I believe that at BronxWorks we incorporated other characteristics similar to ones that contributed to the area's renewal. These include a functional advocacy stance with City government, perseverance during hard times, a belief in the importance of diversity, a reliance on the abilities of community residents, high expectations, community input, efforts to obtain adequate resources, and the development of systems that work.

As I have documented in this book, the high rates of poverty in the South Bronx in the postwar period can be attributed to several forces. One certainly was the pervasive racism and the resultant discrimination that people of color faced. African Americans and Puerto Ricans often could not rent in good buildings until the 1970s or later. Most higher-paying jobs were unavailable, with the exception of limited civil service employment. Factory jobs became increasingly scarce. Children faced unequal treatment in schools. Residents lacked the opportunities that previous groups had, making upward mobility harder.

Destructive governmental policies played a major role in the decline. Robert Moses's highways, particularly the Cross Bronx Expressway and the entrance ramps for long bridges, destroyed healthy neighborhoods. The construction of large numbers of public housing buildings also destroyed neighborhoods but, once completed, became an important housing resource. The saturation of undesirable facilities, such as waste transfer stations, incinerators, and other facilities that rely on heavy truck traffic, degraded the health of residents. As in many cities throughout the United States, people who are poor are relegated to areas with environmental hazards and polluting highways. Despite its problems, the South Bronx served as a refuge for people displaced from other areas of the city, either by urban renewal projects or by increasingly expensive rents.

There was a period of time when some neighborhoods were integrated, and it's clear that people valued living in neighborhoods of racial diversity. But then the racial/ethnic changes happened very fast, too fast, leaving a void in the social fabric. Many local institutions such as community and youth centers, social service organizations, synagogues, and hospitals closed. It was years before new groups took their place. Organizations that survived, including schools and some churches, had to adapt to serving new groups, many of whom spoke other languages. The sense of having a cohesive community that supported families suffered and took decades to rebuild.

The extent of the destruction from fires in the 1970s was unprecedented. People died. Thousands of families became homeless. Children were traumatized. Whole neighborhoods were destroyed. Many of the causes of the fires can be traced back to discriminatory government policies and the devaluation of the lives of people of color. Poor neighborhoods did not receive their equitable share of governmental resources. The disinvestment of public services during NYC's fiscal crisis, compounded by chronic under-resourcing, was the final blow. Fire stations were closed and those that remained lost capacity. Garbage piled up from cuts to sanitation. City workers were laid off, library hours were cut, and arts, music, counseling, and athletic programs were cut from schools. Drugs flooded into poor neighborhoods and young men were sent to prison for long sentences. We saw how a devastated community destroys lives. And of course, residents were blamed for the deplorable conditions in their neighborhoods.

But things changed. As I've shown, community leaders arose, such as Evelina Antonetty, Ramón Jiménez, Genevieve Brooks, Father Louis Gigante, Joyce Davis, Louella Hatch, Maria Torres, Hetty Fox, Aurelia Greene, Austin Jacobo, David Shuffler, Yolanda Garcia, and many others, demonstrating the impact individuals can have. They organized people to demand services that met their needs. As individuals and through nascent organizations, they fought for better schools, access to food for their children, medical care, parks, and sports fields. They squatted in abandoned buildings. They turned vacant lots into community gardens. They started community-based agencies that provided preschool and after-school programs, including programs that were missing from schools, such as arts and music. They saved their community college and got a desperately needed new hospital. They fought against their negative, biased portrayal in the media. They showed that communities, if organized, have power.

Nonprofit housing organizations formed and started finding ways to rehabilitate housing. These included SEBCO, Banana Kelly, Mid Bronx Desperados, Mid-Bronx Senior Citizens Council, Mount Hope Housing, SoBro, New Settlement Apartments, WHEDco, South Bronx Churches, and others. Nonprofit building ownership proved to be a viable alternative to for-profit ownership, as a way to keep rents more affordable over the long haul. As conditions started to improve, residents, particularly in Hunts Point, started tackling environmental issues, such as air quality, truck traffic, and the creation of new parks. They had notable successes. However, government and businesses need to do much more to decrease pollution in the air and water and to ensure healthy neighborhoods. The current asthma rates are unacceptable.

Over recent decades, tens of thousands of immigrants from Latin America and West Africa moved to the South Bronx. Unlike in many other places, they were accepted by the existing residents and, rather than forming their own geographical communities, generally mixed in with the rest of the population. Residents are proud of the Bronx's diversity. Immigrants' energy and drive added to the economy as they worked hard to support their families. Immigrants have enriched the culture through music and the arts. This embrace of immigrants helped bring the South Bronx back.

Progressive government policies started helping in the mid-1980s. NYC committed $5 billion to rebuild devastated communities. Leaders in the Bronx successfully fought for the borough's fair share. The City wisely decided to support nonprofits in playing a lead role in rehabbing and managing housing that had been abandoned. Productive partnerships between community groups and government formed, allowing for real progress.

Over the years (and it takes years), Bronx-based human services agencies—such as United Bronx Parents, BronxWorks, the Point, East Side House Settlement, Casita Maria, New Settlement Apartments, and Mid-Bronx Senior Citizens Council, and others—developed capacity to provide important programs to children and families, strengthening the social fabric of the community. As they gained experience, they had a better chance of competing for funds. Some city agencies, nudged by Bronxites, looked methodically at where their funds were going and targeted their resources more fairly. These investments in communities matter a great deal.

Model programs with measurable outcomes, some piloted at BronxWorks, demonstrated that difficult social issues can be solved. Young people have tremendous potential that is often squandered if systems fail them. Supportive schools and programs help young people succeed, even those several years behind academically. Teen pregnancy can be reduced if girls and boys can see a realistic path to educational and personal success. Both high school and college graduation rates can be increased, dramatically increasing people's earning power. Unemployed residents can be helped to find and retain employment. Jobs taking care of frail elderly people is a need that will only grow as baby boomers age. Immigrants gain increased earning capacity when they learn English, either through ESL programs or on their own. Even people living on the streets for many years can transition to stable, domiciled lives, which improves the living environment for others as well as for themselves. Helping people who are elderly and/or have chronic illnesses lead healthier lives saves health-care dollars. Keeping people in their own homes and out of nursing homes also saves considerable Medicaid funds. In order to have real impact, BronxWorks worked for years to establish services and programs that could help tens of thousands. Other agencies also innovated in significant ways, in areas of youth services, drug treatment, mental health, and workforce development.

Fighting against monied interests had mixed results. The battle against the negative portrayal of the community in the movie *Fort Apache the Bronx* secured minor concessions. NWBCCC successfully confronted bankers who were not investing in the community and landlords who were not maintaining their buildings, taking the fight, if necessary, to their place of residence. Public shaming worked in that instance. Community protesters did get luxury developers to stop rebranding Mott Haven as the "piano district," and similarly groups got the City to stop referring to the Jerome Avenue rezoning area as "Cromwell." Organizations fighting for strong, enforceable community benefits agreements due from major construction projects could secure only minor concessions. The fight to keep the truck traffic from FreshDirect out of Mott Haven was lost, as elected officials valued the jobs the company would bring.

The important battle against increasing displacement of people of low and moderate incomes is now being fought. The economic and human costs of displacement and resultant homelessness are too high to ignore. Other cities are facing this crisis and are also searching for solutions. Government intervention is crucial to counter the influence of powerful real estate interests. Government can do much more to support construction of low-income housing, provide needed funding to maintain both public housing and government-supported housing, and adequately fund rent voucher programs such as Section 8. Also in the government's purview are more effective controls on rent increases of all types, including increases from major capital improvements and increases when apartments are re-rented to new tenants.

Today the South Bronx is at a tipping point: will it go the way of Brooklyn and parts of Queens in being a site of gentrification, pushing out many low-income people in the process? Or will it develop in a more equitable manner, with the needs of its population driving the agenda?

As a longtime activist, I hope I've communicated the large trends as well as the countless small stories that weave a tale of an area struggling to reclaim itself in the context of neglect, disinvestment, drugs, and racism. I've emphasized the experiences of people—mostly poor, mostly disempowered, mostly invisible in the larger tapestry of the New York landscape—whom I grew to care deeply about. I hope I've illuminated their realities in a realistic and complex manner. It's been truly an honor to have had the opportunity to spend my working life serving the people of the South Bronx. I also hope I've communicated the main lesson I've learned over five decades on the ground: that collective voices working through organizations can effect positive change. Community activism matters.

PRESERVING BRONX CULTURAL HISTORY

I have briefly described a few of the cultural gifts that people of the South Bronx have given to the broader society. The arts are an economic engine while they enrich the lives of many. For example, who can discount the role of hip hop, developed in the Bronx in the 1970s, in creating a sense of community, even in hard times. The musical innovations of artists such as DJ Kool Herc, Grandmaster Flash, and the Cold Crush Brothers—to name just a few—became a worldwide force. Other forms of African American, Latin, and Caribbean music blended, fused, and morphed into new musical genres. People danced in the street and held parties in the park. People developed a strong sense of pride in being from the Bronx.

While the culture continues to absorb new influences and the population changes, sometimes incrementally and sometimes dramatically, significant efforts are being made to preserve important African American and Latino arts, traditions, and history. There is concern that the important cultural contributions, which were never fully appreciated by the broader society, could be lost. NYC Council Member Vanessa Gibson comments:

With the growing population, it is important to preserve the character of the district. There is a lot of history of Morrisania that people, particularly young people, don't know. We want to preserve that history and make it available to young people.

I have been involved with the renaming of streets for some Bronx jazz musicians, including Maxine Sullivan, Elmo Hope, and recently Donald Byrd. Byrd gave a lot to bebop. Byrd, whose group was the Blackbyrds, died in 2013. He lived in that community for years. He had a PhD in music and was a professor of music at many colleges.[1]

In May 2017, the street near 1520 Sedgwick Avenue was renamed Hip Hop Boulevard. Called the birthplace of hip hop, it was home to DJ Kool Herc, who, with the help of his sister, organized hip hop parties in the community room of the building.[2] Mike Amadeo, owner of the historic Latin music store Casa Amadeo, already had a street named after him.

A new thousand-unit building called Bronx Point will house the Universal Hip Hop Museum. Using sophisticated technology, the museum seeks to preserve the history of hip hop, with a focus on its early pioneers.[3]

In early 2017, WHEDco broke ground on its newest project, a 305-unit affordable housing complex named Bronx Commons that will house the Bronx Music Hall. Elena Martínez will be codirector of the music hall along with Bobby Sanabria:

> The Bronx is still thought of in terms of negative stereotypes such as crime. We want to make sure that our music and dance legacy get out there too. People know the Bronx as the birthplace of hip hop, but it has such an incredible music and cultural legacy that is largely unknown. We will offer classes, performances, open the space up to the community, allow groups to rehearse, and have space for meetings. We will have permanent exhibits on the history and chronology of music, and archives.[4]

Casita Maria, Dancing in the Streets, and the Bronx Music Heritage Center are establishing a South Bronx Cultural Trail, based on the work of City Lore, to broaden the appreciation of contributions the South Bronx has made to the larger culture. Someday, hopefully, markers will designate historic sites (some mentioned elsewhere in this book) such as Casa Amadeo, the Hunts Point Palace, 52 Park, PS 52, United Bronx Parents,

The Fourth Annual Parranda con Paranda—a holiday celebration that brings together the Puerto Rican and Garifuna cultures—took place on December 17, 2016, at Bronx Music Heritage Center. Bobby Sanabria (foreground) is pictured here with other musicians including James Lovell, Alex Kwabena Colon, Nelson Cabassa, Lucy Blanco, Mateo Gonzalez, Ines Mangual, Oxil Febles, and several members of the Chief Joseph Chatoyer Dance Company, including its director, Felix Gamboa. Photo credit: Elena Martínez/Bronx Music Heritage Center.

the sculpture *Puerto Rican Sun,* the mural *Homage to the People of the Bronx: Double Dutch at Kelly Street,* and others.

Vivian Vázquez and two colleagues created a powerful documentary, *Decade of Fire,* that examines the experiences of people who lived through that very difficult time and the conditions and policies that led to the borough's tragic decline. It also profiles activists who fought for change. The visual scenes of the fires and the interviews are very moving and compelling. Elena Martínez and Steve Zeitlin produced an important documentary that was shown on public TV, called *From Mambo to Hip Hop: A South Bronx Tale,* that details the roots of both genres in the South Bronx.[5]

Fordham University and Lehman College have made a remarkable contribution to preserving life stories of people from the Bronx. Fordham's three hundred Bronx African American oral histories are available on the university's website.[6] Plans are underway to expand Fordham's oral history project to other populations. Lehman College has taped oral histories of four hundred people, many of which have been transcribed.

Casita Maria and the Bronx Music Heritage Center acknowledged the contributions of sisters Elba Cabrera, Evelina Antonetty, and Lillian López with two exhibits and receptions called *Las Tres Hermanas: Art and Activism* in June 2017. Over two hundred family members and admirers greeted Ms. Cabrera, the only surviving sister, who was known as "La Madrina de las Artes" (godmother of the arts). Her sister Lillian was the first Puerto Rican administrator in the library system, and Evelina (highlighted in chapter 4) was a leading advocate for bilingual education and school nutritional programs. Streets have been named after Evelina and her daughter, Lorraine Montenegro.

The South Bronx's many casitas (little houses with gardens) are another example of preserving culture. Bronx Council on the Arts displayed an exhibition about casitas at the Smithsonian in 1991. As Bill Aguado states,

> a casita presents a memory, a history of a life that once was, that is rarely found even in Puerto Rico anymore. Nineteen have been recorded in the Bronx. There are probably more.[7]

Hostos Center for the Arts and Culture, which is focused on Latin and Bronx artists, frequently features jazz performances as well as theater and dance. In 2017 it presented a three-day festival, "Tito Puente Retrospective—Puente for a New Generation," including performances by a twenty-piece band. The festival was covered by the *New York Times* in an article titled "Bringing Tito Puente's Fire to a New Generation."[8]

In 2017 and 2018, Bobby Sanabria conducted the twenty-one-piece Multiverse Big Band in reimagining the music of Leonard Bernstein's *West Side Story.* The original music was expanded to include elements of Venezuelan joropo; Puerto Rican bomba and plena; Dominican merengue; Brazilian samba and samba canção; Cuban mambo, cha-cha-chá, bolero, and son montuno; West African–rooted bembé; and American funk and swing. Performances were held at Jazz at Lincoln Center, the Hostos Center, and other venues.[9] This represents an example of Bronx musical innovation that preserves elements of traditional music while merging diverse genres.

The South Bronx's many arts and literary organizations help preserve the culture through the creation of photographs, music, stories, paintings, and performances that depict life in the Bronx. That culture helped sustain the South Bronx when formidable odds were stacked against it. The values of family, community, social activism, perseverance, generosity, welcoming the stranger, and hard work will continue to guide people in the future.

Joyce Davis sums up how many people feel about the Bronx:

> The Bronx was so pretty, so beautiful, brighter than Brooklyn, wonderful architecture. For me, there is nothing like it. Brooklyn has nice people but it is not like the Bronx, the beautiful borough.[10]

Epilogue

As the Bronx continues to evolve and change, so do the lives of its residents. Some of the people featured in this book have moved into new positions. Ralph Acevedo is now the district manager of Community Board 2 in the Bronx. Bill Aguado is serving as executive director of En Foco; he received an honorary doctorate from Lehman College in recognition of his contributions to Bronx arts. Jeniffer Montaño is now a fourth- and fifth-grade bilingual teacher, working a few blocks from where she lives in the South Bronx; she has earned both a bachelor's and a master's degree in bilingual education. Rosalina Luongo is the director of BronxWorks' Morris Senior Center. Deon Shaw is working and loves her new apartment; her son is happy to have his own room. Freddy Ferrer is cochairman of Mercury LLC and vice chair of the Metropolitan Transportation Authority. Vivian Vázquez's documentary *Decade of Fire* premiered in November 2018.

Hostos Community College was named one of the top ten finalists in 2015 for the prestigious Aspen Prize for Community College Excellence. Its graduation rate, which increases yearly, is above the national average for community colleges, and it provides a means of upward mobility for thousands of Bronx residents. Bronx River Alliance hopes to settle into its new home, River House (cited as NYC's greenest building), in the near future. The Bronx Children's Museum's building is also under construction. Bronx arts groups are thriving, offering exciting exhibits and performances.

BronxWorks expanded its focus on health and nutrition, as well as services for people who are homeless and for children. Funds were successfully raised to complete the renovation of the community center's roof, furnace, elevator, and swimming pool. Under Eileen Torres's leadership, BronxWorks won the 2013 New York Nonprofit Excellence Award.

Most of the activists continue their battles. CASA, led by Fitzroy Christian and Carmen Vega Rivera, is still fighting for low-income tenants, monitoring the effects of the Jerome Avenue rezoning, and evaluating the implementation of the right-to-counsel and Certificate of No Harassment legislation. Paul Lipson continues to work on environmental, economic development, and health issues, including those related to heavy truck traffic. Maria Torres is involved with matters related to the development called the Peninsula. Mychal Johnson is undertaking a community planning project in Mott Haven. Harry DeRienzo stepped down as executive director of Banana Kelly but will stay on for a while as a consultant. Jeanette Puryear continues to lead Mid-Bronx Senior Citizens Council.

Marshall Green expanded his staff of lawyers at the Legal Aid Society to fill the need created by the right to counsel in housing court. Other areas of NYC are being rezoned to encourage the construction of more housing, some of it technically "affordable." It remains to be seen if this will help or hurt the overall housing picture for lower-income families.

Aurelia Greene and Carmen Cordova retired from government service. Carmen had moved to a house in the suburbs. Sadly, she died in January 2019, shortly before this book was published. John Sanchez, Linda Cox, and Nancy Biberman also retired from their agencies. Daniel Díaz, Maggie Greenfield, and Davon Russell, respectively, were promoted to lead those agencies.

Other people profiled in this book have also died. Lorraine Montenegro died in Puerto Rico shortly after Hurricane Maria and is considered to be one of the casualties of the storm and the government's poor response to it. Both a street and the Lorraine Montenegro Women and Children's Program Facility (opened in June 2018) have been named in her honor;

the facility allows children to stay with their mothers who are undergoing treatment for drug addiction. Max Blauner also passed away, and his obituary mentioned the Living Legend Award he received from BronxWorks. Gail Blauner, his daughter, is active in real estate in the Bronx and named the building that houses BronxWorks drop-in center after her dad. Ed Kaufman died several years ago.

For many of us, life continues pretty much on its same path. Elba Cabrera is active with Hostos Community College and with Bronx arts groups. Kathryn Speller gets out less than she used to but is still very interested in community issues. Sallie Smith is active in her community and senior center. Norma Pérez is busy and doing well. Carolyn Pelzer has now worked for BronxWorks for over twenty-five years. Many of the senior staff, such as Julie Belizaire Spitzer, John Weed, Bibi Karin, Ken Small, Scott Auwarter, and Maria Rivera, continue to provide excellent leadership. It constantly amazes me that Julie is raising four daughters, including triplets, and works more than full time, putting in long hours.

When I was working at a frenetic pace, I couldn't image what retirement would be like. Fortunately, I was invited to join two boards, Hostos Community College's Foundation Board and the Bronx River Alliance's board of directors. I also continued my board membership with the Nonprofit Coordinating Committee, a citywide group that works on behalf of nonprofits. I am delighted to be affiliated with these important organizations and I find the involvement rewarding. It has been hugely satisfying to talk in depth with the hundred-plus people interviewed for this book and to write about their lives and important contributions. The stories of people from the South Bronx are a source of ongoing inspiration.

Acknowledgments

A great many people were incredibly generous with their time and knowledge, which was key to making this book possible. Well over a hundred people agreed to be interviewed, and many shared very personal stories. Some I have known for years and consider friends. Others I met during the course of working on the book, as people introduced me to others. A few didn't know me at all and just trusted my word as to why I was asking them so many questions. I thank all of them and hope they enjoy reading all the stories, including their own.

Three women really extended themselves for the book, believing in the significance of this work. Kathryn Speller, a colleague for forty years, met with me many times during the past four years. Her insights, based on her career and involvement in community issues for more than fifty years, led me to explore many of the points she raised during our conversations. Carmen Cordova, a close friend, met with me several times to share her story. She took this project so seriously that she interviewed her mother in Puerto Rico about her memories of coming to the Bronx in the early 1950s, including all the places they lived and the challenges they faced. I regret not being able to use all of the material she provided. The third, Sallie Smith, knew CAB/BronxWorks from its early days. Her memories, along with Kathryn's and my own, and her files were key to describing the West Bronx of the '70s. Sallie provided me with an important document, a study of the housing situation on Grand Concourse written in 1967.

Staff of BronxWorks deserve special recognition and profound thanks on two accounts. First and most importantly, I couldn't possibly have made a success of the agency without the skills and support of the thousands of staff I had the pleasure of working with and learning from over the years. Many stand out and several are acknowledged in chapter 7. I wish I could individually thank them all. Stories provided by a few appear in various places in this book. I greatly appreciate the support Eileen Torres, BronxWorks' executive director, lent to the project, but even more I appreciate the terrific job she is doing running BronxWorks.

I also owe a deep debt of gratitude to everyone who served on the board of directors of BronxWorks over the years, many of whom supported the agency for twenty years or more. Special thanks to Sean Delany, Emily Menlo Marks, Marshall Green, Jean Smith, Lena Townsend, Bruce Phillips, Mark Kemeny, Judith Leonard, John Fouhey, and Bill Aguado. In earlier years, board members who made special contributions were Gemma Hessian, Richard Rivera, Joe Ithier, Lorenzo Barcelo, Dorothy Henderson, and Ilda Rosario. I also thank and value my colleagues from City and State government and from NYC's other settlement houses, as well as elected officials who supported our work.

I am extremely grateful to Naomi Schneider, the editor of this book. I still don't really understand what caused her to take a chance on me. I had never written much except funding proposals and letters of reference for employees. Naomi worked with me to shape the manuscript over the course of four years. Benjy Malings, her editorial assistant, was always very helpful and encouraging, as were all other University of California staff.

Dr. David Gómez, the president of Hostos Community College, read and favorably commented on the book proposal, agreed to be quoted in the book, wrote the Foreword, and reviewed the manuscript when it was in near final form. He gave generously of his time and wisdom despite the pressures of his job, which included expanding the college and significantly improving its graduation rate. I am deeply indebted to him. William Casari, who functions as Hostos's archivist, provided information for the section on the history of Hostos and a historical photo.

Dr. Robert Courtney Smith, a professor at Baruch College, kindly provided the initial introduction to Naomi Schneider, who had published his book *Mexican New York: Transnational Lives of New Immigrants*. Additionally, he made helpful recommendations on the manuscript. I am also grateful to two other professors from Baruch College who reviewed and recommended the book proposal. One is Jack Krauskopf, who had previously served as commissioner of the NYC Human Resources Administration and as dean of the Robert J. Milano Graduate School of Management and Urban Policy at the New School. Jack was supportive during my entire career. Michael Seltzer, who has an extensive background in human services, knew BronxWorks when he was the president of Philanthropy New York. I am fortunate to have served on boards with both Jack and Michael.

On topics that I was less familiar with—the arts and the environment—key people provided invaluable assistance. Paul Lipson contributed much of the information on environmental justice advocacy, as well as helping with a conceptual framework for some issues. Elena Martínez and Dr. Mark Naison generously shared their extensive knowledge of Bronx music and culture. Elena offered historical photos and leads to other photos (as did Paul). Mark also reviewed the manuscript, encouraging me to add more material on music, and provided ideas. Bill Aguado, over the course of several interviews, provided history of Bronx arts and arts groups as well as details on his own amazing career.

Maria Torres of the Point deserves special thanks for her insights, stories, and introductions to other key people. Elba Cabrera shared extensive information on her sister Evelina López Antonetty, as well as her own impressive background. Activists Carmen Vega Rivera and Fitzroy Christian welcomed me to CASA meetings and provided background information on CASA's wide-ranging advocacy. Harry DeRienzo of Banana Kelly provided history of early nonprofit housing developers and of recent housing-related battles. Carolyn Pelzer shared her remarkable story over the course of two interviews.

Many thanks to Sotero Ortiz (BG183) for the artwork he created for the cover, for his photo, and for his interview. It was fun to get to know more about street art during the course of writing this book. The story of Tats Cru is an important part of the history of Bronx hip-hop culture.

Nilka Martell, Mark Rosenthal, Jerry Shroder, CASA, Hostos Community College Archives, Muhamadou Salieu Suso, NYC Housing Partnership, Martha Cooper, Carmen Cordova, Jim Henderson, Joe Conzo Jr., and Francisco Reyes II generously provided photos. I also thank the people in the photos who allowed their images to be used in the book.

Toni Downes, who worked as executive director before me, was very helpful in sharing the early history of CAB. Toni, like Carmen, was very supportive during the entire time I was writing the manuscript. Gene Oliva, a family friend who never tires of telling stories of his childhood in the West Bronx, gave helpful background information.

Often interviews had to be edited for space, but I tried to keep the content the same. All efforts were made during the writing of this book to be as accurate as possible, but if there are errors, they are my own and I regret them and take full responsibility.

My colleague Vivian Vázquez was working on her documentary *Decade of Fire* during the same period I was working on this book. It was always interesting to share a meal with her and compare notes, as well as seeing rough cuts of her film.

My son Kamau Karanja was the first person outside of the editorial staff to read sections of the book. After reading three chapters in 2015, he wrote: "Hi mom, this looks really good. The writing is really professional and the storyline holds together really nicely. You have come a really long way from the earlier drafts. Keep going!" This encouragement was much appreciated.

Several family members and friends provided moral support and practical help. My son Jimmy McLaughlin helped me at times when I was stuck with computer issues. When I was at BronxWorks, I always had smart young assistants who did tasks for me on the computer. Writing a book on a computer required a whole new set of skills, which I slowly (at times painfully) acquired. My friend Carter, an artist, helped me understand what the publisher needed in terms of submitting photographs and also helped me with computer skills. My friend Phoebe Hoss and her daughter Katie made suggestions for the title of the book, which led to the chosen title, just two weeks before Phoebe died. Abby Tannenbaum gave me writing tips. I also appreciate the people at Apple and Microsoft, whose names I don't know, who during many long phone conversations and several visits to the Apple store finally figured out why my relatively new Mac couldn't properly run Word. I have to acknowledge my daughter Johnicka, for always thinking I could do anything. My sister-in-law Patty bought me a warm lap blanket and lap desk so I could work sitting on an old comfortable chair in a cold part of our house. Thanks to everyone who read draft chapters for content and also as proofreaders, including Joan Byron, Harry DeRienzo, Toni Downes, Maryanne Ure, Tom McLaughlin, Barbara Watts Pafumi, Jimmy McLaughlin, Carter, and, of course, my husband Jim.

Jim deserves much special credit and thanks. He is supportive, caring, and helpful. He does all the cooking for us and chauffeurs me at times when I can't drive. He puts my needs and wants first, especially when they relate to working on "the book." My friends and colleagues know how special he is. They always say, "How's Jim?" or "Say hi to Jim" or, in the case of Kathryn Speller, "Say hey to Jim."

Abbreviations

CAB	Citizens Advice Bureau (renamed BronxWorks)
CASA	Community Action for Safe Apartments
CDC	Community development corporation
DACA	Deferred Action for Childhood Arrivals
ESL	English as a second language
GED	General equivalency diploma
HOT	BronxWorks' Homeless Outreach Team
HPD	NYC Department of Housing Preservation and Development
HRA	NYC Human Resources Administration
IS	Intermediate School (followed by an identifying number)
JCTS	Jill Chaifetz Transfer School
LEED	Leadership in Energy and Environmental Design
MOM	Mothers on the Move
NSA	New Settlement Apartments
NWBCCC	Northwest Bronx Community and Clergy Coalition
NYCHA	New York City Housing Authority
PS	Public School (followed by an identifying number)
PTA	Parent-teacher association

SEBCO   South East Bronx Community Organization

SHF   Settlement Housing Fund

SNAP   Supplemental Nutrition Assistance Program for low-income families and individuals (formerly called "food stamps")

SSI   Supplemental Security Income

UBP   United Bronx Parents

WHEDCo   Women's Housing and Economic Development Corporation

YMHA   Young Men's Hebrew Association

YMPJ   Youth Ministries for Peace and Justice

Glossary

bodega	Small, corner convenience store.
City	When capitalized, City refers to the New York City government.
community board	Advisory unit of local government; the unpaid members are appointed by elected officials.
community development corporation	A nonprofit, community-based agency that sponsors housing and and/or other economic development projects.
community district	New York City is divided into fifty-nine community districts, twelve of which are in the Bronx; six comprise the South Bronx.
Con Ed	The power/utility company.
congregate shelter	A shelter in which the person or family does not have private living space but shares space with others.
Gracie Mansion	Official residence of the mayor of New York City.
green card	Lawful permanent residency card.
gypsy cab	An informal term for a cab not fully licensed to pick up passengers from the street.
Medicaid	Federal health insurance program for low-income people.

Section 8	Federally funded housing voucher for low-income people.
settlement house	Community-based, nonprofit agency that provides services and programs to a geographic area.
special ed	Special education for students with special needs.
State	When capitalized, State refers to the New York State government.
sweat equity	Investment of a person's labor, giving them an ownership stake in a project.
tier I shelter	A congregate shelter for families housing men, women, and children.
tier II shelter	A shelter for families in which each family has their own living space.
U visa	A visa for victims of certain crimes that can, under some circumstances, lead to qualification for a green card.
welfare	Used interchangeably with the term public assistance; administered by the New York City Human Resources Administration.
Wite-Out	Brand name for typewriter correction fluid and tape.

Notes

1. Speller 2015 interview.
2. Ryley et al. 2015.
3. Plitt 2017.
4. Statistical Atlas 2015.
5. Office of the Mayor n.d.
6. College Gridirons n.d.
7. Bronx Times n.d.
8. Sisk 2010.
9. Parrott 2009.
10. NYC Economic Development Corporation 2016.
11. Office of the New York State Comptroller 2014.
12. Sisk 2010.
13. A recent study cited in the *Journal of the American Medical Association* (Raj Chetty et al. 2016) and quoted in the *New York Times* (Sanger-Katz 2016) found that poor people in NYC have a longer life expectancy than poor people in most cities in the country. Reasons offered are public health initiatives to combat smoking and obesity as well as a high level of local government funding.
14. Landmarks Preservation Commission 1981; Stewart 2017.
15. NYC Parks n.d., "Pelham Bay Park Highlights—Siwanoy Trail."

16. Jonnes 2002: 11–26.

17. Garcia 2011.

18. Rosenblum 2009: 5, 25.

19. For descriptions of the West Bronx during this period, see Jonnes (2002: 51–58, 278–279) and NYC Department of City Planning (n.d.: 9–10), "Scope of Environmental Impact Statement/Jerome Avenue."

20. Oliva 2015 interview.

21. Freilich 2015 interview.

22. Canada 2017 interview.

23. Naison and Gumbs 2016: 65–67.

24. Oliva 2015 interview.

25. Freilich 2015 interview.

26. NYC Department of City Planning 2017.

27. Flood 2010b.

28. Flood 2010b.

29. Goodman 2017.

30. Cordova 2015 interview.

CHAPTER TWO. HOW THE SOUTH BRONX BECAME THE POOREST CONGRESSIONAL DISTRICT

1. Riccio 2013.

2. Sheehan 2014 interview.

3. Speller 2015 interview.

4. Sheehan 2014 interview.

5. Jonnes 2002: 117–119.

6. New York Times Editorial Board 2018.

7. New York State Committee on Discrimination in Housing 1953; Pear 1992; New York State Committee on Discrimination in Housing 1953; Rothstein 2012.

8. Jonnes 2002: 118.

9. Sanchez 2016 interview.

10. Howell 2015 interview.

11. Echevarria 2015 interview.

12. Naison and Gumbs 2016: 145.

13. Sanabria 2017 interview.

14. Caro 1975: 6.

15. Ibid.: 850–894.

16. Rayman 2017.

17. Caro 1975: 1151.

18. Cabrera 2015 interview.

19. Frey 2015 interview.

20. Library of Congress n.d.

21. Soto 2015 interview.

22. Cordova 2015 interview.

23. Gates 2013; BlackPast n.d.; Jonnes 2002: 98.

24. U.S. Census Bureau 2016.

25. Speller 2015 interview.

26. S. Smith 2015 interview.

27. Speller 2015 interview.

28. Naison and Gumbs 2016: 4.

29. S. Smith 2015 interview.

30. Here I have combined the statements of four women at the Morris Senior Center with whom I talked informally on June 16, 2015.

31. Badger et al. 2018.

32. Cordova 2015 interview.

33. Evans 2015.

34. Naison and Gumbs 2016: 2.

35. Cabrera 2015 interview.

36. Seltzer 2016 interview.

37. Gonzalez 2004: 118.

38. These statements were made by three women with whom I talked informally at two senior centers on June 10 and 16, 2015.

39. Butos 2016 interview.

40. Cordova 2015 interview.

41. da Costa Nunez and Sribnick 2013: 226.

42. Speller 2015 interview.

43. Gardner 2013.

44. Gonzalez 2004: 119.

45. Speller 2015 interview.

46. Cordova 2015 interview.

47. Rivera 2015 interview.

48. Cordova 2015 interview.

49. Ellison 2015.

50. Blad 2017.

51. J. Smith 2015 interview.

52. Cordova 2015 interview.

53. Vázquez 2015 interview.

54. E. Torres 2015 interview.

55. Soto 2015 interview.

56. Jenkins 2014.

57. Canada 2017 interview.

58. Jones 2009: 81.
59. Flores 2016 interview.
60. Davis 2016 interview.
61. Speller 2015 interview.
62. New York Civil Liberties Union 2009.
63. Samaha 2014.
64. Lipson 2015 interview.
65. Vázquez 2015 interview.
66. Phillips-Fein 2017: 22.
67. Riper 1975.
68. Blumenthal 2002.
69. Oreskes 1988; Freudenberg 2006; Phillips-Fein 2013.
70. Doyle 2016 interview.
71. Sotomayor 2013.
72. Spitzer 2016 interview.
73. Cordova 2015 interview.
74. E. Torres 2015 interview.
75. Naison and Gumbs 2016: 66.
76. Cruz 2016 interview.
77. Carrión 2016 interview.

CHAPTER THREE. WHY THE SOUTH BRONX BURNED

Epigraphs: Ortiz 2016 interview; Flores 2016 interview.
1. Gonzalez 2004: 124.
2. NYC Department of City Planning 2017.
3. Flood 2010b.
4. BBC 1972; Gainey 2017 interview.
5. Jonnes 2002: 261.
6. McFadden 1975.
7. Pelzer 2016 interview.
8. Hill 2014 (interview with Morris Greenstein): 14–16.
9. DeRienzo 2008: 158.
10. Hill 2014 (interview with Morris Greenstein): 15.
11. American Jewish Congress 1967.
12. Ibid. My thanks to Sallie Smith for providing a copy of the report.
13. New York Times 1983; Frey 2015 interview.
14. S. Smith 2015 interview.
15. Vázquez 2015 interview.
16. Rodríguez 2015 interview.
17. Glantz and Martinez 2018; Badger 2015; Bouie 2015.

18. Hill 2014 (interview with Morris Greenstein): 14–17; Frey 2015 interview.
19. Ibid.
20. Rodríguez 2015 interview.
21. DeRienzo 2008: 164.
22. Rodríguez 2015 interview.
23. DeRienzo 2015 interview.
24. Vázquez 2015 interview.
25. Rodríguez 2015 interview.
26. Flood 2010b.
27. Jonnes 2002: 266.
28. Ibid.: 259–260.
29. Treaster 1975. However, during the blackout of July 13, 1977, there was widespread looting of stores and businesses in NYC and many were set on fire.
30. New York Times 1979.
31. Flood 2010b ; Wallace and Wallace 2001: 29–40.
32. Flores 2016 interview.
33. Shaw 2016 interview.
34. Ortiz 2016 interview.
35. Wallace and Wallace 2001: 24–26.
36. NYC Rent Guidelines Board 1996: 127.
37. Jonnes 2002: 281–287; Rosenblum 2009: 193–195.

CHAPTER FOUR. PEOPLE FIGHT BACK:
1960S AND 1970S

1. Luongo 2015 interview.
2. Phillips-Fein 2017: 207–208. Planned shrinkage never became official City policy and was disavowed by Mayor Abe Beame (Jonnes 2002: 299).
3. Cabrera 2015 interview.
4. Vázquez 2015 interview.
5. Cabrera 2015 interview.
6. Goldman 2016 interview.
7. Ferrer 2016 interview.
8. Cabrera 2015 interview.
9. Conzo 2018 interview.
10. Greene 2016 interview.
11. Matthews 2014.
12. For more detailed information on Ramón Velez, see Jonnes 2002: 164–174.
13. Goldman 2016 interview.
14. Brody 2017.

15. Zehnder 2016 interview.
16. Cabrera 2015 interview.
17. Gonzalez 1995; Aronczyk 2014.
18. Melendez 2017 interview.
19. Moyer 2016 interview.
20. Cabrera 2015 interview.
21. Hostos Community College n.d.; Gómez 2015 interview; Casari 2016.
22. Sotomayor 2013: 113.
23. Gómez 2015 interview.
24. Ibid.
25. Ibid.
26. Marion Streater Johnson interview 2017.
27. Hostos Community College n.d.
28. Melendez 2017 interview.
29. See chapter 1.
30. Verel 2016; Gonzalez 2009; Naison and Gumbs 2016: 68–73.
31. Mary Mitchell Family and Youth Center 2006; Pace 2002.
32. Speller 2015 interview.
33. Vázquez 2015 interview.
34. Gonzalez 2017; Samuels 2011; Nicholson 2015.
35. Mallozzi 2012.
36. Ortiz 2016 interview.
37. Kelley 2015 interview.
38. Jonnes 2002: 190–191, 256–258.
39. Frey 2015 interview.
40. Strelnick 2016 interview.
41. Urban Health Plan 2017.
42. Speller 2015 interview.
43. Kaufman 1974.
44. Downes 2014 interview.
45. Siegal 1974.
46. Bird 1976.
47. da Costa Nunez and Sribnick 2013.
48. Moritz 2015.
49. Hall 2014.
50. Reyes 2016 interview.
51. Greene 2016 interview.
52. S. Smith 2015 interview.
53. Conzo 2018 interview.
54. Levin 2015 interview.
55. DeRienzo 2015 interview.

56. Banana Kelly Community Improvement Association 2017.
57. DeRienzo 2015 interview.
58. Jonnes 2002: 302; Gonzalez 2004: 132; Redfearn 2007.
59. Gonzalez 2004: 133.
60. Jonnes 2002: 249–252.
61. Frey 2015 interview.
62. Davis 2016 interview.
63. Speller 2015 interview.
64. Furman Center n.d.
65. Levin 2015 interview.
66. Furman Center 2017; Rodríguez 2015 interview.
67. Levin 2015 interview.
68. Furman Center 2017.
69. City Lore n.d. "Hunts Point Palace."
70. Naison and Gumbs 2016: 50–51.
71. Ibid.: 38.
72. Mark Naison, email to author, January 29, 2018.
73. Ibid.; Fernandez 2006.
74. Biography.org 2016.
75. E. Martínez 2017 interview.
76. Roberts 2005.
77. Sanabria 2017 interview.
78. Amadeo 2017 interview.
79. Socialism and Democracy Online 2011.
80. RollingStone.com 2018.
81. Nossiter 1995.
82. Socialism and Democracy Online 2011.
83. OldSchoolHipHop.com 2010.
84. E. Martínez 2017 interview.
85. Mark Naison email to author, April 12, 2018.
86. Christian 2016 interview.
87. City Lore n.d. "Casita Rincón Criollo."
88. Bronx Museum of the Arts 2017.
89. Flores 2016 interview.
90. Conzo 2018 interview.
91. Levin 2015 interview.
92. Goldberger 1979.
93. Vega-Rivera 2016 interview.
94. Aguado 2015 interview.

CHAPTER FIVE. PROGRESS, BUT PLAGUES DESCEND
ON THE SOUTH BRONX: 1980S

1. Velázquez 2015 interview.
2. Dunlap 1982.
3. Quindlen 1982; Jonnes 2002: 410–411; Munch n.d.
4. Bady n.d.
5. E. Torres 2015 interview.
6. S. Smith 2015 interview.
7. Finder 1990.
8. Green 2016 interview.
9. Silverman 2016 interview.
10. Strelnick 2016 interview.
11. Basler 1986.
12. Neighborhood Stabilization Program, NYC Commission on Human Rights 1986.
13. Ibid.
14. Frey 2015 interview.
15. da Costa Nunez 2013: 228–229.
16. Dreier 2011.
17. Oser 1989; Jonnes 2002: 337.
18. Acosta and Acosta 2016 interview.
19. Strelnick 2016 interview.
20. Lynn 1991.
21. U.S. House of Representatives n.d.
22. Carrión 2016 interview.
23. Greene 2016 interview.
24. Velasquez 2007.
25. Sotomayor 1988.
26. Ferrer 2016 interview.
27. Doyle 2016 interview.
28. Velázquez 2015 interview.
29. Doyle 2016 interview.
30. Speller 2015 interview.
31. Auwarter 2016 interview.
32. Pérez 2016 interview.
33. Washington 2016 interview.
34. Karim 2016 interview.
35. Washington 2016 interview.
36. Martínez 2017 interview.
37. NYC Parks n.d., "Playground 52"; Gonzalez 2013.
38. Martínez 2017 interview.

39. Karanja 2015 interview.

40. Acevedo 2016 interview.

41. M. Torres 2016 interview.

42. Thomas 2012. For detailed information on Bronx immigrants' countries of origin, see NYC Department of City Planning 2013: 29–35.

43. Caro-López 2010.

44. Velez 2016 interview.

45. Block 2009.

46. Aduna 2016 interview.

47. Florida 2015.

48. Roberts 2017.

49. Gladstone 2017.

50. Ortiz 2016 interview.

51. Nossiter 1995.

52. Ortiz 2016 interview.

53. M. Torres 2016 interview.

54. Aguado 2015 interview.

55. Flores 2016 interview.

CHAPTER SIX. NOT YET PARADISE, BUT WE'VE COME A LONG WAY: 1990S

Epigraph: Pelzer 2016 interview.

1. Levin 2015 interview.

2. Weed 2016 interview.

3. Pelzer 2016 interview.

4. Weed 2016 interview.

5. Pelzer 2016 interview.

6. Weed 2016 interview.

7. Pelzer 2016 interview.

8. Furman Center 2006.

9. Ferrer 2016 interview.

10. Furman Center 2006.

11. Velázquez 2015 interview.

12. Ferrer 2016 interview.

13. Bronx Center Steering Committee 1993: 37.

14. DeRienzo 2008: 82; Gonzalez 2004: 140–141; Rothstein 1994.

15. Pelzer 2016 interview.

16. Dillon 1995.

17. Pelzer 2016 interview.

18. Weintraub 2014 interview.

19. NYC Department of City Planning n.d., "Change in Total Population, 1990 and 2000 New York City and Boroughs."

20. DiNapoli 2013b.

21. Office of the New York State Comptroller 2015.

22. Fiscal Policy Institute 2011.

23. NYC Department of City Planning 2002.

24. Block 2009.

25. Margarita 2016 interview.

26. Juana 2016 interview.

27. Kabba 2016 interview.

28. Butos 2016 interview.

29. Aicha 2016 interview; Isabella 2016 interview; Nadege 2016 interview; Yusra 2016 interview.

30. Leland 2017.

31. Office of the Bronx District Attorney, Darcel D. Clark 2016.

32. Chauhan and Kois 2012.

33. Sharkey 2017.

34. E. Torres 2015 interview.

35. Celona 2015.

36. The Garifuna are an Afro-Caribbean people from coastal regions of Central America who have a distinct language and cultural traditions.

37. Pace 2002.

38. Sanabria 2017 interview.

39. For many years, each member of the state legislature had funds—so-called member items—they could distribute to community groups to run programs in their area. The amount of the funds varied from member to member. The total distributed in fiscal year 1989–90 was over $13 million. These grants have generally been eliminated.

40. Rubel 1997.

41. M. Torres 2016 interview.

42. Chidren's Aid Society 2017.

43. Turner 2016 interview.

44. Vázquez 2015 interview.

45. Tibbets 2016 interview.

46. Smart 2016 interview.

47. Lewis 2016 interview.

48. Rivera 2016 interview.

49. Aduna 2016 interview.

50. Manny 2016 interview.

51. NYC Department of City Planning 2017.

52. NYC Economic Development Corporation 2016; Crean 2015; Kane and Crespo 2016.

53. Strelnick 2016 interview.
54. Lipson 2015 interview.
55. Biberman 2017 interview.
56. Smalls 1997; E. Gonzalez 2004: 143.
57. Ferrer 2016 interview.

CHAPTER SEVEN. MANY FACES OF SUCCESS:
2000–2018

Epigraphs: Manny 2016 interview; Suso 2017 interview; Sanabria 2017 interview; M. Torres 2016 interview; Shuffler 2016 interview; Montaño 2017 interview; Wright 2017 interview; Velázquez 2015 interview.
1. DiNapoli 2013a.
2. Shuffler 2016 interview.
3. DeKadt 2011.
4. Díaz 2016.
5. Stewart 1999; Martinez 2000.
6. Cox 2016 interview.
7. Shuffler 2016 interview.
8. Valencia 2016.
9. Waterfront Alliance 2017.
10. Lipson 2015 interview.
11. Robbins 2015; Hispanic Research Inc. 2014; Block 2009.
12. Sanger-Katz 2016; Alcorn 2012; Strelnick 2016 interview.
13. Strelnick 2016 interview.
14. LaMantia 2015.
15. Vázquez 2015 interview.
16. New York Times Editorial Board 2014.
17. Montaño 2017 interview.
18. Algar 2016; Breslow 2012.
19. Wright 2017 interview.
20. Lahey 2014.
21. Goldstein 2016.
22. Doyle 2016 interview.
23. M. Torres 2016 interview. Also see Whitehead 2012.
24. Speller 2015 interview.
25. Wright 2017 interview.
26. Shaw 2016 interview.
27. Badger 2015b.
28. Alston 2017; Semuels 2016; Ehrenfreund 2016; Moore 2017; Gordon 2016; Edin and Shaefer 2016.

29. Powell 2016.
30. Williams 2006; Hu 2006; Dwyer 2009; Gonen 2018.
31. New York City Bar 2010; Hauser 2017.
32. Brown 2009.
33. New York City Bar 2010; Egbert 2009.
34. Fairbanks 2017 interview. Also see Warerkar 2017.
35. NYC Parks 2017.
36. Murray 2014.
37. Inside Philanthropy 2017.
38. Akhtar 2017.
39. Sanabria 2017 interview.
40. Suso 2017 interview.
41. Sanabria 2017 interview.
42. Shaw 2016 interview.
43. Manny 2016 interview.
44. Acevedo 2016 interview.
45. Manny 2016 interview.
46. Beekman 2011; Mallozzi 2015.
47. Secret 2011.
48. Carrión 2016 interview.

CHAPTER EIGHT. "THE BRONX WAS THE LAST PLACE": REFLECTIONS ON DISPLACEMENT AND GENTRIFICATION

Epigraphs: Martínez 2017 interview; M. Torres 2016 interview; Aguado 2015 interview.
1. Lightfeldt 2015.
2. Zimmer 2016.
3. Regional Plan Association 2017.
4. Plitt 2015.
5. Flores 2016 interview.
6. Hu 2015; Rivlin-Nadler 2017; Maurer 2017.
7. Weiss 2018; Conde 2018.
8. Hu 2013; Jacobs 2015.
9. Bakalar 2017.
10. Mychal Johnson 2017 interview.
11. Empire State Development 2016.
12. Montaño 2017 interview.
13. Lightfeldt 2015.
14. Census reporter 2016a, 2016b.

15. Kenisa 2017 interview.
16. Barker 2018.
17. Sen and Gates 2018.
18. Bagli 2017.
19. NYC Department of Housing Preservation and Development 2017.
20. Cusano 2016.
21. DeRienzo 2017.
22. Christian 2016 interview.
23. Vázquez 2015 interview.
24. Bronx Photo League 2016.
25. Savitch-Lew 2017.
26. Doyle 2016 interview.
27. Savitch-Lew 2017.
28. Hughes 2017.
29. Commercial Observer Editors 2015.
30. Egbert 2008.
31. Dominus 2008.
32. Samtani 2013.
33. Geiger 2014.
34. Souccar 2017.
35. Furman Center 2016; Roberts 2011.
36. Lewis 2017.
37. Newman and Wyly 2006.
38. Stewart 2017b.
39. NYC Office of Civil Justice 2016; Pastor 2015.
40. NYC Department of Homeless Services 2017.
41. Institute for Children, Poverty, and Homelessness 2017.
42. Stewart 2018.
43. Serpas 2016.
44. City-Data.com 2016.
45. Knafo 2015.
46. Regional Plan Association 2017.
47. Fayyad 2017.
48. Bloom 2015; Harris 2015.
49. NYC Housing Authority 2017.
50. Ferré-Sadurní and Goodman 2018.
51. Furman Center 2016.
52. Frey 2015 interview.
53. CASA 2017.
54. Cintron 2017 interview.
55. Khawaja 2017.
56. New York Times 2017.

57. Magistro 2017 interview.
58. Doyle 2016 interview.
59. Biberman 2017 interview.
60. NYC Office of Civil Justice 2016.
61. Wills 2013.
62. Murphy 2017.
63. Tobias 2017.
64. CASA 2017.
65. Christian 2016 interview.
66. Goodman 2016.
67. Brenzel 2017.
68. Frey 2015 interview.
69. Mays 2018.
70. Mychal Johnson 2017 interview.
71. M. Torres 2016 interview.

CHAPTER NINE. LESSONS LEARNED

1. Gibson 2017 interview.
2. Fermino 2016.
3. Pastor 2017.
4. Martínez 2017 interview.
5. Pareles 2006.
6. Fordham University 2018.
7. Aguado 2015 interview.
8. Russonello 2017.
9. Hostos Center for the Arts and Culture 2018.
10. Davis 2016 interview.

Interviews

All interviews were conducted by the author.

Acevedo, Ralph, 2016 (June 10)
Acosta, José, and Leticia Acosta, 2016 (November 28)
Aduna, Ata, 2016 (March 14)
Aguado, Bill, 2015 (December 11)
Aicha, 2016 (October 26)
Amadeo, Miguel, 2017 (February 22)
Auwarter, Scott, 2016 (September 6)
Biberman, Nancy, 2017 (February 16)
Butos, Isabel, 2016 (August 12)
Cabrera, Elba, 2015 (October 6)
Canada, Joan, 2017 (February 7)
Carrión, Gladys, 2016 (October 20)
Casari, William, 2016 (December 19)
Christian, Fitzroy, 2016 (April 8)
Cintron, Marlene, 2017 (September 13)
Conzo, Joe, Jr., 2018 (May 18)
Cordova, Carmen, 2015 (June 5)
Cox, Linda, 2016 (December 15)

Cruz, Nicolas, 2016 (August 10)
Davis, Joyce, 2016 (January 5)
DeRienzo, Harry, 2015 (June 3)
Downes, Toni, 2014 (April 3)
Doyle, Jack, 2016 (November 5)
Echevarria, Gladys, 2015 (June 10)
Fairbanks, James, 2017 (November 1)
Ferrer, Fernando (Freddy), 2016 (July 25)
Flores, Ricky, 2016 (February 26)
Freilich, Stan, 2015 (May 19)
Frey, William, 2015 (December 24)
Gainey, Susan, 2017 (August 2)
Gibson, Vanessa, 2017 (September 15)
Goldman, Kathy, 2016 (October 14)
Gómez, David, 2015 (January 3)
Green, Marshall, 2016 (September 7)
Greene, Aurelia, 2016 (November 30)
Howell, Dorothy, 2015 (June 10)
Isabella, 2016 (October 26)

Johnson, Marion Streater, 2017 (February 6)

Johnson, Mychal, 2017 (September 17)

Juana, 2016 (October 19)

Kabba, 2016 (March 15)

Karanja, Kamau, 2015 (September 24)

Karim, Bibi, 2016 (September 22)

Kelley, Damyn, 2015 (September 15)

Kenisa, 2017 (April 7)

Levin, Nicole, 2015 (September 17)

Lewis, Lauret, 2016 (August 12)

Lipson, Paul, 2015 (December 22)

Luongo, Rosalina, 2015 (June 16)

Magistro, Peter, 2017 (March 6)

Manny, 2016 (September 30)

Margarita, 2016 (October 19)

Martínez, Elena, 2017 (February 4)

Melendez, Miguel (Mickey), 2017 (September 22)

Montaño, Jeniffer, 2017 (May 9)

Moyer, Peter, 2016 (October 4)

Nadege, 2016 (October 26)

Naison, Mark, 2015 (June 17)

Oliva, Eugene, 2015 (May 25)

Ortiz, Sotero (BG183), 2016 (September 29)

Pelzer, Carolyn, 2016 (September 2)

Pérez, Norma, 2016 (May 18)

Reyes, Joseph, 2016 (October 4)

Rivera, Divina, 2015 (June 16)

Rodríguez, Irma, 2015 (April 30)

Sanabria, Bobby, 2017 (February 7)

Sanchez, John, 2016 (September 22)

Seltzer, Michael, 2016 (January 18)

Shaw, Deon, 2016 (November 28)

Sheehan, Mary, 2014 (May 13)

Shuffler, David, 2016 (December 12)

Silverman, Marcella, 2016 (August 16)

Smart, Solomon, 2016 (August 12)

Smith, Jean, 2015 (April 30)

Smith, Sallie, 2015 (June 18)

Soto, Eric, 2015 (June 23)

Speller, Kathryn, 2015 (May 28)

Spitzer, Julie Belizaire, 2016 (March 1)

Strelnick, Hal, 2016 (November 21)

Suso, Muhamadou Salieu, 2017 (February 19)

Tibbets, Jeanne, 2016 (October 18)

Torres, Eileen, 2015 (August 18)

Torres, Maria, 2016 (February 18)

Turner, Johnicka, 2016 (September 27)

Vázquez, Vivian, 2015 (March 31)

Vega-Rivera, Carmen, 2016 (March 11)

Velázquez, Guillerma, 2015 (November 7)

Velez, Domitilo, 2016 (August 12)

Washington, 2016 (October 18)

Weed, John, 2016 (August 19)

Weintraub, Leta, 2014 (March 31)

Wright, Donnisha, 2017 (February 23)

Yusra, 2016 (October 26)

Zehnder, Linda, 2016 (December 12)

Bibliography

Akhtar, Allana. 2017. "How Cardi B Escaped Poverty to Become the First Female Rapper in 19 Years to Top the Charts." *Time,* September 27. Accessed February 18, 2018. http://time.com/money/4959065/how-cardi-b-escaped-poverty-to-become-the-first-female-rapper-in-19-years-to-top-the-charts/.

Alcorn, Ted. 2012. "Redefining Public Health in New York City." *The Lancet,* June 2. Accessed December 8, 2017. http://www.thelancet.com/journals/lancet/article/PIIS0140–6736%2812%2960879–4/fulltext.

Alda, Arlene. 2015. *Just Kids from the Bronx.* New York: Henry Holt.

Algar, Selim. 2016. "These Neighborhoods Have the Best HS Graduation Rates." *New York Post,* May 11. Accessed December 8, 2017. https://nypost.com/2016/05/11/these-neighborhoods-have-the-best-hs-graduation-rates/.

Alston, Philip. 2017. "Statement on Visit to the USA, by Professor Philip Alston, United Nations Special Rapporteur on Extreme Poverty and Human Rights." United Nations Human Rights Office of the High Commissioner, December 15. Accessed January 26, 2018. http://www.ohchr.org/EN/NewsEvents/Pages/DisplayNews.aspx?NewsID=22533&LangID=E.

American Jewish Congress. 1967. "The Grand Concourse, Promise and Challenge: A Study of Social and Physical Conditions in the Grand Concourse Area of the Bronx with Recommendations for Community Action." American Jewish Congress, Commission on Community Relations, New York. Unpublished neighborhood study.

Aronczyk, Amanda. 2014. "The Revolutionaries Who Rescued a Hospital."
    WNYC, June 2. Accessed November 24, 2017. http://www.wnyc.org/story
    /lab-coat-afro-and-shades-taking-lincoln-hospital/.
Badger, Emily. 2015a. "Redlining: Still a Thing." *Washington Post,* May 28.
    Accessed November 19, 2017. https://www.washingtonpost.com/news/wonk
    /wp/2015/05/28/evidence-that-banks-still-deny-black-borrowers-just-
    as-they-did-50-years-ago/?utm_term=.9a693e57e56a.
———. 2015b. "When Work Isn't Enough to Keep You Off Welfare and Food
    Stamps." *Washington Post,* April 14. Accessed December 8, 2017. https://www
    .washingtonpost.com/news/wonk/wp/2015/04/14/when-work-isnt-enough-
    to-keep-you-off-welfare-and-food-stamps/?utm_term=.648d0b16bf7d.
———. 2017. "The Unsung Role That Ordinary Citizens Played in the Great
    Crime Decline." *New York Times,* November 8. Accessed December 1, 2017.
    https://www.nytimes.com/2017/11/09/upshot/the-unsung-role-that-ordinary-
    citizens-played-in-the-great-crime-decline.html?_r=0.
Badger, Emily, Claire Cain Miller, Adam Pearce, and Kevin Quealy. 2018.
    "Extensive Data Shows Punishing Reach of Racism for Black Boys." *New
    York Times,* March 19. Accessed March 19, 2018. https://www.nytimes.com
    /interactive/2018/03/19/upshot/race-class-white-and-black-men.html.
Bady, David. n.d. "Andrew Freedman Home for Men and Women." Lehman
    College. Accessed November 27, 2017. http://www.lehman.edu/vpadvance
    /artgallery/arch/buildings/freedman.html.
Bagli, Charles V. 2017. "New York Secures the Most Affordable Housing Units in
    27 Years." *New York Times,* January 11. Accessed December 9, 2017. https://
    www.nytimes.com/2017/01/11/nyregion/de-blasio-affordable-housing
    .html?_r=0.
Bakalar, Nicholas. 2017. "Air Pollution May Harm Babies Even Before They Are
    Born." *New York Times,* December 5. Accessed May 27, 2018. https://www
    .nytimes.com/2017/12/05/well/family/air-pollution-may-harm-babies-even-
    before-they-are-born.html.
Banana Kelly Community Improvement Association. 2017. "Banana Kelly
    History." Accessed November 25, 2017. http://www.bkcianyc.org/history/#.
    Whok5LaZPVo.
Barker, Kim. 2018. "The Eviction Machine Churning through New York City."
    New York Times, May 20. Accessed May 20, 2019. https://www.nytimes
    .com/interactive/2018/05/20/nyregion/nyc-affordable-housing.html.
Basler, Barbara. 1986. "Bronx Shelter to Close; Hazards Cited by State." *New
    York Times,* May 9. Accessed November 27, 2017. http://www.nytimes
    .com/1986/05/09/nyregion/bronx-shelter-to-close-hazards-cited-by-state
    .html.
Baum, Dan. 2016. "Legalize It All." *Harpers,* April. Accessed May 28, 2018.
    https://harpers.org/archive/2016/04/legalize-it-all/.

BBC. 1972. "Man Alive: The Bronx Is Burning FDNY (Complete) 1972."
    YouTube. Accessed November 18, 2017. https://www.youtube.com/watch?v=
    ygF3NJvy3bY.

Beekman, Daniel. 2011. "Boxer Gets Help off Mat, into Apartment." *New York
    Daily News,* April 16. Accessed December 10, 2017. http://www.nydailynews
    .com/new-york/champion-boxer-iran-barkley-ropes-homelessness-nonprofit-
    article-1.114693.

Biography.org. 2016. "Eddie Palmieri Biography: Songwriter, Pianist (1936–)."
    Accessed March 5, 2018. https://www.biography.com/people/eddie-palmieri-
    402802.

Bird, David. 1976. "Why the Fight for 'Deplorable' Fordham Hospital." *New York
    Times,* April 23. Accessed November 25, 2017. http://www.nytimes.com
    /1976/04/23/archives/why-the-fight-for-deplorable-fordham-hospital.html.

BlackPast. n.d. "The Great Migration 1915–1960." Accessed November 16, 2017.
    http://www.blackpast.org/aah/great-migration-1915–1960.

Blad, Evie. 2017. "Teachers' Lower Expectations for Black Students May Become
    'Self-Fulfilling Prophecies,' Study Finds." *Education Week,* October 24.
    Accessed March 22, 2018. http://blogs.edweek.org/edweek/rulesforengagement
    /2017/10/teachers_lower_expectations_for_black_students_may_become_
    self-fulfilling_prophecies_researchers_say.html.

Block, Dorian. 2009. "Census Says African, Hispanic Immigrants Flocking to
    Bronx Boro." *New York Daily News,* February 3. Accessed November 27,
    2017. http://www.nydailynews.com/new-york/bronx/census-african-hispanic-
    immigrants-flocking-bronx-boro-article-1.388678.

Bloom, Ester. 2015. "When Neighborhoods Gentrify, Why Aren't Their Public
    Schools Improving?" *The Atlantic,* October 7. Accessed December 10, 2017.
    https://www.theatlantic.com/business/archive/2015/10/gentrification-
    schools/408568/.

Blumenthal, Ralph. 2002. "Recalling New York at the Brink of Bankruptcy."
    New York Times, December 5. Accessed November 17, 2017. http://www
    .nytimes.com/2002/12/05/nyregion/recalling-new-york-at-the-brink-of-
    bankruptcy.html.

Bob Herbert's Op-Ed TV. 2018. "Bob Herbert's Op-Ed TV: Why Do So Many
    African Students Call CUNY's Bronx Community College Home?" *CUNY
    TV,* April 23. Accessed May 18, 2018. http://www.cuny.tv/show/opedtv
    /PR2007219.

Bouie, Jamelle. 2015. "A Tax on Blackness: Racism Is Still Rampant in Real
    Estate." *Slate,* May 13. Accessed November 19, 2017. http://www.slate.com
    /articles/news_and_politics/politics/2015/05/racism_in_real_estate_land-
    lords_redlining_housing_values_and_discrimination.html.

Brenzel, Kathryn. 2017. "De Blasio Changes Housing Goals at the Expense of
    the Middle Class: City Adds New Requirements for Developers Receiving

Certain Subsidies." *The Real Deal,* July 25. Accessed December 10, 2017. https://therealdeal.com/2017/07/25/de-blasio-changes-housing-goals-at -the-expense-of-the-middle-class/.

Breslow, Jason. 2012. "Dropout Nation by the Numbers: Dropping Out of High School." *PBS,* September 12. Accessed December 8, 2017. https://www.pbs .org/wgbh/frontline/article/by-the-numbers-dropping-out-of-high-school/.

Brody, Jane E. 2017. "Feeding Young Minds: The Importance of School Lunches." *New York Times,* June 5. Accessed December 15, 2017. https:// www.nytimes.com/2017/06/05/well/feeding-young-minds-the-importance-of-school-lunches.html?_r=0.

Bronx Center Steering Committee. 1993. "The Bronx Center: A Report to Bronx Borough President Fernando Ferrer from the Bronx Center Steering Committee." Unpublished planning report.

Bronx Community College. n.d. Bronx Community College website. Accessed November 24, 2017. https://www.bcc.cuny.edu.

Bronx Museum of the Arts. 2017. "Bronx Museum of the Arts: History." Accessed November 26, 2017. http://www.bronxmuseum.org/about/.

Bronx Photo League. 2016. *Jerome Ave.* Bronx, NY: Bronx Documentary Center Editions.

Bronx Times. n.d. Census. Accessed November 5, 2017. http://www.bronx.com /census.html.

Brown, Eliot. 2009. "Rezoning Would Transform South Bronx Swath Near Yankee Stadium." *Observer,* February 2. Accessed December 8, 2017. http:// observer.com/2009/02/rezoning-would-transform-south-bronx-swath-near-yankee-stadium/.

Brown, Emma. 2016. "Yale Study Suggests Racial Bias among Preschool Teachers." *Washington Post,* September 27. Accessed March 22, 2018. https://www.washingtonpost.com/news/education/wp/2016/09/27/yale-study-suggests-racial-bias-among-preschool-teachers/?utm_term=.3dfad94a061c.

Caro, Robert. 1975. *The Power Broker: Robert Moses and the Fall of New York.* New York: Vintage Books.

Caro-López, Howard. 2010. "Dominicans in New York City 1990–2008." Center for Latin American, Caribbean and Latino Studies, City University of New York, October. http://clacls.gc.cuny.edu/files/2013/10/Dominicans-in-New-York-City-1990–2008.pdf.

CASA. 2017. "New CASA Report Highlights How Tenants Are Fighting Displacement under the Threat of Rezoning." Community Action for Safe Apartments, May 18. Accessed December 10, 2017. https://casapower.org/?s= white+paper+resisting+displacement.

Celona, Larry. 2015. "Fire Kills 87 People at the Happy Land Social Club in the Bronx in 1990." *New York Daily News,* March 17. Accessed December 1, 2017.

http://www.nydailynews.com/new-york/nyc-crime/dozens-die-fire-illegal-bonx-social-club-1990-article-1.2152091.

Census Reporter. 2016a. "NYC-Bronx Community District 4—Concourse, Highbridge & Mount Eden PUMA, NY." Accessed December 10, 2017. https://censusreporter.org/profiles/79500US3603708-nyc-bronx-community-district-4-concourse-highbridge-mount-eden-puma-ny/.

———. 2016b. "NYC-Bronx Community District 5—Morris Heights, Fordham South & Mount Hope PUMA, NY." Accessed December 10, 2017. https://censusreporter.org/profiles/79500US3603707-nyc-bronx-community-district-5-morris-heights-fordham-south-mount-hope-puma-ny/.

Charyn, Jerome. 2015. *Bitter Bronx: Thirteen Stories.* New York: Liveright.

Chauhan, Preeti, and Lauren Kois. 2012. "Homicide by Neighborhood: Mapping New York City's Violent Crime Drop." Research and Evaluation Center, John Jay College of Criminal Justice, City University of New York. Accessed December 1, 2017. https://johnjayrec.nyc/2012/07/19/rec20122-2/.

Chetty, Raj, Michael Stepner, Sarah Abraham, Shelby Lin, Benjamin Scuderi, Nicholas Turner, Augustin Bergeron, and David Cutler. 2016. "The Association between Income and Life Expectancy in the United States, 2001–2014." *Journal of the American Medical Association,* April 11. Accessed November 12, 2017. https://jamanetwork.com/journals/jama/fullarticle/2513561?guestAccessKey=4023ce75-d0fb-44de-bb6c-8a10a30a6173.

Children's Aid Society. 2017. "Carrera Pregnancy Prevention." Accessed December 3, 2017. http://stopteenpregnancy.childrensaidsociety.org/about-us.

City-Data.com. 2016. "Newburgh, New York (NY) Poverty Rate Data." Accessed December 10, 2017. http://www.city-data.com/poverty/poverty-Newburgh-New-York.html.

City Lore. n.d. "Casita Rincón Criollo." *Place Matters.* Accessed November 26, 2017. http://www.placematters.net/node/1445.

———. n.d. "Hunts Point Palace." *Place Matters.* Accessed November 26, 2017. http://www.placematters.net/node/1243.

College Gridirons. n.d. *Yankee Stadium.* Accessed November 6, 2017. http://www.collegegridirons.com/bowlstadiums/YankeeStadium.htm.

Commercial Observer Editors. 2015. "5 Reasons We Love the Bronx." *Commercial Observer,* August 15. Accessed December 10, 2017. https://commercial-observer.com/2015/08/5-reasons-we-love-the-bronx/.

Conde, Ed Garcia. 2018. "Developers behind the 'Piano District' Sell Their Waterfront Property for $165 Million; Highest Sale for Development Site in Bronx History." *Welcome 2 The Bronx,* April 4. Accessed April 16, 2018. https://www.welcome2thebronx.com/2018/04/04/developers-behind-piano-district-sell-waterfront-property-165-million-highest-sale-development-site-bronx-history/.

Crean, Sarah. 2015. "The Bronx Is Breathing." *New York Environment Report,* February 25. Accessed December 5, 2017. http://www.nyenvironmentreport .com/the-bronx-is-breathing/.

Cusano, Arthur. 2016. "Jerome Ave. Rezoning to Enable Taller Buildings, More Residential Housing." *Bronx Times,* September 10. Accessed December 9, 2017. https://www.bxtimes.com/stories/2016/37/37-jerome-2016–09–09-bx.html.

da Costa Nunez, Ralph, and Ethan G. Sribnick. 2013. *The Poor among Us: A History of Family Poverty and Homelessness in New York City.* New York: White Tiger Press.

DeKadt, Maarten. 2011. *The Bronx River: An Environmental and Social History.* New York: History Press and Arcadia.

DelReal, Jose A. 2017. "Ben Carson Calls Poverty 'a State of Mind' during Interview." *Washington Post,* May 24. Accessed December 8, 2017. https:// www.washingtonpost.com/news/post-politics/wp/2017/05/24/ben-carson-calls-poverty-a-state-of-mind-during-interview/?utm_term=.5326d8defa45.

DeRienzo, Harold. 2008. *The Concept of Community: Lessons from the Bronx.* Milan, Italy: IPOC di Pietro Condemi.

———. 2017. "CityViews: Is It Time for a Housing Plan Reset?" *City Limits,* April 5. Accessed December 9, 2017. https://citylimits.org/2017/04/05/ cityviews-is-it-time-for-a-housing-plan-reset/.

Díaz, Rubén, Jr., 2016. Speech at Bronx River Alliance ribbon cutting for new foot bridge over the river (October 6).

Dillon, Sam. 1995. "Alternative Schools; Friction over Experimental Schools." *New York Times,* May 25. Accessed November 29, 2017. http://www.nytimes .com/1995/05/25/nyregion/alternative-schools-friction-over-experimental-schools.html?pagewanted=all.

DiNapoli, Thomas P. 2013a. "An Economic Snapshot of the Bronx." *New York State Controller,* July. Accessed March 23, 2018. https://www.osc.state.ny.us /osdc/rpt4–2014.pdf.

———. 2013b. "The Role of Immigrants in the New York City Economy." *Office of New York State Controller,* November. Accessed November 27, 2017. https://www.osc.state.ny.us/osdc/rpt8–2014_eng.pdf.

Dominus, Susan. 2008. "Big Visions for Building Don't Include People Inside." *New York Times,* March 10. Accessed May 26, 2018.

Dreier, Peter. 2011. "Reagan's Real Legacy." *The Nation,* February 4. https:// www.thenation.com/article/reagans-real-legacy/.

Dunlap, David. 1982. "'Red Caps' Fighting Arson in the Northwest Bronx." *New York Times,* July 19. Accessed November 27, 2017. http://www.nytimes.com /1984/01/09/nyregion/red-caps-fighting-arson-in-the-northwest-bronx.html.

Dwyer, Jim. 2009. "A New Yankee Stadium, the Same Old Politics." *New York Times,* January 13. Accessed December 8, 2017. http://www.nytimes.com /2009/01/14/nyregion/14about.html.

Edin, Kathryn J., and H. Luke Shaefer. 2016. *$2.00 a Day: Living on Almost Nothing in America*. Boston: Houghton Mifflin Harcourt.

Egbert, Bill. 2007. "Bronx Organization Leader Hangs It Up." *New York Daily News,* December 17. Accessed November 25, 2017. http://www.nydailynews .com/new-york/bronx/bronx-organization-leader-hangs-article-1.274993.

———. 2008. "Bank Note (Lots of 'Em) in Big Sale." *New York Daily News,* January 28. Accessed December 10, 2017. http://www.nydailynews.com /new-york/bronx/historic-building-fetches-32-million-article-1.339962.

———. 2009. "Job-Training Funds Diverted." *New York Daily News,* July 14. Accessed December 8, 2017. http://www.nydailynews.com/new-york/bronx /job-training-funds-diverted-robbing-peter-pay-paul-source-article-1.426741.

Ehrenfreund, Max. 2016. "How welfare reform changed American poverty, in 9 charts." *Washington Post,* August 22. Accessed December 8, 2107. https:// www.washingtonpost.com/news/wonk/wp/2016/08/22/the-enduring- legacy-of-welfare-reform-20-years-later/?utm_term=.013487a89d5a.

Ellison, Katherine. 2015. "Being Honest about the Pygmalion Effect." *Discover Magazine,* October 29. Accessed March 21, 2018. http://discovermagazine .com/2015/dec/14-great-expectations.

Empire State Development. 2016. "Annual Report on the State of Small Businesses 2016." Accessed February 24, 2018. https://cdn.esd.ny.gov/Reports /2016_2017/2016_ESD_ANNUAL_REPORT_SMALL_BUSINESS.pdf.

Evans, Howie. 2015. Interview with the Bronx African American History Project. BAAHP Ditigal Archive at Fordham University, October 1. https://fordham .bepress.com/cgi/viewcontent.cgi?article=1198&context=baahp_oralhist.

Fayyad, Abdallah. 2017. "The Criminalization of Gentrifying Neighborhoods." *The Atlantic,* December 20. Accessed December 20, 2017. https://www .theatlantic.com/politics/archive/2017/12/the-criminalization-of-gentrifying- neighborhoods/548837/.

Fermino, Jennifer. 2016. "Bronx Street Renamed to Honor Birth of Hip Hop." *New York Daily News,* February 25. Accessed December 11, 2017. http:// www.nydailynews.com/new-york/bronx-street-renamed-honor-birth-hip-hop- article-1.2544125.

Fernandez, Manny. 2006. "Morrisania Melody." *New York Times,* April 30. Accessed October 30, 2018. https://www.nytimes.com/2006/04/30 /nyregion/thecity/morrisania-melody.html.

Ferré-Sadurní, Luis, and J. David Goodman. 2018. "New York Public Housing Set to Get Federal Monitor and $1 Billion in Repairs." *New York Times,* May 31. Accessed June 15, 2018. https://www.nytimes.com/2018/05/31/nyregion /nycha-federal-monitor-repairs.html.

Finder, Alan. 1990. "When Welfare Pays the Rent." *New York Times,* June 3. Accessed November 27, 2017. http://www.nytimes.com/1990/06/03 /weekinreview/the-region-when-welfare-pays-the-rent.html.

Fiscal Policy Institute. 2011. "Immigrant Small Businesses in New York City." October 3. Accessed February 24, 2018. http://www.fiscalpolicy.org/FPI_ ImmigrantSmallBusinessesNYC_20111003.pdf.

Flood, Joe. 2010a. *The Fires: How a Computer Formula, Big Ideas, and the Best of Intentions Burned Down New York City—and Determined the Future of American Cities.* New York: Riverhead Books.

———. 2010b. "Why the Bronx Burned." *New York Post,* May 16. Accessed November 17, 2017. https://nypost.com/2010/05/16/why-the-bronx-burned/.

Florida, Richard. 2015. "America's Leading Immigrant Cities: Trump Has It Backwards—Large Immigrant Populations Boost Rather Than Hurt U.S. Metros." *CityLab,* September 22. Accessed March 30, 2018. https://www .citylab.com/equity/2015/09/americas-leading-immigrant-cities/406438/.

Fordham University. 2018. Bronx African American History Project: Oral Histories. http://fordham.bepress.com/baahp_oralhist/.

Freudenberg, Nicholas. 2006. "The Impact of New York City's 1975 Fiscal Crisis on the Tuberculosis, HIV, and Homicide Syndemic." National Institutes of Health, March. Accessed November 18, 2017. https://www.ncbi.nlm.nih.gov /pmc/articles/PMC1470515/.

Furman Center. 2006. "Housing Policy in New York City: A Brief History, Working Paper 0 6_0 1." Furman Center for Real Estate and Urban Policy, NYU School of Law. Accessed November 26, 2017. http://furmancenter.org /files/publications/AHistoryofHousingPolicycombined0601_000.pdf.

———. 2016. "The Location of New York City's Expiring Affordable Housing." Furman Center for Real Estate and Urban Policy, NYU School of Law, December 8. Accessed March 29, 2018. http://furmancenter.org/thestoop /entry/coredata-visualization-mapping-expiring-affordable-housing-in-new-york-city.

———. 2017. "Directory of New York City Affordable Housing Programs." Furman Center for Real Estate and Urban Policy, NYU School of Law. Accessed November 26, 2017. http://furmancenter.org/institute/directory/.

Garcia, Sandra E. 2011. "Rich History of Hunts Point." *Bronx Journal,* December 12. Accessed November 14, 2017. http://bronxjournal.com/2011 /12/the-rich-history-of-hunts-point/.

Gardner, Todd. 2013. "The Racial and Ethnic Composition of Local Government Employees in Large Metropolitian Areas, 1960–2010." U.S. Census Bureau, August. Accessed November 16, 2017. https://www2.census.gov/ces /wp/2013/CES-WP-13–38.pdf.

Gates, Henry Louis, Jr. 2013. "African Americans: Many Rivers to Cross." *PBS,* October 3. Accessed November 17, 2017. http://www.pbs.org/black-culture /shows/list/african-american-history-many-rivers-to-cross/.

Geiger, Daniel. 2014. "Architecturally Notable Bronx Building Sold for $114M: A Pair of Firms Snapping Up Outerborough Office Properties Has Struck

Again, Buying the Landmarked Bank Note Building." *Crain's New York Business,* September 15. Accessed December 10, 2017. https://www.crainsnewyork.com/node/139236/printable/print.

Gladstone, Valerie. 2017. "Valerie Capers Hears All." *New York Sun,* August 31. Accessed February 15, 2018. https://www.nysun.com/arts/valerie-capers-hears-all/61720/.

Glantz, Aaron, and Emmanuel Martinez. 2018. "Modern-Day Redlining: How Banks Block People of Color from Homeownership." *Chicago Tribune,* February 17. Accessed March 10, 2018. http://www.chicagotribune.com/business/ct-biz-modern-day-redlining-20180215-story.html.

Goldberger, Paul. 1979. "Exhibit on South Bronx Weaves a Complex Web." *New York Times,* November 30. Accessed November 26, 2017. http://www.nytimes.com/1979/11/30/archives/exhibit-on-south-bronx-weaves-a-complex-web-an-appraisal.html?_r=0.

Goldstein, Dana. 2016. "Bill de Blasio's Pre-K Crusade." *The Atlantic,* September 7. Accessed March 23, 2018. https://www.theatlantic.com/education/archive/2016/09/bill-de-blasios-prek-crusade/498830/.

Gonen, Yoav. 2018. "Firm Owes City $100M for Flopped Yankee Stadium Parking Lots." *New York Post,* October 25. Accessed November 6, 2018. https://nypost.com/2018/10/25/firm-owes-city-100m-for-flopped-yankee-stadium-parking-lots/.

Gonzalez, David. 2009. "Play Street Becomes a Sanctuary." *New York Times,* July 31. Accessed December 10, 2017. http://www.nytimes.com/2009/08/02/nyregion/02ritual.html.

———. 2013. "For Decades, Fighting to Rescue a Bronx Park From Disrepair." *New York Times,* August 4. Accessed November 27, 2017. http://www.nytimes.com/2013/08/05/nyregion/for-decades-fighting-to-rescue-a-bronx-park-from-disrepair.html.

———. 2017. "Benjy Melendez's Legacy: Peace and Hope in the Bronx." *New York Times,* June 4. Accessed November 24, 2017. https://www.nytimes.com/2017/06/04/nyregion/benjy-melendez-bronx.html?_r=0.

Gonzalez, Evelyn. 2004. *The Bronx.* New York: Columbia University Press.

Gonzalez, Juan. 1995. "Lincoln Emancipation Hosp Takeover in '70 Made Medical History." *New York Daily News,* July 18. Accessed November 24, 2017. http://www.nydailynews.com/archives/news/lincoln-emancipation-hosp-takeover-70-made-medical-history-article-1.702378.

Goodman, J. David. 2017. "De Blasio Expands Affordable Housing, but Results Aren't Always Visible." *New York Times,* October 5. Accessed November 14, 2017. https://www.nytimes.com/2017/10/05/nyregion/de-blasio-affordable-housing-new-york-city.html.

———. 2016. "New York Passes Rent Rules to Blunt Gentrification." *New York Times,* March 22. Accessed March 30, 2016. https://www.nytimes

.com/2016/03/23/nyregion/new-york-council-passes-zoning-changes-de-blasio-sought.html.

Gordon, Leslie. 2016. "New Study of Welfare Family Caps Emboldens Anti-Poverty Advocates." *BerkeleyLaw Alumni News,* November 7. Accessed December 8, 2017. https://www.law.berkeley.edu/article/new-study-welfare-family-caps-emboldens-anti-poverty-advocates/.

Hall, Delaney. 2014. "Was the 1977 New York City Blackout a Catalyst for Hip-Hop's Growth?" *Slate,* October 16. Accessed June 13, 2018. http://www.slate.com/blogs/the_eye/2014/10/16/roman_mars_99_percent_invisible_was_the_1977_nyc_wide_blackout_a_catalyst.html.

Hanson, Avis. 2004. Interview 1 with the Bronx African American History Project, June 24. BAAHP Digital Archive at Fordham University. https://fordham.bepress.com/baahp_oralhist/95/.

Harris, Elizabeth. 2015. "School Segregation Persists in Gentrifying Neighborhoods, Maps Suggest." *New York Times,* December 16. Accessed May 28, 2018. https://www.nytimes.com/2015/12/16/nyregion/school-segregation-persists-in-gentrifying-neighborhoodsmaps-suggest.html.

Hauser, Micah. 2017. "Yankee Charity Neglects Its Stadium's Neighbors." *New York Times,* June 26. Accessed October 26, 2018. https://www.nytimes.com/2017/06/27/sports/baseball/yankee-stadium-charity.html.

Hill, Emita Brady. 2014. *Bronx Faces and Voices: Sixteen Stories of Courage and Community.* Lubbock: Texas Tech University Press.

Hispanic Research Inc. 2014. "A Closer Look at the Largest Hispanic City: New York." Accessed December 7, 2017. http://www.hispanicresearch.com/index.php/hispanic-market-data/hispanic-market-profile-and-demographics/112-a-closer-look-at-the-largest-hispanic-city-new-york.

Hostos Center for the Arts and Culture. 2018. "Bobby Sanabria and the MultiVerse Big Band Performing WEST SIDE STORY: Reimagined." Accessed March 26, 2018. https://www.hostos.cuny.edu/culturearts/geninfo/Press%20Release/02%2022%2018%20BOBBY%20SANABRIA%20MULTIVERSE.pdf.

Hostos Community College. n.d. "Hostos Community College History." Accessed November 24, 2017. http://www.hostos.cuny.edu/About-Hostos/The-History-of-Hostos.

Hu, Winnie. 2006. "Yankees Win as Council Approves Stadium." *New York Times,* April 6. Accessed December 8, 2017. http://www.nytimes.com/2006/04/06/nyregion/yankees-win-as-council-approves-stadium.html.

———. 2013. "Residents Sue FreshDirect over Move to the Bronx." *New York Times,* March 4. Accessed December 10, 2017. http://www.nytimes.com/2013/03/05/nyregion/residents-sue-freshdirect-over-move-to-the-bronx.html.

———. 2015. "Bronx Pop-Up Art Show Prompts Criticism That It Invoked Borough's Painful Past." *New York Times,* November 6. Accessed December

10, 2017. https://www.nytimes.com/2015/11/07/nyregion/bronx-pop-art-show-prompts-criticism-that-it-invoked-boroughs-painful-past.html.

Hughes, C. J. 2017. "The Bronx Is Building." *New York Times,* March 3. Accessed December 23, 2017. https://www.nytimes.com/2017/03/03/realestate/the-bronx-is-building.html.

Inside Philanthropy. 2017. "Jennifer Lopez." May 2. Accessed May 28, 2018. https://www.insidephilanthropy.com/glitzy-giving/jennifer-lopez.html.

Institute for Children, Poverty, and Homelessness. 2017. "On the Map: The Atlas of Student Homelessness in New York City 2017." Accessed December 10, 2017. http://www.icphusa.org/new_york_city/map-atlas-student-homelessness-new-york-city-2017/.

Jacobs, Suzanne. 2015. "The South Bronx Isn't Falling for Fresh Direct's Dirty Trucks." *Grist,* March 10. Accessed December 10, 2017. http://grist.org/cities/the-south-bronx-isnt-falling-for-fresh-directs-dirty-trucks/.

Jenkins, P. Nash. 2014. "Heroin Addiction's Fraught History." *The Atlantic,* February 14. Accessed November 17, 2017. https://www.theatlantic.com/health/archive/2014/02/heroin-addictions-fraught-history/284001/.

Jones, Allen. 2009. *The Rat That Got Away: A Bronx Memoir.* New York: Fordham University Press.

Jonnes, Jill. 2002. *South Bronx Rising: The Rise, Fall, and Resurrection of an American City.* New York: Fordham University Press.

Kane, Daniel, and Marcos Crespo. 2016. "Build the Hunts Point Ramps in the South Bronx." *Crain's New York Business,* March 24. Accessed December 5, 2017. http://www.crainsnewyork.com/article/20160324/OPINION/160329941/op-ed-easy-call-build-the-hunts-point-ramps.

Kaufman, Ed. 1974. "Report to the Greater New York Fund." Unpublished report.

Khawaja, Seher. 2017. "CityViews: An Urgent Need to Address Our City's Human Dignity Crisis." *City Limits,* August 14. Accessed December 10, 2017. https://citylimits.org/2017/08/14/cityviews-an-urgent-need-to-address-our-citys-human-dignity-crisis/.

Knafo, Saki. 2015. "Is Gentrification a Human-Rights Violation?" *The Atlantic,* September 2. Accessed December 10, 2017. https://www.theatlantic.com/business/archive/2015/09/gentrification-brooklyn-human-rights-violation/402460/.

Knight, Christina, and Mark Naison. 2016. "How the Bronx Gave Us Hip Hop." *Thirteen,* November 21. Accessed February 15, 2018. http://www.thirteen.org/blog-post/how-the-bronx-gave-us-hip-hop/.

Kozol, Jonathan. 1995. *Amazing Grace: The Lives of Children and the Conscience of America.* New York: Crown.

Krohn-Hansen, Christian. 2013. *Making New York Dominican: Small Business, Politics and Everyday Life.* Philadelphia: University of Pennsylvania Press.

Lahey, Jessica. 2014. "Poor Kids and the 'Word Gap.'" *The Atlantic*, October 16. Accessed December 8, 2017. https://www.theatlantic.com/education/archive/2014/10/american-kids-are-starving-for-words/381552/.

LaMantia, Jonathan. 2015. "For Six Years Running, Bronx Is the Least-Healthy County in NY State: Poverty, Unemployment and Limited Access to Health Care Plague the Borough's Residents." *Crain's New York Business*, March 25. Accessed March 7, 2018. http://www.crainsnewyork.com/article/20150325/HEALTH_CARE/150329911/for-six-years-running-bronx-is-the-least-healthy-county-in-ny-state.

Lamberg, Carol. 2018. *Neighborhood Success Stories: Creating and Sustaining Affordable Housing in New York*. New York: Fordham University Press.

Landmarks Preservation Commission. 1981. "Sunnyslope." July 28. Accessed November 12, 2017. http://s-media.nyc.gov/agencies/lpc/lp/1079.pdf.

Laspina, Fernando. 2017. *Mis Memorias, Mis Raices*. Bronx, NY: Editorial Fundación.

LeBlanc, Adrian Nicole. 2003. *Random Family: Love, Drugs, Trouble, and Coming of Age in the Bronx*. New York: Scribner.

Leland, John. 2017. "David Dinkins Doesn't Think He Failed. He Might Be Right." *New York Times*, November 10. Accessed December 20, 2017. http://stopteenpregnancy.childrensaidsociety.org/about-us.

Lewis, Cora. 2017. "30% of the Black-Owned Businesses in NY Disappeared." *BuzzFeed News*, May 3. Accessed April 15, 2018. https://www.buzzfeed.com/coralewis/in-5-years-new-york-lost-30-of-its-black-owned-businesses?utm_term=.frNr3yr4az#.vllze7zL9V.

Library of Congress. n.d. "Immigration, Puerto Rican, Cuban Migration to a New Land." Accessed November 16, 2017. https://www.loc.gov/teachers/classroommaterials/presentationsandactivities/presentations/immigration/cuban3.html.

Lightfeldt, Alan. 2015. "Bright Lights, Big Rent Burden: Understanding New York City's Rent Affordability Problem." *Easy Street*, March 1. Accessed December 10, 2017. https://streeteasy.com/blog/new-york-city-rent-affordability/.

Lynn, Frank. 1991. "Freed from Prison, Simon Returns to Bronx and Weeps in Joy." *New York Times*, July 12. Accessed November 29, 2017. http://www.nytimes.com/1991/07/12/nyregion/freed-from-prison-simon-returns-to-bronx-and-weeps-in-joy.html.

Mahler, Jonathan. 2005. *Ladies and Gentlemen, the Bronx Is Burning: 1977, Baseball, Politics and the Battle for the Soul of a City*. New York: Picador.

Mallozzi, Vincent M. 2012. "In Bronx Gym, Man Who Went Astray Leads Youths on Straight Path." *New York Times*, December 22. Accessed November 24, 2017. https://cityroom.blogs.nytimes.com/2012/12/27/with-boxing-man-with-troubled-past-teaches-bronx-youths-a-better-way/.

———. 2015. "Iran Barkley and Pamela Graham: A Boxer Marries His Champ."
New York Times, December 4. Accessed December 10, 2017. https://www
.nytimes.com/2015/12/06/fashion/weddings/iran-barkley-boxer-middle-
weight-champion-marries-pamela-graham.html?_r=0.

Martinez, Jose. 2000. "Bronx River Cleanup: National Guard Raising Cars from
Waterway." *New York Daily News,* August 29. Accessed December 7, 2017.
http://www.nydailynews.com/archives/boroughs/bronx-river-cleanup-national-
guard-raising-cars-waterway-article-1.882191.

Mary Mitchell Family and Youth Center. 2006. "Biography of Astin Jacobo."
Accessed December 9, 2017. http://www.themarymitchellfyc.org/biography_
of_astin_jacobo.htm.

Matthews, Dylan. 2014. "Everything You Need to Know about the War on
Poverty." *Washington Post,* January 8. Accessed November 24, 2017.
https://www.washingtonpost.com/news/wonk/wp/2014/01/08
/everything-you-need-to-know-about-the-war-on-poverty/?utm_term=
.56bba01d601e.

Maurer, Mark. 2017. "Chetrit, Somerset Seeking $500M Loan for Bronx
Megaproject Financing Would Be among Largest Ever for Private Resi
Development in the Borough." *The Real Deal,* March 30. Accessed December
10, 2017. https://therealdeal.com/2017/03/30/chetrit-somerset-seeking-
500m-loan-for-bronx-megaproject/.

Mays, Jeffery C. 2018. "More Housing for New York's Homeless? Council Will
Weigh Question Mayor Ignored at His Gym." *New York Times,* October 30.
Accessed November 3, 2018. https://www.nytimes.com/2018/10/30/nyregion
/homeless-nyc-mayor-city-council.html

McFadden, Robert D. 1975. "40 Blazes Erupt in South Bronx Area." *New York
Times,* June 3. Accessed November 19, 2017. http://www.nytimes.com/1975
/06/03/archives/40-blazes-erupt-in-south-bronx-area-40-fires-18-major-
ones-erupt-in.html?_r=0.

Mohr, Nicholasa. 1975. *El Bronx Remembered.* New York: HarperCollins.

Moore, Wes. 2017. "The War on Poverty Has Become a War on the Poor." *Time,*
July 5. Accessed December 8, 2017. http://time.com/4842822/war-on-poverty-
wes-moore/.

Moritz, Owen. 2015. "Looters Prey on the City during the Blackout of 1977." *New
York Daily News,* July 12. Accessed November 25, 2017. http://www
.nydailynews.com/new-york/nyc-crime/looters-prey-city-blackout-1977-article-
1.2284260.

Munch, Janet Butler. n.d. "Bronx Architecture." Lehman College. Accessed
November 27, 2017. http://www.lehman.edu/vpadvance/artgallery/arch
/buildings/ConcoursePlaza.html.

Murphy, Jarrett. 2017. "Reaction to City Announcing Right to Counsel in
Housing Court." *City Limits,* February 13. Accessed December 11, 2017.

https://citylimits.org/2017/02/13/reaction-to-city-announcing-right-to-counsel-in-housing-court/.

Murray, Nick. 2014. "From Corner Delis to Yankee Stadium: Romeo Santos' Historic Bronx Gig." *Rolling Stone,* July 11. Accessed May 26, 2018. https://www.rollingstone.com/music/news/from-corner-delis-to-yankee-stadium-romeo-santos-historic-bronx-gig-20140711.

Naison, Mark, and Bob Gumbs. 2016. *Before the Fires: An Oral History of African American Life in the Bronx from the 1930s to the 1960s.* New York: Fordham University Press.

Neighborhood Stabilization Program, NYC Commission on Human Rights. 1986. "Tenants of the West Bronx on the Way Out, but No Place to Go." New York: Citizens Advice Bureau.

Newman, Kathe, and Elvin K. Wyly. 2006. "The Right to Stay Put, Revisited: Gentrification and Resistance to Displacement in New York City." *Urban Studies* 43: 23–57.

New York City Bar. 2010. "The Role of Community Benefit Agreements in New York City's Land Use Process." *New York City Bar,* March 8. Accessed December 8, 2017. http://www.nycbar.org/pdf/report/uploads/20071844-TheRoleofCommunityBenefitAgreementsinNYCLandUseProcess.pdf.

New York Civil Liberties Union. 2009. "The Rockefeller Drug Laws: Unjust, Irrational, and Ineffective." Accessed November 17, 2017. https://www.nyclu.org/sites/default/files/publications/nyclu_pub_rockefeller.pdf.

New York State Committee on Discrimination in Housing. 1953. "What Price Slum Clearance?" Background memorandum, February 24. Accessed November 15, 2017. https://socialwelfare.library.vcu.edu/programs/housing/price-slum-clearance/.

New York Times. 1979. "Senate Panel Fears Arson Cases Are Nearing an 'Epidemic' Stage." *New York Times,* December 27. Accessed November 18, 2017. http://www.nytimes.com/1979/12/27/archives/senate-panel-fears-arson-cases-are-nearing-an-epidemic-stage-no.html.

New York Times. 1983. "Cuomo Raises Housing Allowance for Recipients of Welfare by 25%." *New York Times,* December 3. Accessed November 19, 2017. http://www.nytimes.com/1983/12/03/nyregion/cuomo-raises-housing-allowance-for-recipients-of-welfare-by-25.html.

New York Times. 2017. "Some Colleges Have More Students from the Top 1 Percent Than the Bottom 60. Find Yours." *New York Times: The Upshot,* January 18. Accessed March 25, 2018. https://www.nytimes.com/interactive/2017/01/18/upshot/some-colleges-have-more-students-from-the-top-1-percent-than-the-bottom-60.html.

New York Times Editorial Board. 2014. "Small Schools Work in New York." *New York Times,* October 17. Accessed December 8, 2017. https://www.nytimes.com/2014/10/18/opinion/small-schools-work-in-new-york.html.

New York Times Editorial Board. 2018. "America's Federally Financed Ghettos."
  New York Times, April 7. Accessed April 7, 2018. https://www.nytimes
  .com/2018/04/07/opinion/sunday/americas-federally-financed-ghettos
  .html?rref=collection%2Fsectioncollection%2Fsunday.

Nicholson, Shan (Director). 2015. *Rubble Kings.* Documentary film. New York:
  Saboteur Media.

Nossiter, Adam. 1995. "Hip-Hop Club (Gang?) Is Banned in the Bronx; Cultural
  Questions about Zulu Nation." *New York Times,* October 4. Accessed
  November 27, 2017. http://www.nytimes.com/1995/10/04/nyregion/hip-hop-
  club-gang-is-banned-in-the-bronx-cultural-questions-about-zulu-nation
  .html?pagewanted=all.

NYC Department of City Planning. 2002. "Decennial Census Counts of Major
  Hispanic Subgroups New York City and Boroughs, 2000, table 14." *NYC
  2000: Results from the 2000 Census.* Accessed November 29, 2017. https://
  www1.nyc.gov/assets/planning/download/pdf/data-maps/nyc-population
  /census2000/nyc20002.pdf.

———. 2013. "The Newest New Yorkers, Chapter 3." December. Accessed
  November 28, 2017. https://www1.nyc.gov/assets/planning/download/pdf
  /data-maps/nyc-population/nny2013/chapter3.pdf.

———. 2017. "New York City Population by Community District." *NYC Open
  Data,* September 29. Accessed November 14, 2017. https://data.cityof-
  newyork.us/City-Government/New-York-City-Population-By-Community-
  Districts/xi7c-iiu2.

———. n.d. "Change in Total Population, 1990 and 2000 New York City and
  Boroughs." *Decennial Census—Census 2000.* Accessed November 29, 2017.
  https://www1.nyc.gov/site/planning/data-maps/nyc-population/census-
  summary-2000.page.

———. n.d. "Scope of Environmental Impact Statement/Jerome Avenue."
  Accessed November 13, 2017. http://www1.nyc.gov/assets/planning/download
  /pdf/applicants/env-review/jerome-avenue/01_deis.pdf?r=1.

NYC Department of Health and Mental Hygiene. 2013. "Federally Funded
  Health Centers in New York City." October. Accessed November 25, 2017.
  http://www1.nyc.gov/assets/doh/downloads/pdf/epi/datatable34.pdf.

NYC Department of Homeless Services. 2017. "Daily report 12/8/17." Accessed
  December 8, 2017. http://www1.nyc.gov/assets/dhs/downloads/pdf
  /dailyreport.pdf.

NYC Department of Housing Preservation and Development. 2017. "MIH
  Mandatory Inclusionary Zoning." *nyc.gov.* Accessed December 10, 2017. http://
  www1.nyc.gov/assets/hpd/downloads/pdf/community/mih-one-pager.pdf.

NYC Economic Development Corporation. 2016. "Hunts Point Peninsula."
  September 12. Accessed November 10, 2017. https://www.nycedc.com
  /project/hunts-point-peninsula.

NYC Housing Authority. 2017. "Report to the Committee on Finance and the Committee on Public Housing on the Fiscal 2018 Executive Budget for New York City Housing Authority." NYC Council, May 18. Accessed December 10, 2017. http://council.nyc.gov/budget/wp-content/uploads/sites/54/2017/03 /NYCHA-exec.pdf.

NYC Office of Civil Justice. 2016. "NYC Office of Civil Justice 2016 Annual Report." NYC Human Resources Administration, June. Accessed December 10, 2017. https://www1.nyc.gov/assets/hra/downloads/pdf/services/civiljustice /OCJ%202016%20Annual%20Report%20FINAL_08_29_2016.pdf.

NYC Parks. 2017. "Tour de Bronx." NYC Department of Parks and Recreation. Accessed December 8, 2017. https://www.nycgovparks.org/events/2017/10/22 /tour-de-bronx.

———. n.d. "Pelham Bay Park Highlights—Siwanoy Trail." NYC Department of Parks and Recreation. Accessed November 12, 2017. https://www.nycgovparks .org/parks/pelham-bay-park/highlights/11658.

———. n.d. "Playground 52." NYC Department of Parks and Recreation. Accessed November 27, 2017. https://www.nycgovparks.org/parks /playground-52-lii/history.

NYC Rent Guidelines Board. 1996. "Housing NYC: Rents, Markets and Trends '96." Accessed November 17, 2017. http://www.nycrgb.org/downloads/research /pdf_reports/96book.pdf.

Office of the Bronx District Attorney, Darcel D. Clark. 2016. "Statistics and Reports: Decline in Crime." Accessed November 30, 2017. http://bronxda .nyc.gov/html/reports/decline.shtml.

Office of the Mayor. n.d. "Bill de Blasio." Accessed November 17, 2017. http:// www1.nyc.gov/office-of-the-mayor/.

Office of the New York State Comptroller. 2014. "Housing Affordability in New York State." March 10. Accessed November 9, 2017. https://www.osc.state .ny.us/reports/housing/affordable_housing_ny_2014.pdf.

———. 2015. "DiNapoli: New York City's Immigrant Population Playing Increased Role in Economy." November 5. Accessed November 13, 2017. https://www.osc.state.ny.us/press/releases/nov15/110515.htm.

OldSchoolHipHop.com. 2010. "Cold Crush Brothers." January 7. Accessed May 30, 2018. http://www.oldschoolhiphop.com/artists/emcees/coldcrushbrothers .htm.

Oreskes, Michael. 1988. "Fiscal Crisis Still Haunts the Police." *New York Times*, July 6. Accessed November 18, 2017. http://www.nytimes.com/1985/07/06 /nyregion/fiscal-crisis-still-haunts-the-police.html?pagewanted=all.

Oser, Alan S. 1989. "PERSPECTIVES: South Bronx Homes; the Housing Shift Near Charlotte Street." *New York Times,* March 19. Accessed November 27, 2017. http://www.nytimes.com/1989/03/19/realestate/perspectives-south-bronx-homes-the-housing-shift-near-charlotte-street.html?pagewanted=all.

Pace, Eric. 2002. "Astin Jacobo, 73, Unofficial Mayor of a Bronx Neighborhood." *New York Times,* March 30. Accessed December 11, 2017. http://www .nytimes.com/2002/03/30/nyregion/astin-jacobo-73-unofficial-mayor-of-a-bronx-neighborhood.html.

Pareles, Jon. 2006. "Mambo and Hip-Hop: Two Bronx Sounds, One Sense of Dignity." *New York Times,* September 14. Accessed December 11, 2017. http:// www.nytimes.com/2006/09/14/arts/television/14pare.html.

Parrott, James. 2009. "Impact of Economic Crisis on Nonprofits in the Bronx." Fiscal Policy Institute, March 13. Accessed November 14, 2017. http://www .fiscalpolicy.org/FPI_EconomicCrisisAndBronxNonprofits_20090313.pdf.

Pastor, Kate. 2015. "Deepening Housing Crisis Plays Out in Bronx Courthouse." *City Limits,* February 4. Accessed December 10, 2017. https://citylimits .org/2015/02/04/deepening-housing-crisis-plays-out-in-bronx-courthouse/.

———. 2017. "Hip-Hop Museum Coming to New Bronx Point Mega-Development." *DNAinfo,* September 26. Accessed December 11, 2017. https://www .dnainfo.com/new-york/20170922/concourse/new-development-bronx-point-housing-hip-hop-museum-theater.

Pear, Robert. 1992. "Bias Is Admitted by New York City in Public Housing." *New York Times,* July 1. Accessed November 15, 2007. http://www.nytimes.com /1992/07/01/nyregion/bias-is-admitted-by-new-york-city-in-public-housing .html?pagewanted=all.

Phillips-Fein, Kim. 2013. "The Legacy of the 1970s Fiscal Crisis: Nearly Forty Years after Ford Told New York to Drop Dead, the City Is Still Here—but Forever Changed." *The Nation,* April 16. Accessed November 18, 2017. https://www.thenation.com/article/legacy-1970s-fiscal-crisis/.

———. 2017. *Fear City: New York's Fiscal Crisis and the Rise of Austerity Politics.* New York: Henry Holt.

Plitt, Amy. 2015. "Developers Try to Rebrand the South Bronx to Disastrous Effect." *Curbed New York,* November 2. Accessed December 10, 2017. https:// ny.curbed.com/2015/11/2/9905036/developers-try-to-rebrand-the-south-bronx-to-disastrous-effect.

———. 2017. "The Richest Neighborhoods in New York City." *Curbed New York,* June 27. Accessed November 6, 2017. https://ny.curbed. com/2017/6/27/15881706/nyc-richest-neighborhoods-manhattan-brooklyn.

Powell, Michael. 2016. "Grumbling about Socialism, the Yankees Profit from It." *New York Times,* April 16. Accessed December 8, 2017. https://www.nytimes .com/2016/04/17/sports/baseball/grumbling-about-socialism-the-yankees-profit-from-it.html?_r=0.

Quindlen, Anna. 1982. "About New York." *New York Times,* October 6. Accessed November 27, 2017. http://www.nytimes.com/1982/10/06/nyregion/about-new-york.html.

Rayman, Graham. 2017. "Cross Bronx Expressway Named Most Congested City Roadway in U.S." *New York Daily News,* February 20. Accessed February 3, 2018. http://www.nydailynews.com/new-york/cross-bronx-expressway-named-congested-city-roadway-u-s-article-1.2977466.

Redfearn, Jennifer. 2007. "Sins of the Father." *Village Voice,* January 16. Accessed November 26, 2017. https://www.villagevoice.com/2007/01/16/sins-of-the-father-3/.

Regional Plan Association. 2017. "Pushed Out: Housing Displacement in an Unaffordable Region." Regional Plan Association, March. http://library.rpa.org/pdf/RPA-Pushed-Out-Housing-Displacement-in-an-Unaffordable-Region.pdf.

Riccio, James A. 2013. "Conditional Cash Rewards—Family Rewards." MSRC, September. Accessed November 15, 2017. https://www.mdrc.org/publication/conditional-cash-transfers-new-york-city.

Riper, Frank Van. 1975. "Ford to City: Drop Dead." *New York Daily News,* October 29. Accessed November 17, 2017. http://www.nydailynews.com/new-york/president-ford-announces-won-bailout-nyc-1975-article-1.2405985.

Rivlin-Nadler, Max. 2017. "Here Is the South Bronx's 1,300-Unit Gentrification Death Star." *Village Voice,* March 9. Accessed December 10, 2017. https://www.villagevoice.com/2017/03/09/here-is-the-south-bronxs-1300-unit-gentrification-death-star/.

Robbins, Liz. 2015. "Influx of West Africans in the Bronx Spurs Demand for Interpreters." *New York Times,* November 26. Accessed December 7, 2017. https://www.nytimes.com/2015/11/27/nyregion/influx-of-west-africans-in-the-bronx-spurs-demand-for-interpreters.html.

Roberts, Sam. 2011. "Striking Change in Bedford-Stuyvesant as the White Population Soars." *New York Times,* August 4. Accessed December 10, 2017. http://www.nytimes.com/2011/08/05/nyregion/in-bedford-stuyvesant-a-black-stronghold-a-growing-pool-of-whites.html.

———. 2016. "People Fled the Bronx in the 1970s. Now Its Population Is Booming." *New York Times,* September 15. Accessed December 7, 2017. https://www.nytimes.com/2016/09/16/nyregion/as-new-york-city-grows-the-bronx-especially-is-booming.html.

———. 2017. "Dave Valentin, a Grammy Award–Winning Latin Jazz Flutist, Dies at 64." *New York Times,* March 8. Accessed March 5, 2018. https://www.nytimes.com/2017/03/08/arts/music/dave-valentin-dead-latin-jazz-flutist.html.

Roberts, Talibah. 2005. Interview with the Bronx African American History Project, March 15. BAAHP Digital Archive at Fordham. https://fordham.bepress.com/baahp_oralhist/196/.

RollingStone.com. 2018. "Afrika Bambaataa Bio." Accessed June 1, 2018. https://www.rollingstone.com/music/artists/afrika-bambaataa/biography.

Rosenblum, Constance. 2009. *Boulevard of Dreams.* New York: New York University Press.

Rosenthal, Mel. 2001. *In the South Bronx of America.* Evanston, IL: Curbstone Press.

Rothstein, Mervyn. 1994. "A Renewal Plan in the Bronx Advances." *New York Times,* July 10. Accessed November 29, 2017. http://www.nytimes.com/1994 /07/10/realestate/a-renewal-plan-in-the-bronx-advances.html?pagewanted= all.

Rothstein, Richard. 2012. "Race and Public Housing: Revisiting the Federal Role." Economic Policy Institute, December 2. Accessed November 16, 2017. http://www.epi.org/publication/race-public-housing-revisiting-federal-role/.

Rubel, David. 1997. "Unequal Slices: A Study of the Distribution of Government and Private Funding Sources to New York City Neighborhood Service Providers and Community Districts." Accessed December 3, 2017. http:// www.davidrubelconsultant.com/publications/MHC%20Unequal%20 Slices%20Study%20Working%20Paper%20Version.pdf.

Russonello, Giovanni. 2017. "Bringing Tito Puente's Fire to a New Generation." *New York Times,* April 25. Accessed December 11, 2017. https://www .nytimes.com/2017/04/25/arts/music/tito-puente-50-years-of-el-rey.html.

Ryley, Sarah, Erik Badia, Ginger Adams Otis, and Larry McShane. 2015. "Parents in South Bronx School District, NYC's Worst, Struggle to Find Promising Options." *New York Daily News,* March 15. http://www .nydailynews.com/new-york/education/failing-south-bronx-schools-affected-student-life-home-article-1.2150189.

Samaha, Albert. 2014. "Cheaper, More Addictive, and Highly Profitable: How Crack Took Over NYC in the '80s." *Village Voice,* August 12. Accessed November 17, 2017. https://www.villagevoice.com/2014/08/12/cheaper-more-addictive-and-highly-profitable-how-crack-took-over-nyc-in-the-80s/.

Samtani, Hiten. 2013. "City's Human Resources Administration Inks 175K SF Lease in Bronx's Hunts Point." *The Real Deal,* January 11. Accessed December10,2017.https://therealdeal.com/2013/01/11/hra-inks-175k-square-foot-lease-in-bronxs-hunts-point/.

Samuels, Tanyanika. 2011. "Former Bronx Gang Members Mark 40th Anniversary of Truce That Led to Decline of Street Violence in the 1970s." *New York Daily News,* December 8. http://www.nydailynews.com/new-york/bronx /bronx-gang-members-mark-40th-anniversary-truce-led-decline-street-violence-1970s-article-1.988287.

Sanger-Katz, Margot. 2016. "Poor New Yorkers Tend to Live Longer Than Other Poor Americans." *New York Times,* April 11. Accessed December 8, 2017. https://www.nytimes.com/2016/04/11/upshot/poor-new-yorkers-tend-to-live-longer-than-other-poor-americans.html.

Savitch-Lew, Abigail. 2017. "The High-Income Neighborhoods the City Could Look to Rezone." *City Limits,* May 10. Accessed December 10, 2017. https:// citylimits.org/2017/05/10/the-high-income-neighborhoods-the-city-could-look-to-rezone/.

Secret, Mosi. 2011. "Smaller Shelters and Persuasion Coax Homeless off Bronx Streets." *New York Times,* October 18. Accessed December 10, 2017. http:// www.nytimes.com/2011/10/18/nyregion/nyc-makes-progress-helping-bronxs-chronic-homeless-adults.html.

Sell, Meredith. 2014. "How New York City Beat Arson." *City Limits,* May 14. Accessed November 27, 2017. https://citylimits.org/2014/05/14/how-new-york-city-beat-arson/.

Semuels, Alana. 2016. "The End of Welfare as We Know It: America's Once-Robust Safety Net Is No More." *The Atlantic,* April 1. Accessed December 8, 2017.https://www.theatlantic.com/business/archive/2016/04/the-end-of-welfare-as-we-know-it/476322/.

Sen, Mandu, and Moses Gates. 2018. "The High Cost of Bad Landlords: Impacts of Irresponsible Building Ownership in New York City." Regional Plan Association, October. Accessed November 2, 2018. http://library.rpa.org /pdf/RPA_Cost_of_Bad_Landlords.pdf.

Serpas, Sarah. 2016. "For Low-Income People of Color in NYC, Segregation Is a Regional Problem." *City Limits,* August 1. Accessed December 10, 2017. https://citylimits.org/2016/08/01/for-low-income-people-of-color-in-nyc-segregation-is-a-regional-problem/.

Sharkey, Patrick. 2017. "Community and the Crime Decline: The Causal Effect of Local Nonprofits on Violent Crime." *American Sociological Review,* October 25. Accessed December 1, 2017. http://journals.sagepub.com/eprint /VThwp5JSFz7eNKF5GkxW/full.

Siegal, Allan M. 1974. "Bringing Help to Neighborhoods." *New York Times,* December 15. Accessed November 25, 2017. http://www.nytimes.com/1974 /12/15/archives/at-the-holiday-season-remember-the-neediest-cases-bringing-help-to.html.

Sisk, Richard. 2010. "South Bronx Poorest District in Nation, 38% Live below Poverty Line." *New York Daily News,* September 29.

Smalls, F. Romall. 1997. "The Bronx Is Named an 'All-America' City." *New York Times,* July 20. Accessed December 5, 2017. http://www.nytimes.com/1997 /07/20/nyregion/the-bronx-is-named-an-all-america-city.html.

Smith, Dennis. 1973. *Report from Engine Co. 82.* New York: Pocket Books.

Smith, Robert Courtney. 2006. *Mexican New York: Transnational Lives of New Immigrants.* Berkeley: University of California Press.

Socialism and Democracy Online. 2011. "From Doo Wop to Hip Hop: The Bittersweet Odyssey of African-Americans in the South Bronx" [written by Mark Naison]. *Journal of the Research Group on Socialism and Democracy*

Online, April 16. Accessed February 15, 2018. http://sdonline.org/36
/from-doo-wop-to-hip-hop-the-bittersweet-odyssey-of-african-
americans-in-the-south-bronx/.

Sotomayor, John. 1988. "Ferrer Urges Bronx Housing Renewal." *New York
Times,* March 2. http://www.nytimes.com/1988/03/02/nyregion/ferrer-urges-
bronx-housing-renewal.html.

Sotomayor, Sonia. 2013. *My Beloved World.* New York: Alfred A. Knopf.

Souccar, Miriam Kreinin. 2017. "The Bronx Is Booming: Film Studio Breaks
Ground in Soundview." *Crain's New York Business,* June 5. Accessed December
10, 2017. http://www.crainsnewyork.com/article/20170605/ENTERTAIN
MENT/170609957/new-bronx-film-studio-breaks-ground-in-soundview.

Spittal, Amelia, and Abigail Savitch-Lew. 2017. "Report: Rents Rose, but So Did
Poverty." *City Limits,* June 9. Accessed December 10, 2017. https://citylimits
.org/2017/06/09/report-rents-rose-but-so-did-poverty/.

Statistical Atlas. 2015. "Race and Ethnicity in the South Bronx, New York, New
York." April 28. Accessed November 6, 2017. https://statisticalatlas.com
/neighborhood/New-York/New-York/South-Bronx/Race-and-Ethnicity.

Stewart, Barbara. 1999. "In Bronx, a Plan for Reeling in Fish, Not Cars." *New
York Times,* November 20. Accessed December 7, 2017. http://www.nytimes
.com/1999/11/20/nyregion/in-bronx-a-plan-for-reeling-in-fish-not-cars.html.

Stewart, Nikita. 2017a. "Adding Pantries and Spice to New York's Hungry
Neighborhoods." *New York Times,* September 11. https://www.nytimes
.com/2017/09/11/nyregion/new-york-food-pantries.html.

———. 2017b. "New Homeless Shelters Are Coming to New York City: Which
Neighborhoods Are Likely to Get Them?" *New York Times,* July 22. Accessed
December 10, 2017. https://www.nytimes.com/interactive/2017/07/22
/nyregion/nyc-homeless-shelter-maps.html.

———. 2018. "Homeless People Outside New York City Are Pushing for More
Help." *New York Times,* April 4. Accessed April 15, 2018. https://www
.nytimes.com/2018/04/04/nyregion/homeless-people-new-york.html.

Tempey, Nathan. 2017. "Thousands of Rent-Stabilized Apartments at Risk as
NYC Phases Out Controversial Homeless Shelter Program." *Gothamist,*
June 29. Accessed December 10, 2017. http://gothamist.com/2017/06/29
/cluster_site_rent_stabilized.php.

Thomas, Kevin J. A. 2012. "A Demographic Profile of Black Caribbean Immigrants in the United States." Migration Policy Institute, April. Accessed
November 27, 2017. https://www.migrationpolicy.org/research/CBI-
demographic-profile-black-caribbean-immigrants.

Tobias, Jimmy. 2017. "These Cities Are about to Make It Harder for Landlords
to Evict People." *The Nation,* August 28. Accessed April 10, 2018. https://
www.thenation.com/article/these-cities-are-about-to-make-it-harder-for-
landlords-to-evict-people/.

Treaster, Joseph B. 1975. "8 Landlords and Associates Are Indicted in Bronx Fires." *New York Times,* June 12. Accessed November 19, 2017. http://www .nytimes.com/1975/06/12/archives/8-landlords-and-associates-are-indicted-in-bronx-fires-8-indicted.html.

Ultan, Lloyd. 2009. *The Northern Borough: A History of the Bronx.* Bronx, NY: Bronx County Historical Society.

Urban Health Plan. 2017. "Urban Health Plan history." Accessed November 25, 2017. https://www.urbanhealthplan.org/history/.

U.S. Census Bureau. 2016. "QuickFacts: Bronx County (Bronx Borough), New York." Accessed November 16, 2017. https://www.census.gov/quickfacts/fact /table/bronxcountybronxboroughnewyork/BZA110215.

U.S. House of Representatives. n.d. "Garcia, Robert." Accessed November 29, 2017. http://history.house.gov/People/Detail/13625.

Valencia, Milton J. 2016. "After 30 Years, Court Marks Boston Harbor Cleanup." *Boston Globe,* August 16. Accessed December 7, 2017. https://www .bostonglobe.com/metro/2016/08/06/three-decades-later-court-celebrates-end-boston-harbor-cleanup-era/EFKyY9F63azlbFU5BBR1fK/story.html.

Vázquez, Charlie, and Kim Vaquedano (Editors). 2014. *Bronx Memoir Project.* New York: Bronx Council on the Arts.

Velasquez, Carlos. 2007. *The Political Icon: José E. Serrano.* New York: Galos.

Verel, Patrick. 2016. "Bronx Black History: Hetty Fox, Portrait of a Tireless Activist." *Fordham News,* February 1. Accessed December 10, 2017. https:// news.fordham.edu/arts-and-culture/bronx-black-history-hetty-fox-portrait-of-a-tireless-activist/.

Wallace, Deborah, and Rodrick Wallace. 2001. *A Plague on Your Houses: How New York Was Burned Down and National Public Health Crumbled.* New York: Verso.

Warerkar, Tanay. 2017. "Promised South Bronx Parkland Could Become Affordable Housing Instead." *Curbed New York,* May 8. Accessed December 8, 2017. https://ny.curbed.com/2017/5/8/15578078/yankee-stadium-bronx-park-affordable-housing.

Waterfront Alliance. 2017. "The South Bronx Rediscovers Its River." June. Accessed December 7, 2017. http://waterfrontalliance.org/2017/06/09 /more-waterfront-access-for-the-south-bronx/.

Weiss, Lois. 2018. "Brookfield Buys Bronx Residential Project for $165M." *New York Post,* April 3. Accessed April 7, 2018. https://nypost.com/2018/04/03 /brookfield-buys-bronx-residential-project-for-165m/.

Whitehead, Kim. 2012. "Sharon De La Cruz, Artist and Activist from the Point, Honored for Community Work in the Bronx." *New York Daily News,* February 23. Accessed December 8, 2017. http://www.nydailynews.com/new-york /bronx/sharon-de-la-cruz-artist-activist-point-honored-community-work-bronx-article-1.1026377.

Williams, Timothy. 2006. "Bronx Board Is Shuffled after Rejecting New Stadium." *New York Times*, June 19. Accessed December 8, 2017. http://www.nytimes.com/2006/06/19/nyregion/19stadium.html.

Wills, Kerry. 2012. "William Hodson Community Center, Nation's First Place for Seniors, Still Vibrant as It Gears Up for 70th Anniversary." *New York Daily News*, November 29. Accessed December 2, 2017. http://www.nydailynews.com/new-york/bronx/william-hodson-community-center-mission-ageless-article-1.1209034.

———. 2013. "Bronx Tenant Organizers Say Scales Tipped to Landlords." *New York Daily News*, March 18. Accessed December 11, 2017. http://www.nydailynews.com/new-york/bronx/bronx-tenant-organizers-scales-tipped-landlords-article-1.1290150.

Worth, Robert. 1999. "Guess Who Saved the South Bronx? Big Government." *Washington Monthly*, April. Accessed November 13, 2017. http://www.unz.org/Pub/WashingtonMonthly-1999apr-00026.

Wright, Cecil. 2016. *21 Days to Freedom*. New York: Createspace.

Zimmer, Amy. 2016. "Most New Yorkers Are Roughly 1 Paycheck Away from Homelessness: Study." *DNAinfo*, November 25. Accessed December 10, 2017. https://www.dnainfo.com/new-york/20161125/central-harlem/emergency-savings-nyc-residents-rent-food-homeless.

Zong, Jie, and Jeanne Batalova. 2016. "Caribbean Immigrants in the United States." *Migration Policy Institute*, September 14. Accessed November 27, 2017. https://www.migrationpolicy.org/article/caribbean-immigrants-united-states.

Index

Milton Keynes UK
Ingram Content Group UK Ltd.
UKHW022314250224
438379UK00007B/876